FANTASTIC FOUR 4

FOUREVER

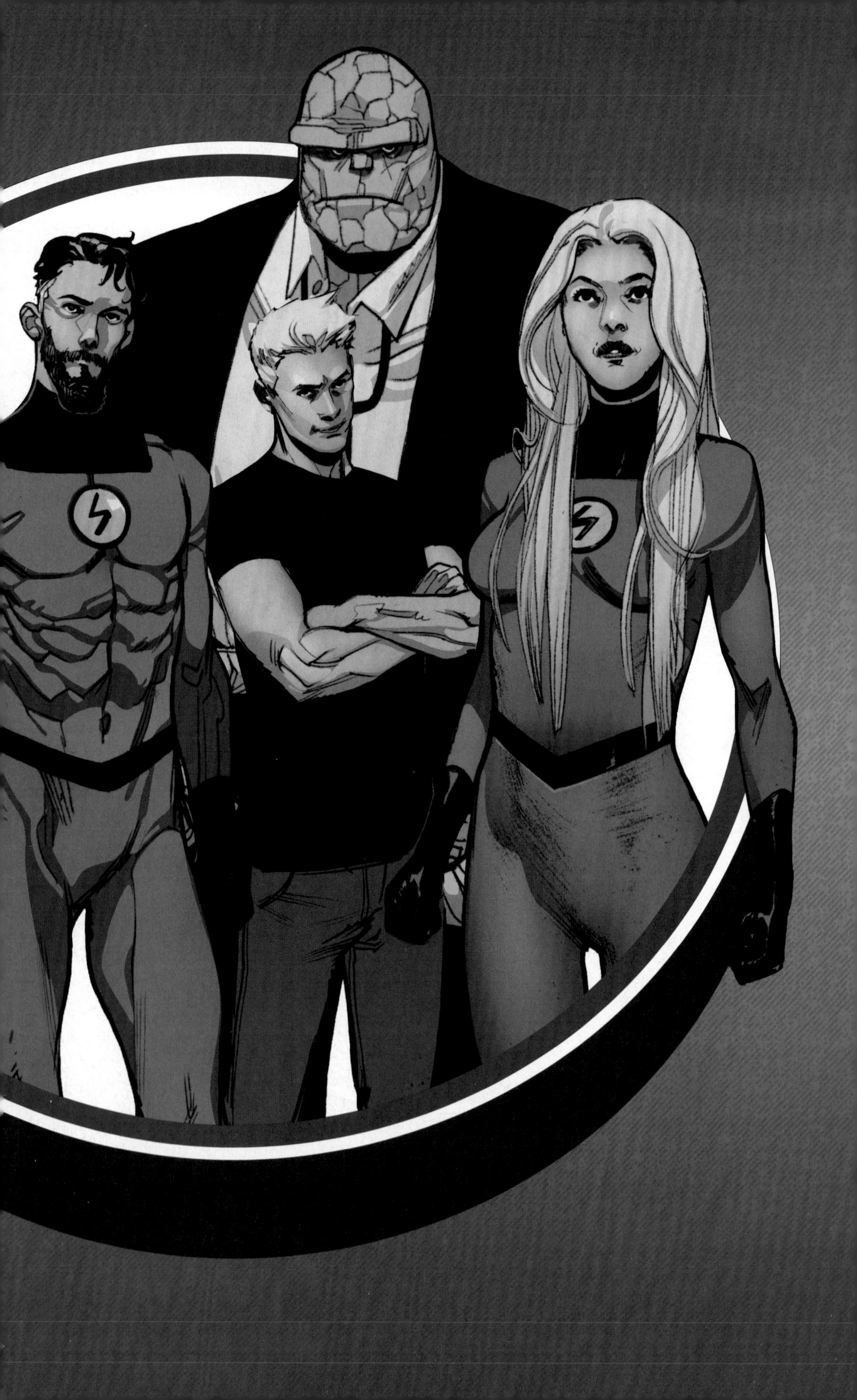

A brilliant scientist — his best friend — the woman he loved — and her fiery-tempered kid brother! Together, they braved the unknown terrors of outer space, and were changed by cosmic rays into something more than merely human! They became the...

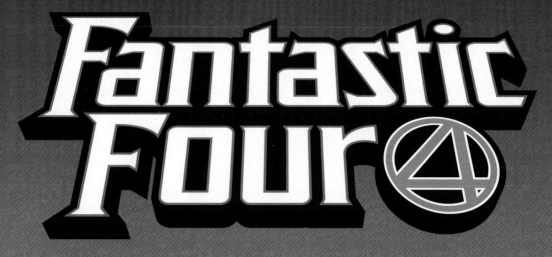

Fantastic Four

The world believes that Reed and Sue Richards, along with the Future Foundation, sacrificed themselves to stop a universal catastrophe. Ben Grimm, A.K.A. the Thing, also believes them to be dead. But Johnny Storm hasn't given up hope that the rest of his family is out there...somewhere...

FOUREVER

Dan Slott
WRITER

ISSUES #1-3

Sara Pichelli with Nico Leon (#3)
PENCILERS

Sara Pichelli with Elisabetta D'Amico (#1-3) & Nico Leon (#3)
INKERS

Marte Gracia
COLOR ARTIST

"OUR DAY OF DOOM AND VICTORY"

Simone Bianchi
ARTIST

Simone Bianchi & Marco Russo
COLOR ARTISTS

"WHAT THE POP?!"

Skottie Young
ARTIST

Jeremy Treece
COLOR ARTIST

ISSUE #4

Stefano Caselli & Nico Leon
ARTISTS

Erick Arciniega
COLOR ARTIST

VC's Joe Caramagna
LETTERER

Esad Ribić
COVER ART

Alanna Smith
ASSOCIATE EDITOR

Tom Brevoort
EDITOR

The Fantastic Four created by Stan Lee & Jack Kirby

COLLECTION EDITOR Jennifer Grünwald
ASSISTANT EDITOR Caitlin O'Connell
ASSOCIATE MANAGING EDITOR Kateri Woody
EDITOR, SPECIAL PROJECTS Mark D. Beazley

VP PRODUCTION & SPECIAL PROJECTS Jeff Youngquist
SVP PRINT, SALES & MARKETING David Gabriel
BOOK DESIGNER Adam Del Re

EDITOR IN CHIEF C.B. Cebulski
CHIEF CREATIVE OFFICER Joe Quesada
PRESIDENT Dan Buckley
EXECUTIVE PRODUCER Alan Fine

FANTASTIC FOUR VOL. 1: FOUREVER. Contains material originally published in magazine form as FANTASTIC FOUR #1-4. First printing 2019. ISBN 978-1-302-91349-6. Published by MARVEL WORLDWIDE, INC., a subsidiary of MARVEL ENTERTAINMENT, LLC. OFFICE OF PUBLICATION: 135 West 50th Street, New York, NY 10020. **Printed in Canada.** DAN BUCKLEY, President, Marvel Entertainment; JOHN NEE, Publisher; JOE QUESADA, Chief Creative Officer; TOM BREVOORT, SVP of Publishing; DAVID BOGART, SVP of Business Affairs & Operations, Publishing & Partnership; DAVID GABRIEL, SVP of Sales & Marketing, Publishing; JEFF YOUNGQUIST, VP of Production & Special Projects; DAN CARR, Executive Director of Publishing Technology; ALEX MORALES, Director of Publishing Operations; DAN EDINGTON, Managing Editor; SUSAN CRESPI, Production Manager; STAN LEE, Chairman Emeritus. For information regarding advertising in Marvel Comics or on Marvel.com, please contact Vit DeBellis, Custom Solutions & Integrated Advertising Manager, at vdebellis@marvel.com. For Marvel subscription inquiries, please call 888-511-5480. **Manufactured between 1/11/2019 and 2/12/2019 by SOLISCO PRINTERS, SCOTT, QC, CANADA.**

10 9 8 7 6 5 4 3 2 1

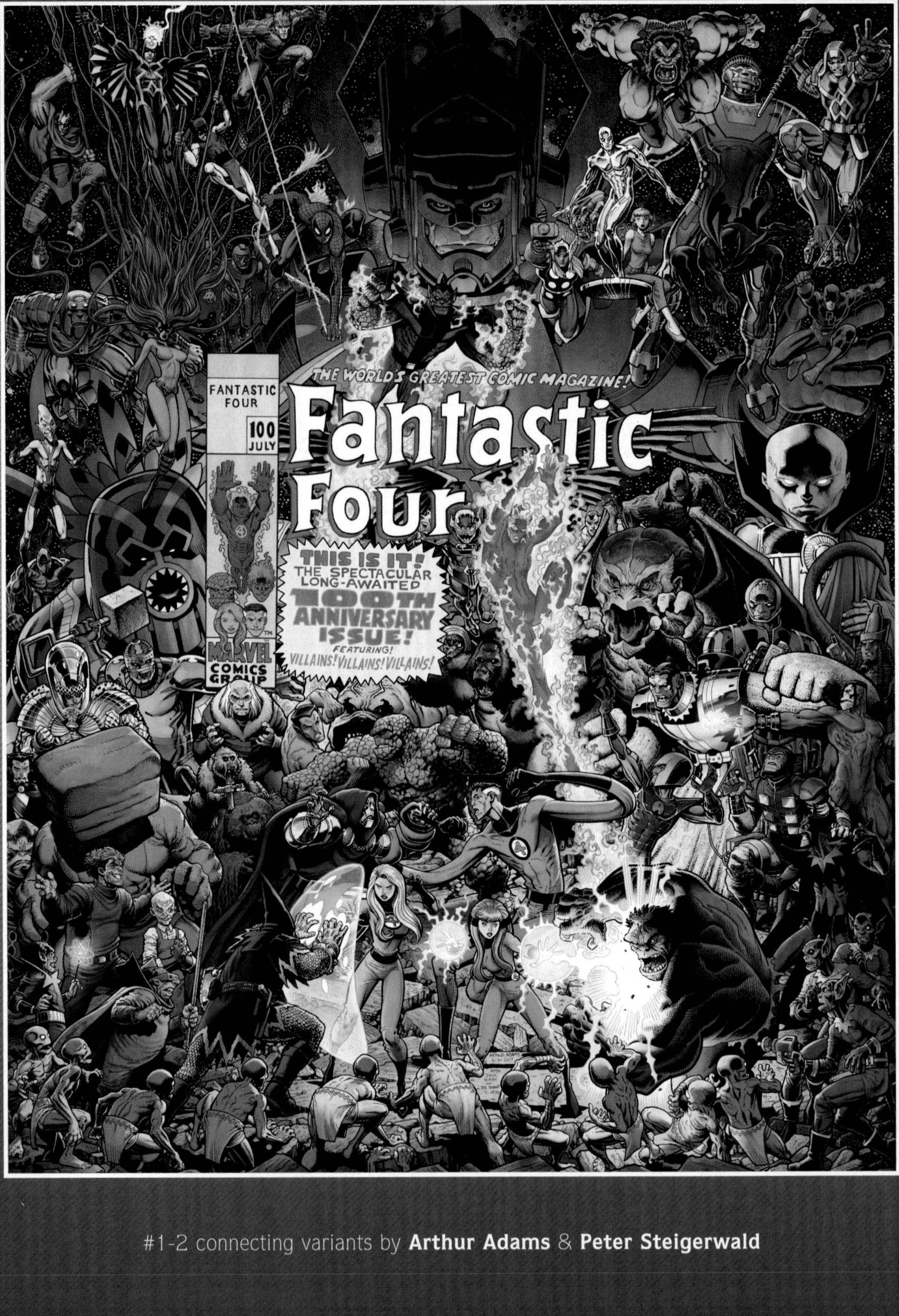
FANTASTIC FOUR
100
JULY
MARVEL COMICS GROUP
THE WORLD'S GREATEST COMIC MAGAZINE!
Fantastic Four
THIS IS IT! THE SPECTACULAR LONG-AWAITED 100TH ANNIVERSARY ISSUE!
FEATURING! VILLAINS! VILLAINS! VILLAINS!

#1-2 connecting variants by **Arthur Adams** & **Peter Steigerwald**

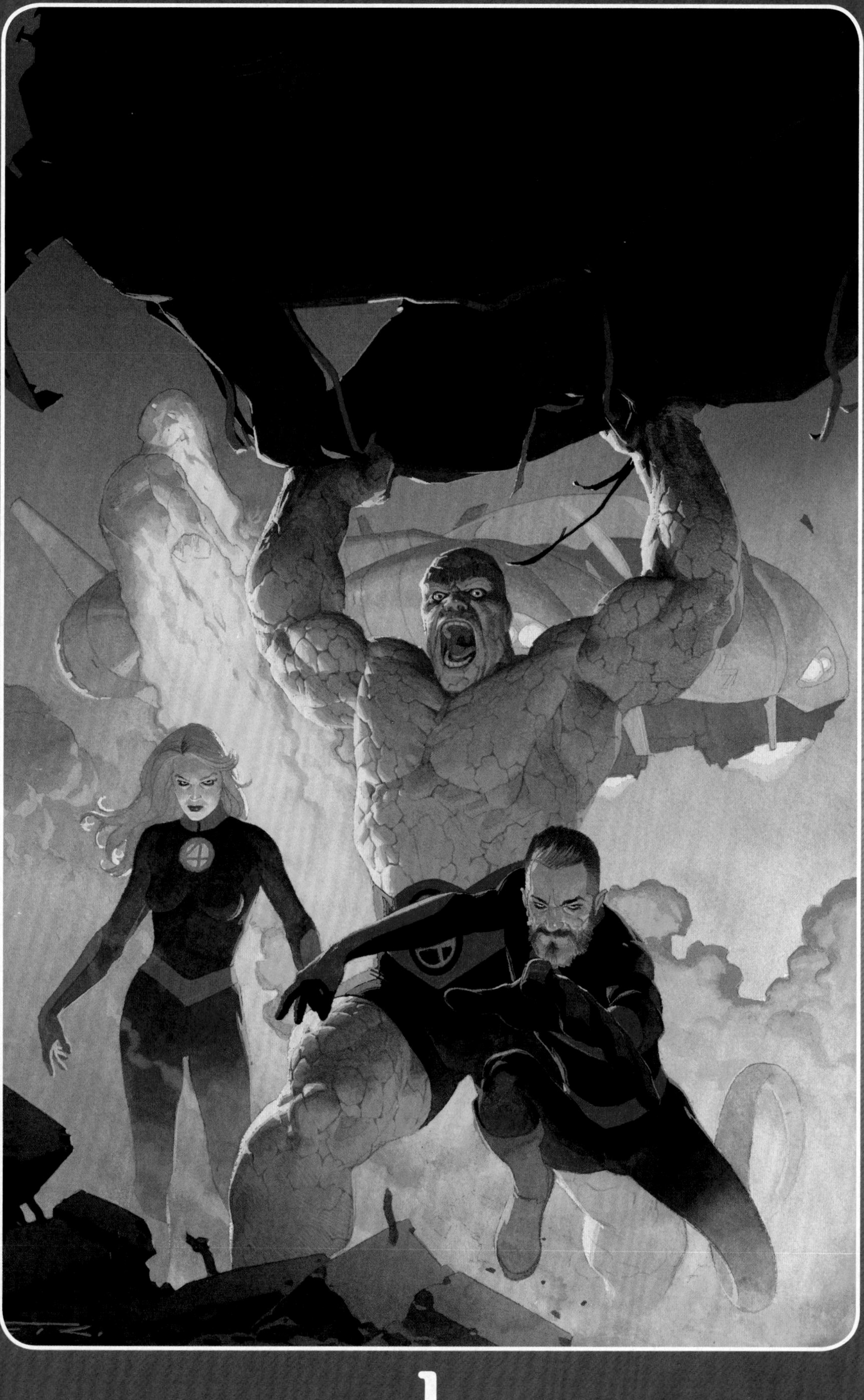

1

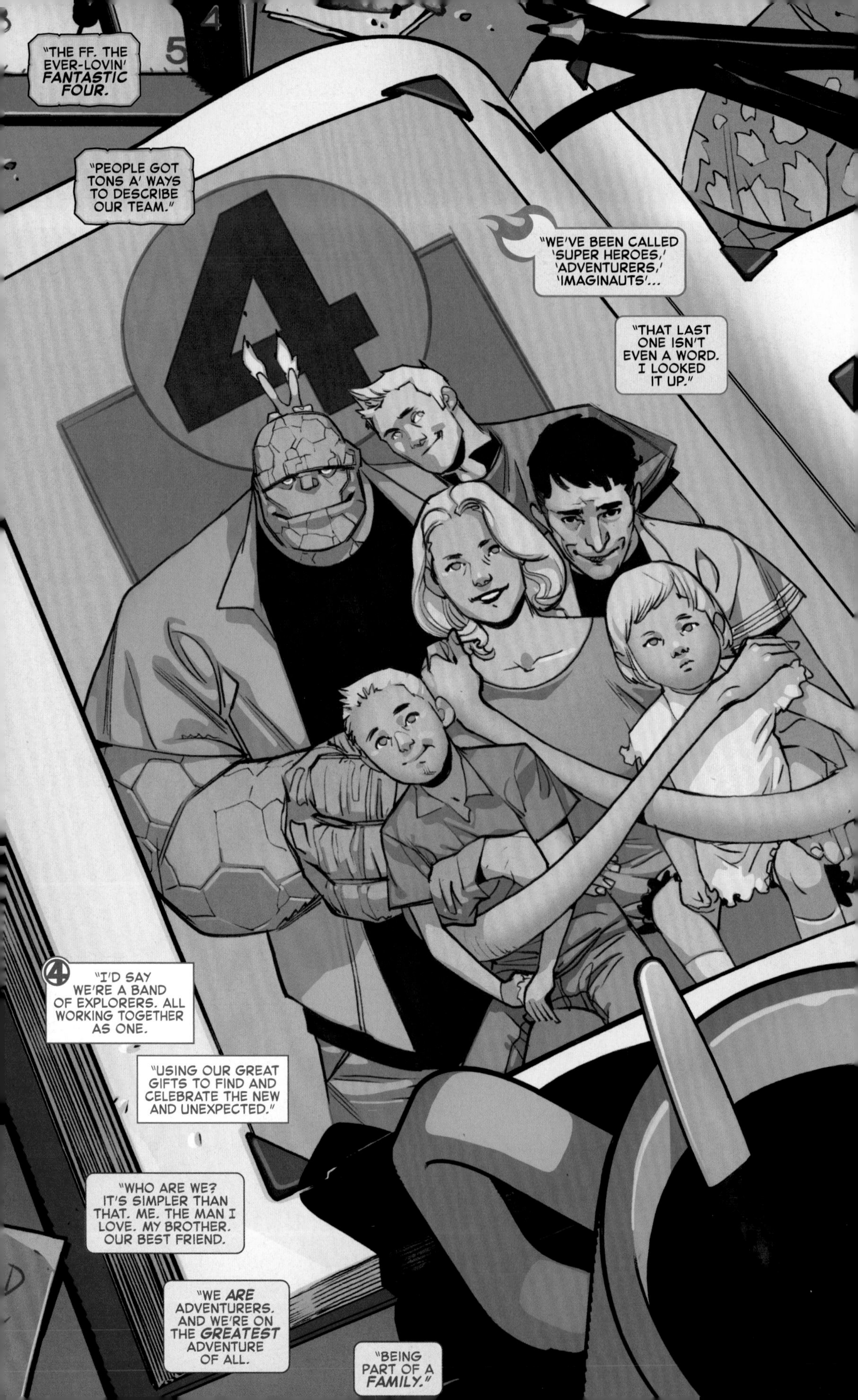
"THE FF. THE EVER-LOVIN' FANTASTIC FOUR.
"PEOPLE GOT TONS A' WAYS TO DESCRIBE OUR TEAM."
"WE'VE BEEN CALLED 'SUPER HEROES,' 'ADVENTURERS,' 'IMAGINAUTS'...
"THAT LAST ONE ISN'T EVEN A WORD. I LOOKED IT UP."
"I'D SAY WE'RE A BAND OF EXPLORERS. ALL WORKING TOGETHER AS ONE.
"USING OUR GREAT GIFTS TO FIND AND CELEBRATE THE NEW AND UNEXPECTED."
"WHO ARE WE? IT'S SIMPLER THAN THAT. ME. THE MAN I LOVE. MY BROTHER. OUR BEST FRIEND.
"WE ARE ADVENTURERS. AND WE'RE ON THE GREATEST ADVENTURE OF ALL.
"BEING PART OF A FAMILY."

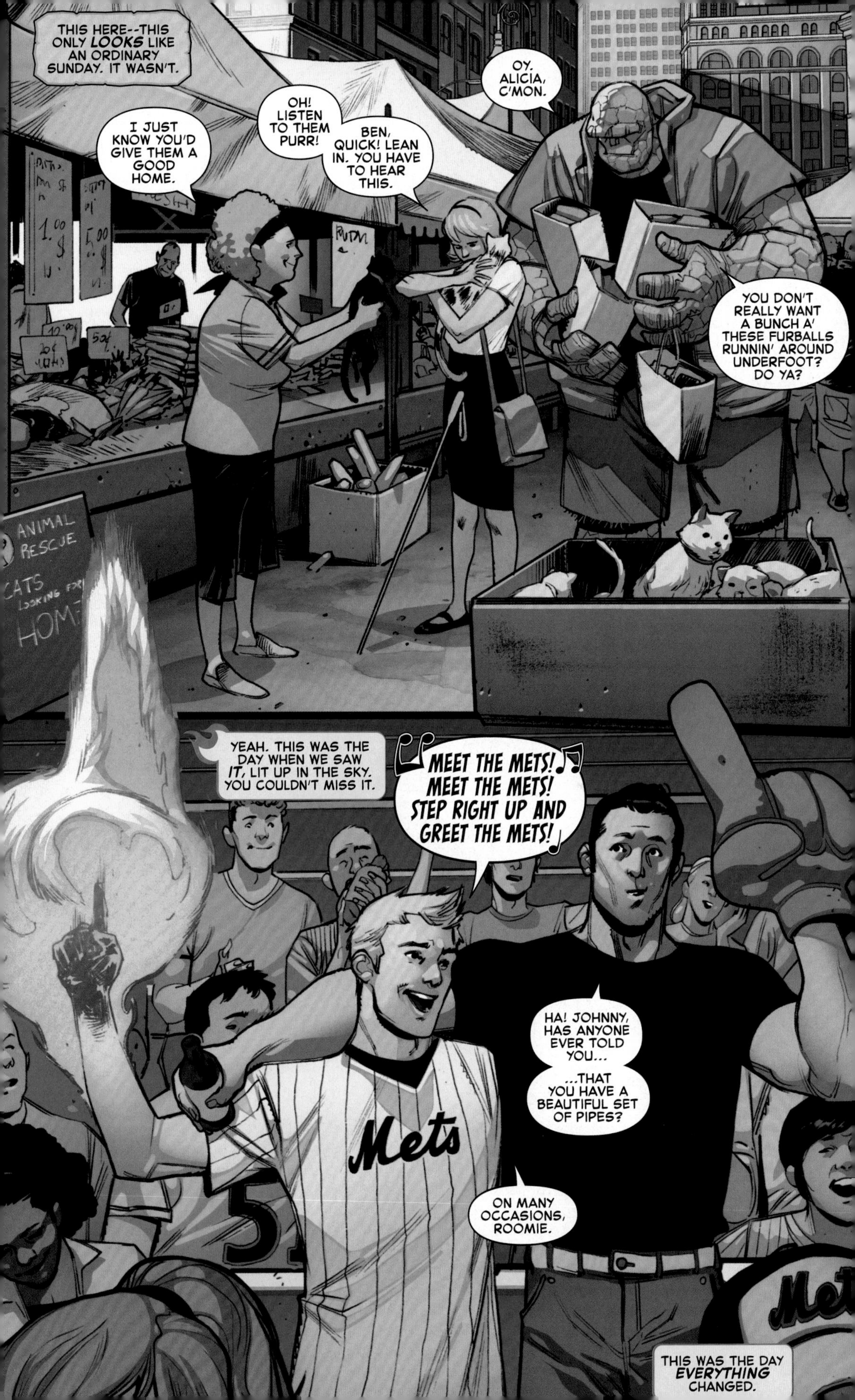
THIS HERE--THIS ONLY LOOKS LIKE AN ORDINARY SUNDAY. IT WASN'T.
I JUST KNOW YOU'D GIVE THEM A GOOD HOME.
OH! LISTEN TO THEM PURR!
BEN, QUICK! LEAN IN. YOU HAVE TO HEAR THIS.
OY. ALICIA, C'MON.
YOU DON'T REALLY WANT A BUNCH A' THESE FURBALLS RUNNIN' AROUND UNDERFOOT? DO YA?
ANIMAL RESCUE
CATS LOOKING FOR HOME
YEAH. THIS WAS THE DAY WHEN WE SAW IT, LIT UP IN THE SKY. YOU COULDN'T MISS IT.
MEET THE METS! MEET THE METS! STEP RIGHT UP AND GREET THE METS!
HA! JOHNNY, HAS ANYONE EVER TOLD YOU...
...THAT YOU HAVE A BEAUTIFUL SET OF PIPES?
Mets
ON MANY OCCASIONS, ROOMIE.
THIS WAS THE DAY EVERYTHING CHANGED.

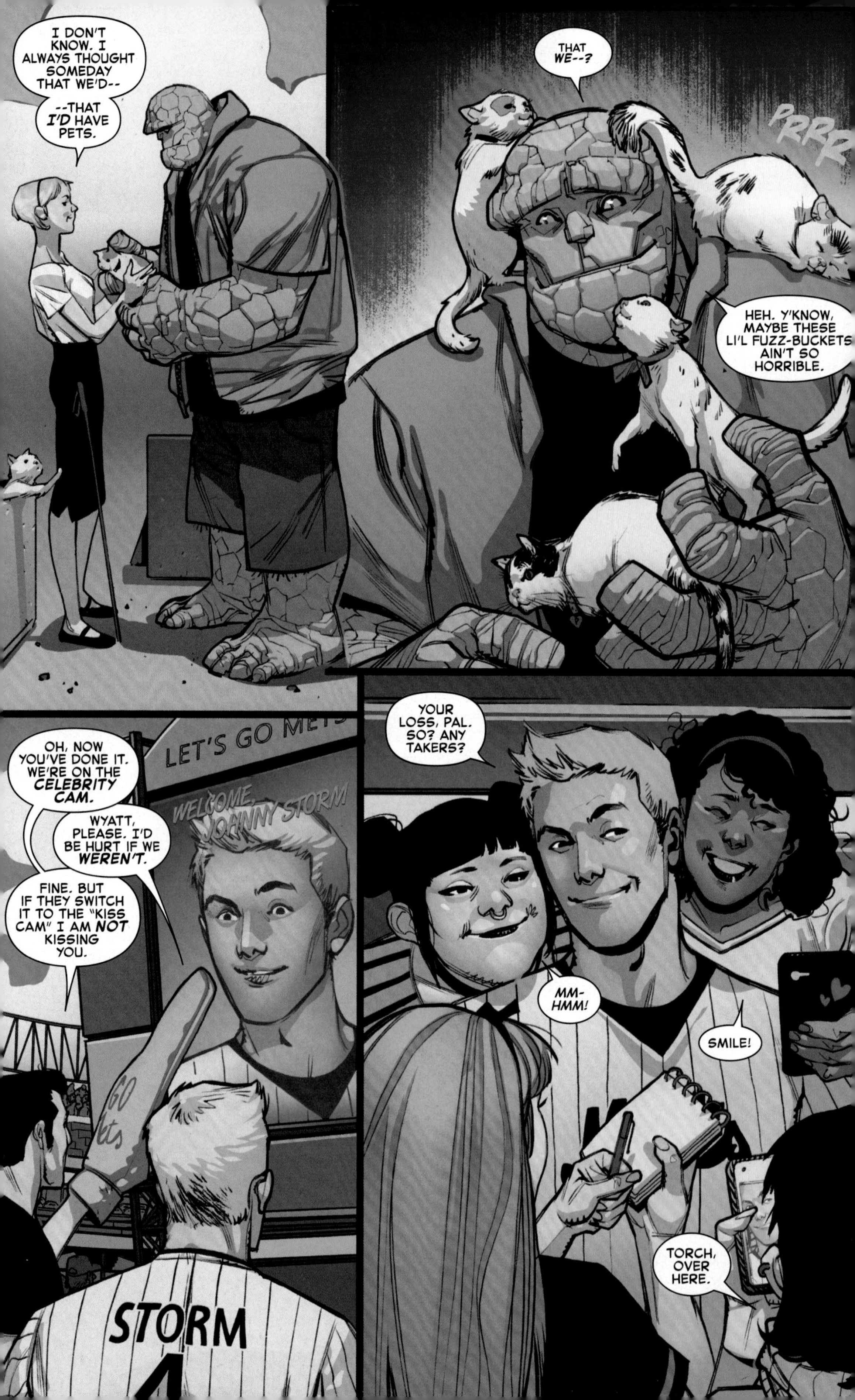
I DON'T KNOW. I ALWAYS THOUGHT SOMEDAY THAT WE'D--
--THAT I'D HAVE PETS.
THAT WE--?
PRRR
HEH. Y'KNOW, MAYBE THESE LI'L FUZZ-BUCKETS AIN'T SO HORRIBLE.
LET'S GO METS
WELCOME, JOHNNY STORM
OH, NOW YOU'VE DONE IT. WE'RE ON THE CELEBRITY CAM.
WYATT, PLEASE. I'D BE HURT IF WE WEREN'T.
FINE. BUT IF THEY SWITCH IT TO THE "KISS CAM" I AM NOT KISSING YOU.
GO Mets
STORM
YOUR LOSS, PAL. SO? ANY TAKERS?
MM-HMM!
SMILE!
TORCH, OVER HERE.

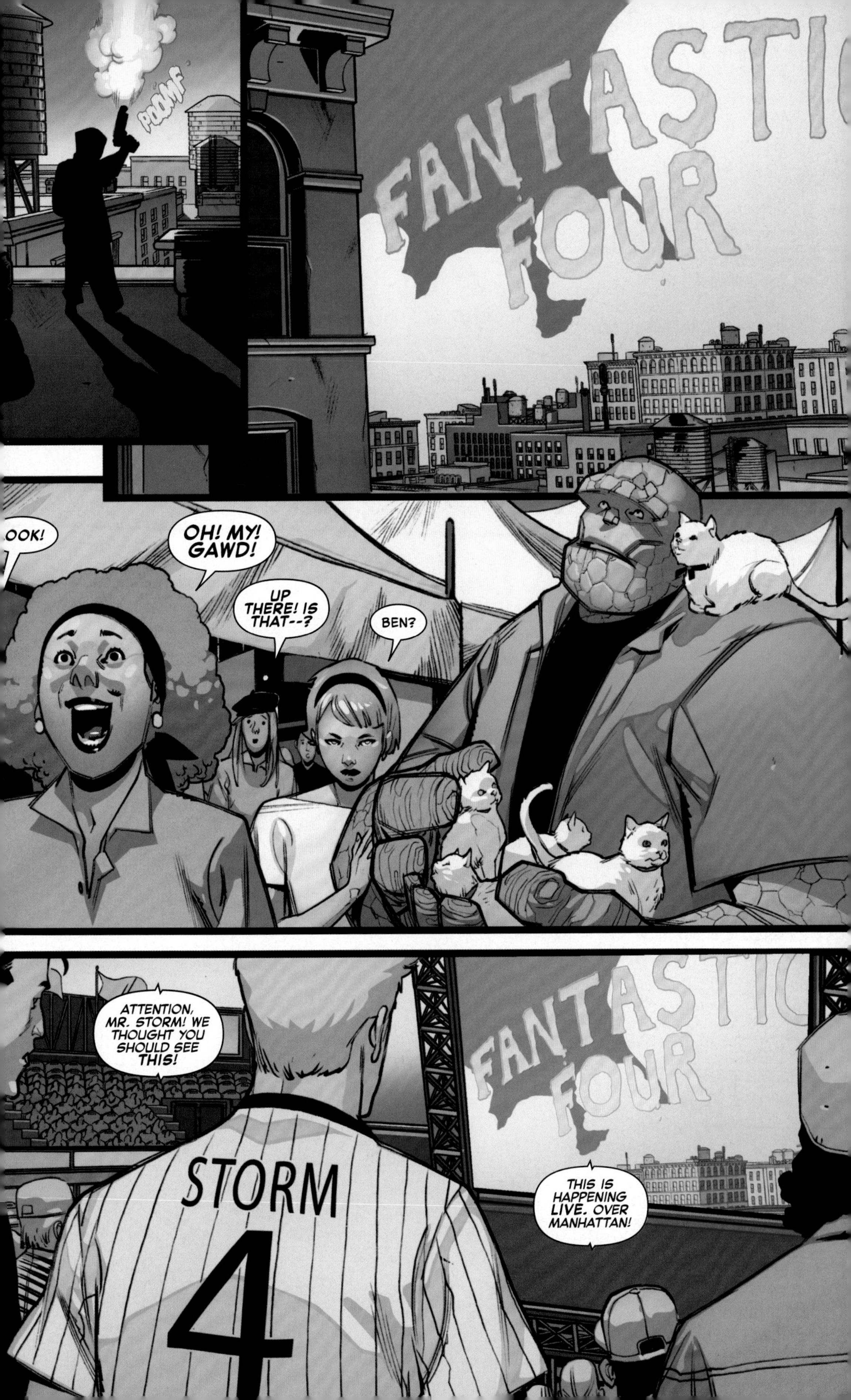
POOMF
OOK!
OH! MY! GAWD!
UP THERE! IS THAT--?
BEN?
ATTENTION, MR. STORM! WE THOUGHT YOU SHOULD SEE THIS!
STORM 4
THIS IS HAPPENING LIVE. OVER MANHATTAN!

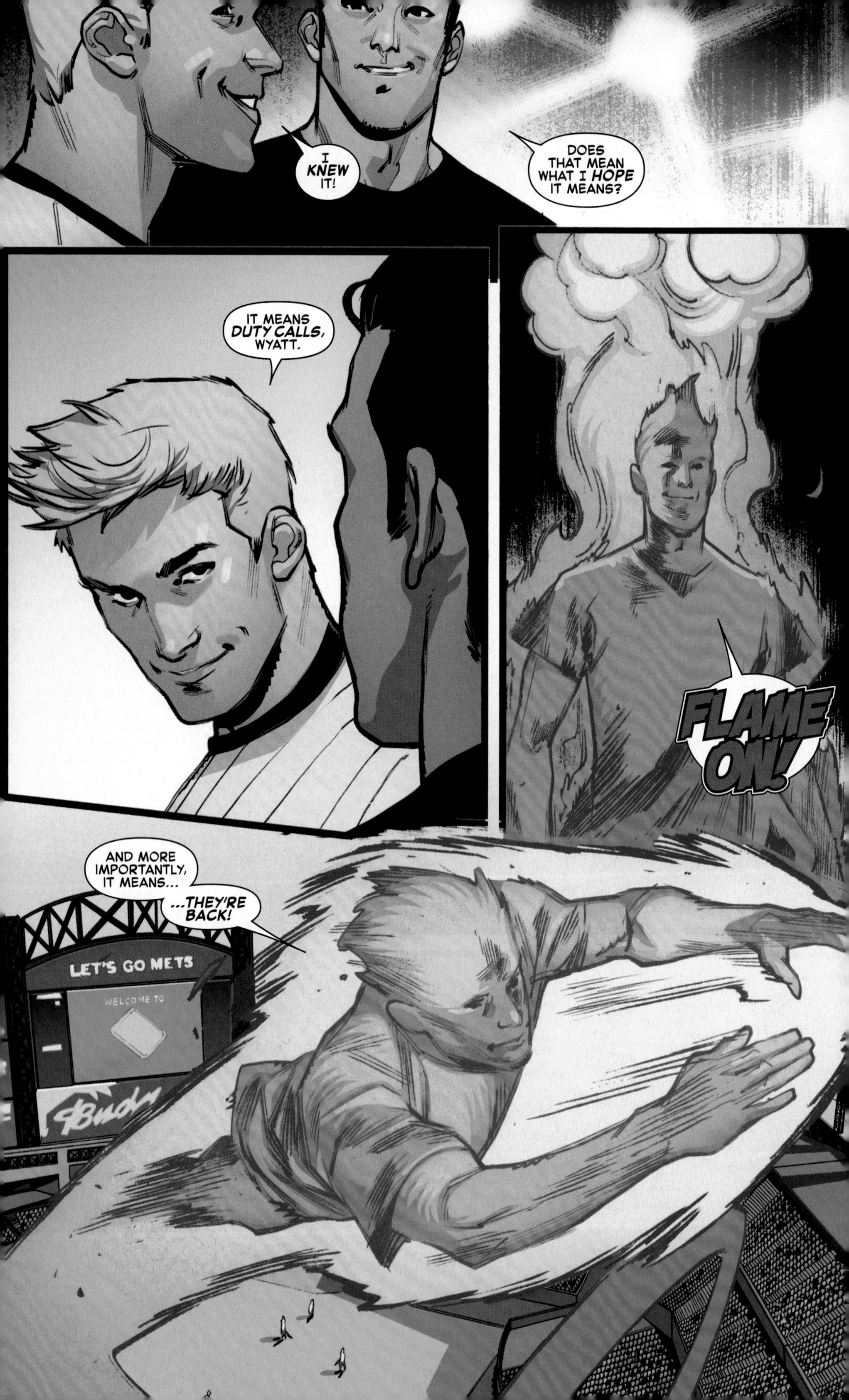
I KNEW IT!
DOES THAT MEAN WHAT I HOPE IT MEANS?
IT MEANS DUTY CALLS, WYATT.
FLAME ON!
AND MORE IMPORTANTLY, IT MEANS...
...THEY'RE BACK!
LET'S GO METS
WELCOME TO

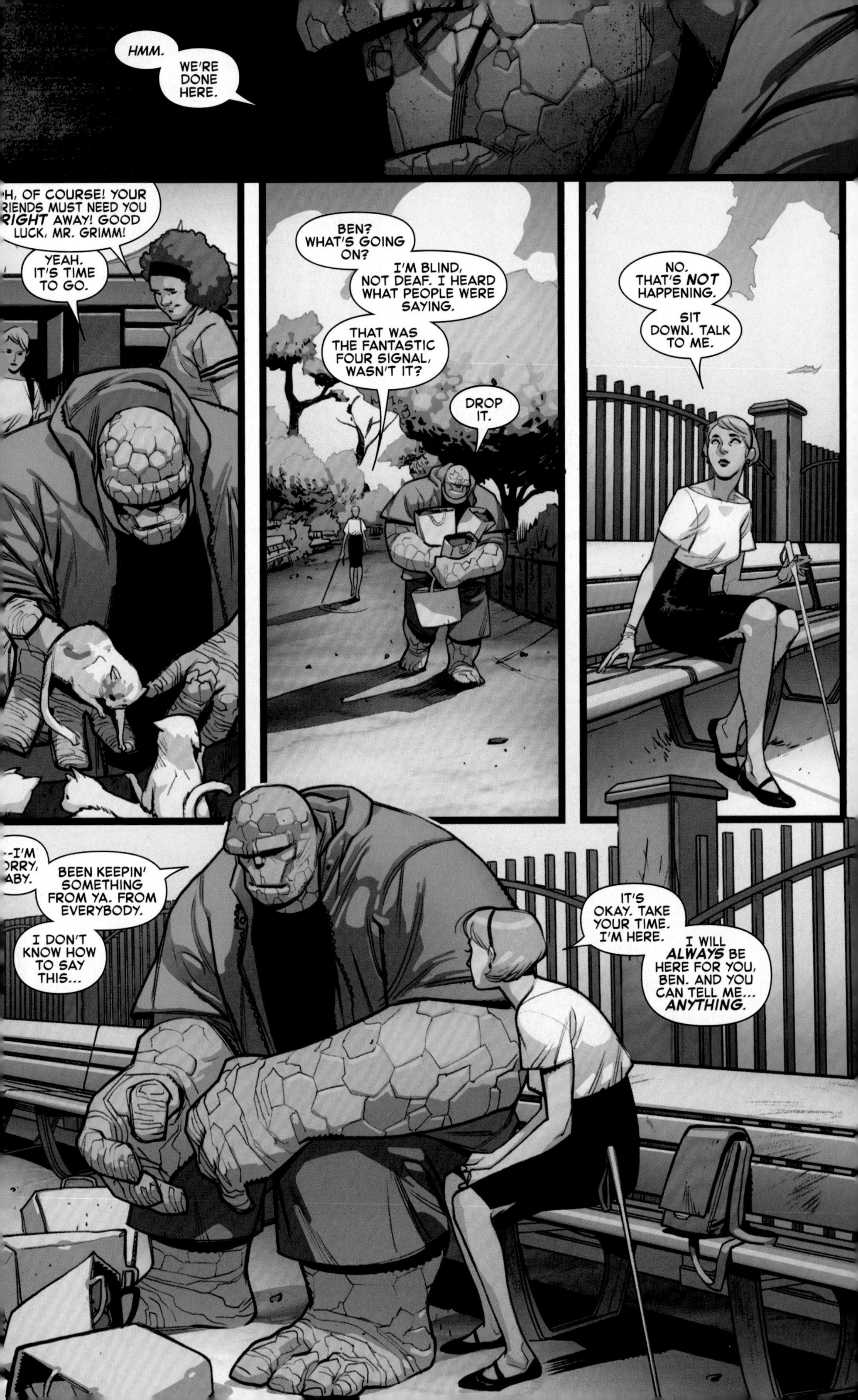
HMM.
WE'RE DONE HERE.
H, OF COURSE! YOUR RIENDS MUST NEED YOU RIGHT AWAY! GOOD LUCK, MR. GRIMM!
YEAH. IT'S TIME TO GO.
BEN? WHAT'S GOING ON?
I'M BLIND, NOT DEAF. I HEARD WHAT PEOPLE WERE SAYING.
THAT WAS THE FANTASTIC FOUR SIGNAL, WASN'T IT?
DROP IT.
NO. THAT'S NOT HAPPENING.
SIT DOWN. TALK TO ME.
--I'M ORRY, ABY.
BEEN KEEPIN' SOMETHING FROM YA. FROM EVERYBODY.
I DON'T KNOW HOW TO SAY THIS...
IT'S OKAY. TAKE YOUR TIME. I'M HERE.
I WILL ALWAYS BE HERE FOR YOU, BEN. AND YOU CAN TELL ME... ANYTHING.

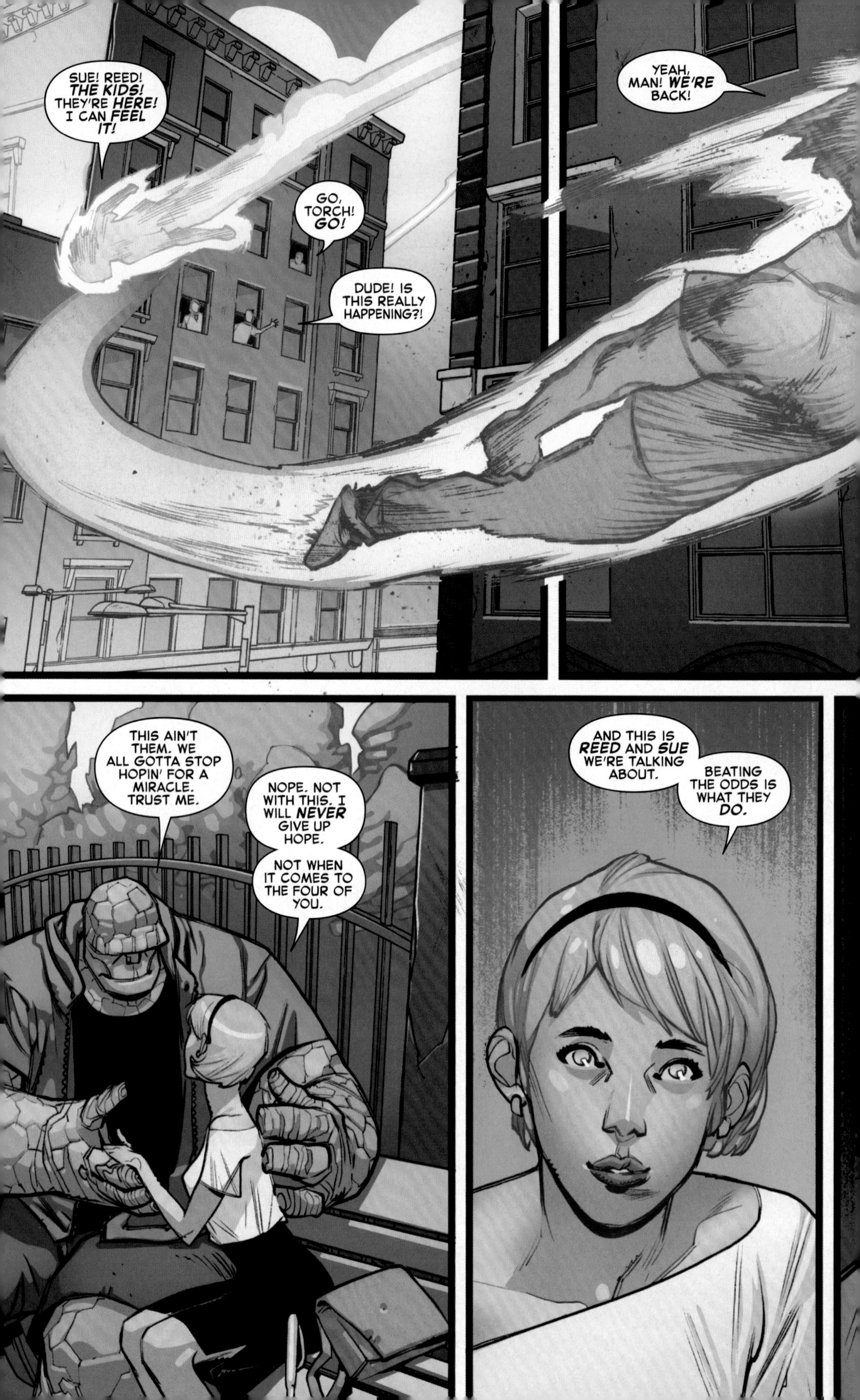

SUE! REED! THE KIDS! THEY'RE HERE! I CAN FEEL IT!
GO, TORCH! GO!
DUDE! IS THIS REALLY HAPPENING?!
YEAH, MAN! WE'RE BACK!
THIS AIN'T THEM. WE ALL GOTTA STOP HOPIN' FOR A MIRACLE. TRUST ME.
NOPE. NOT WITH THIS. I WILL NEVER GIVE UP HOPE.
NOT WHEN IT COMES TO THE FOUR OF YOU.
AND THIS IS REED AND SUE WE'RE TALKING ABOUT.
BEATING THE ODDS IS WHAT THEY DO.

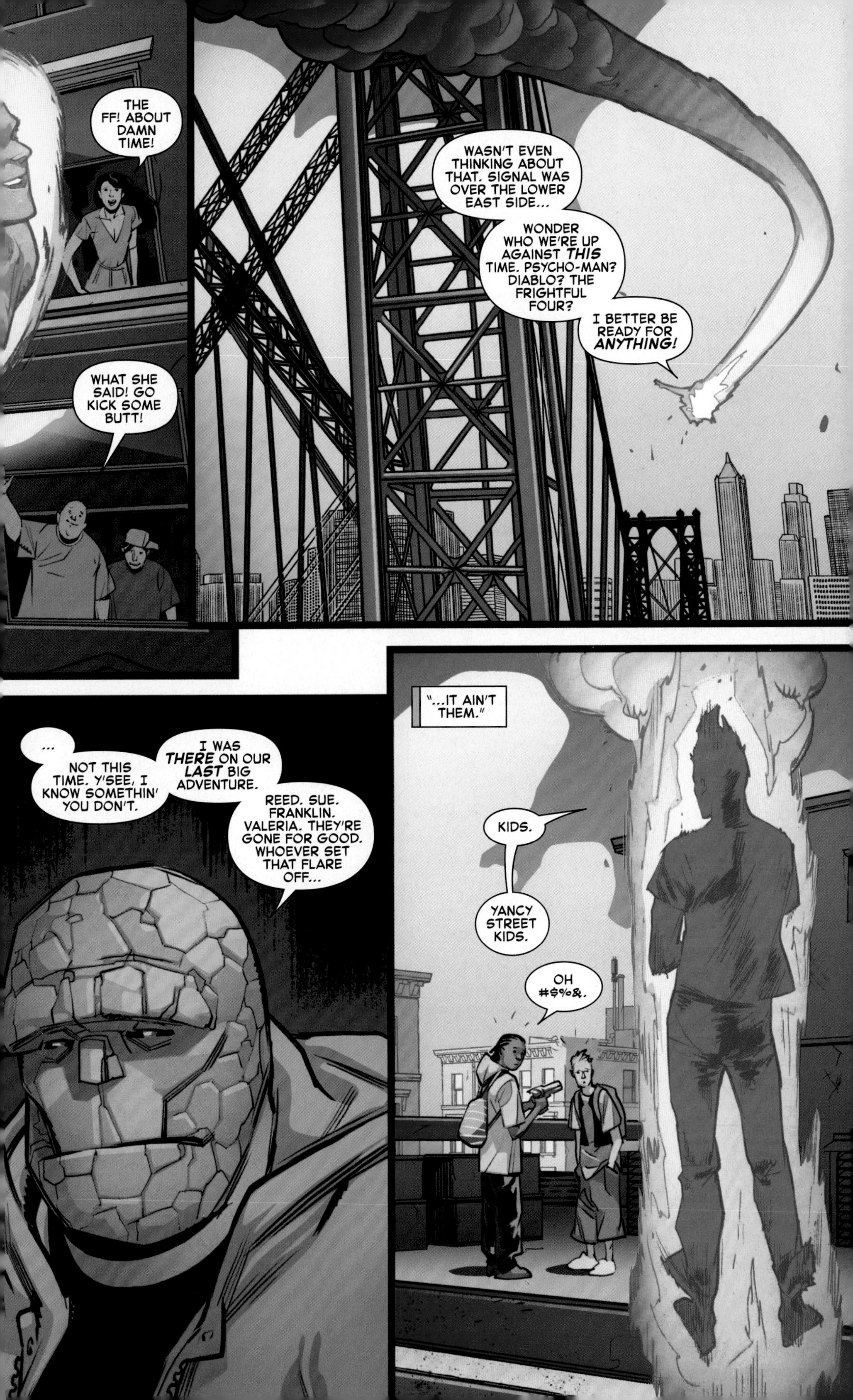
THE FF! ABOUT DAMN TIME!
WHAT SHE SAID! GO KICK SOME BUTT!
WASN'T EVEN THINKING ABOUT THAT. SIGNAL WAS OVER THE LOWER EAST SIDE...
WONDER WHO WE'RE UP AGAINST THIS TIME. PSYCHO-MAN? DIABLO? THE FRIGHTFUL FOUR?
I BETTER BE READY FOR ANYTHING!
...
NOT THIS TIME. Y'SEE, I KNOW SOMETHIN' YOU DON'T.
I WAS THERE ON OUR LAST BIG ADVENTURE.
REED. SUE. FRANKLIN. VALERIA. THEY'RE GONE FOR GOOD. WHOEVER SET THAT FLARE OFF...
"...IT AIN'T THEM."
KIDS.
YANCY STREET KIDS.
OH #$%&.

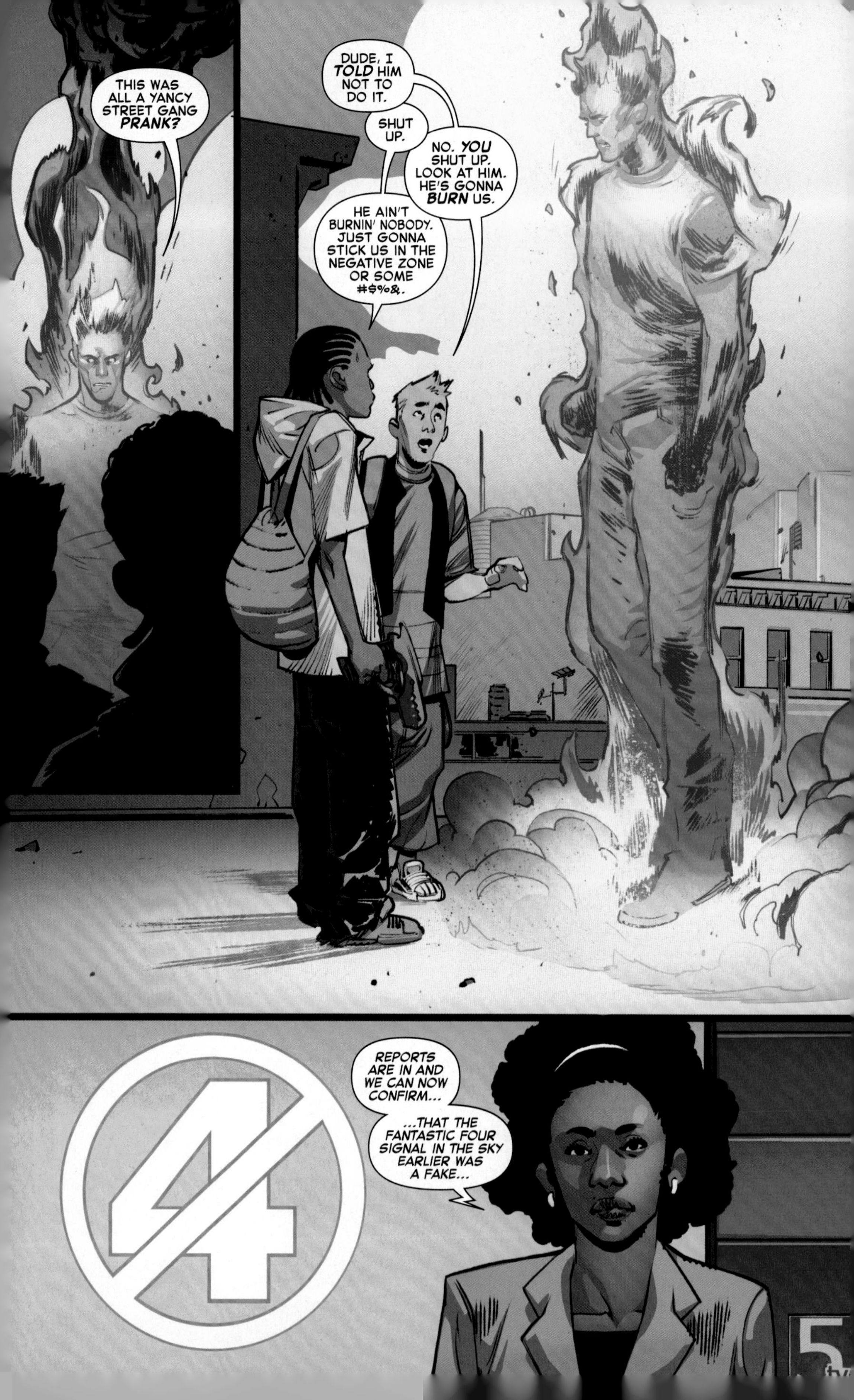
THIS WAS ALL A YANCY STREET GANG PRANK?
DUDE, I TOLD HIM NOT TO DO IT.
SHUT UP.
NO. YOU SHUT UP. LOOK AT HIM. HE'S GONNA BURN US.
HE AIN'T BURNIN' NOBODY. JUST GONNA STICK US IN THE NEGATIVE ZONE OR SOME #$%&.
REPORTS ARE IN AND WE CAN NOW CONFIRM...
...THAT THE FANTASTIC FOUR SIGNAL IN THE SKY EARLIER WAS A FAKE...

FOUR NO MORE

...TURNING TODAY INTO A BITTER REMINDER THAT HALF OF THE WORLD'S GREATEST SUPER HERO TEAM REMAINS MISSING.

THIS COULD NOT COME AT A WORSE TIME...

...AS NEXT WEEK MARKS THE ANNIVERSARY OF THE HISTORIC FLIGHT...

...WHEN REED RICHARDS, SUE STORM, HER BROTHER JOHNNY AND PILOT BEN GRIMM LAUNCHED THEIR ROCKET INTO SPACE...

...WERE BOMBARDED BY STRANGE COSMIC RAYS AND SOON FOUND THEMSELVES TRANSFORMED...

...INTO FOUR OF EARTH'S FINEST CHAMPIONS.

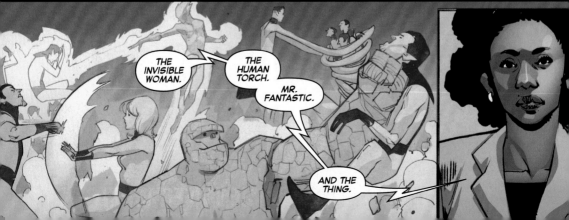

THE INVISIBLE WOMAN.

THE HUMAN TORCH.

MR. FANTASTIC.

AND THE THING.

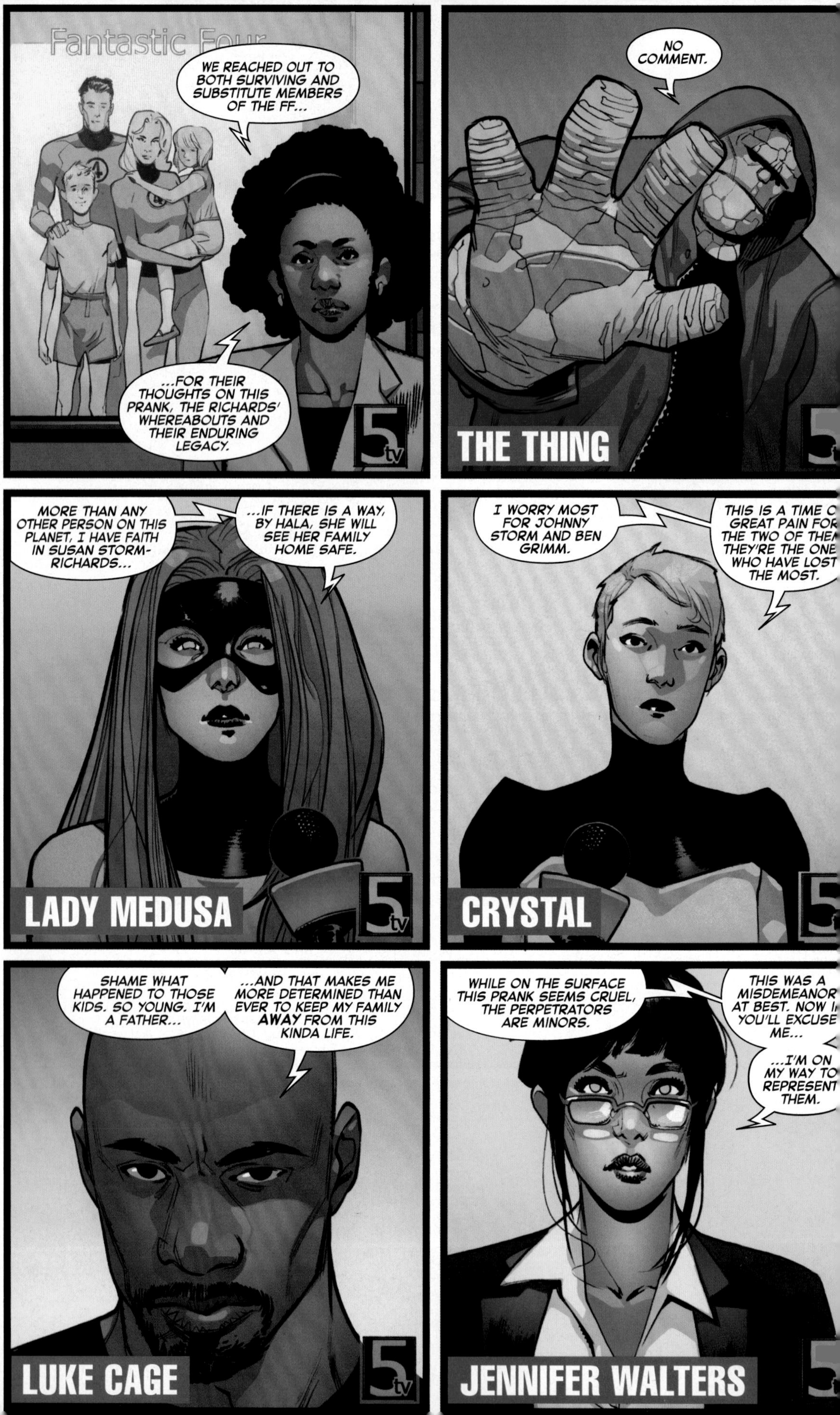

Fantastic Four
WE REACHED OUT TO BOTH SURVIVING AND SUBSTITUTE MEMBERS OF THE FF...
...FOR THEIR THOUGHTS ON THIS PRANK, THE RICHARDS' WHEREABOUTS AND THEIR ENDURING LEGACY.
5tv
NO COMMENT.
THE THING
MORE THAN ANY OTHER PERSON ON THIS PLANET, I HAVE FAITH IN SUSAN STORM-RICHARDS...
...IF THERE IS A WAY, BY HALA, SHE WILL SEE HER FAMILY HOME SAFE.
LADY MEDUSA
5tv
I WORRY MOST FOR JOHNNY STORM AND BEN GRIMM.
THIS IS A TIME O GREAT PAIN FOR THE TWO OF THEM THEY'RE THE ONE WHO HAVE LOST THE MOST.
CRYSTAL
SHAME WHAT HAPPENED TO THOSE KIDS. SO YOUNG. I'M A FATHER...
...AND THAT MAKES ME MORE DETERMINED THAN EVER TO KEEP MY FAMILY AWAY FROM THIS KINDA LIFE.
LUKE CAGE
5tv
WHILE ON THE SURFACE THIS PRANK SEEMS CRUEL, THE PERPETRATORS ARE MINORS.
THIS WAS A MISDEMEANOR AT BEST. NOW I YOU'LL EXCUSE ME...
...I'M ON MY WAY TO REPRESENT THEM.
JENNIFER WALTERS

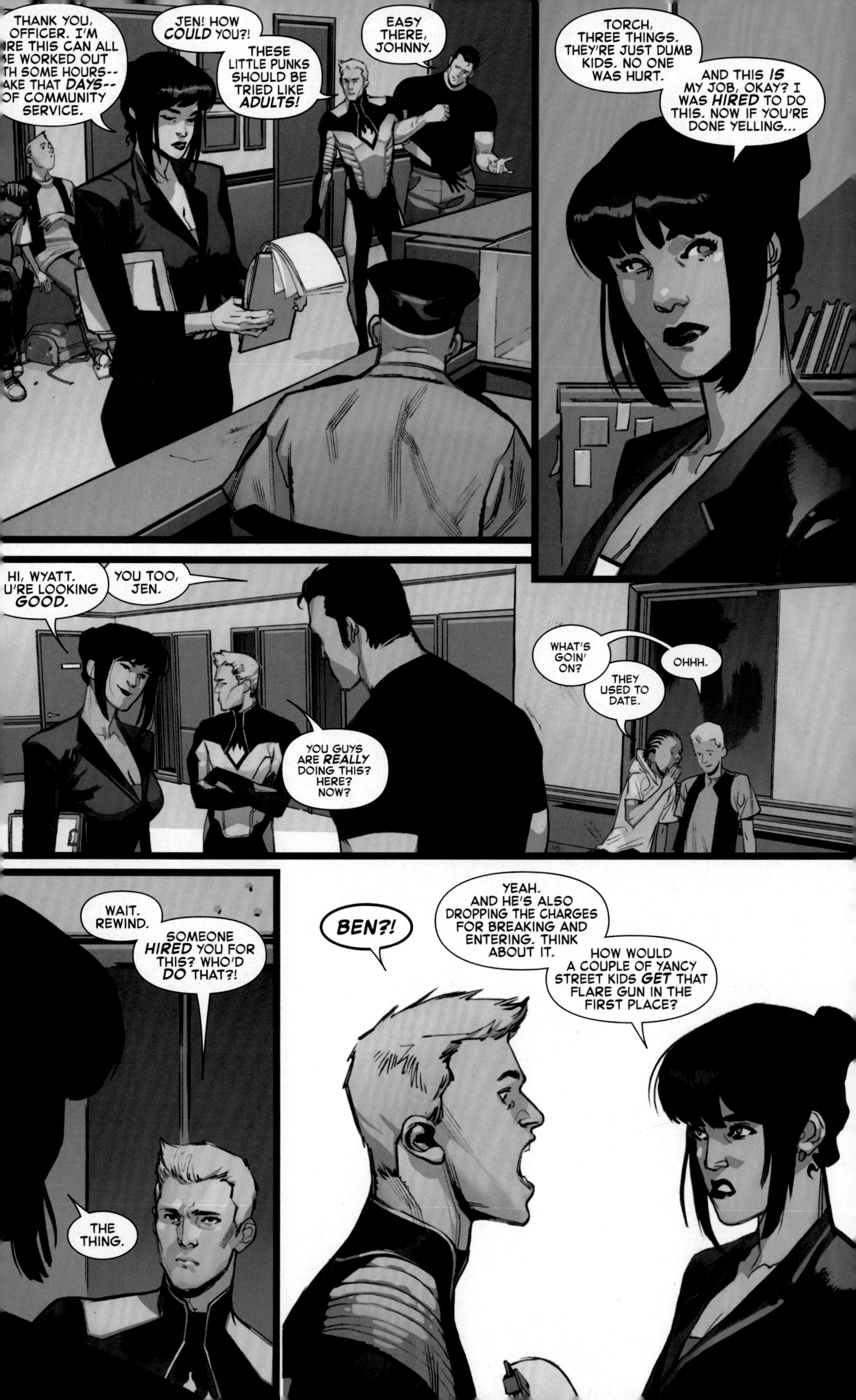
THANK YOU, OFFICER. I'M ...RE THIS CAN ALL ...E WORKED OUT ...TH SOME HOURS-- ...AKE THAT DAYS-- OF COMMUNITY SERVICE.
JEN! HOW COULD YOU?!
THESE LITTLE PUNKS SHOULD BE TRIED LIKE ADULTS!
EASY THERE, JOHNNY.
TORCH, THREE THINGS. THEY'RE JUST DUMB KIDS. NO ONE WAS HURT.
AND THIS IS MY JOB, OKAY? I WAS HIRED TO DO THIS. NOW IF YOU'RE DONE YELLING...
HI, WYATT. ...U'RE LOOKING GOOD.
YOU TOO, JEN.
YOU GUYS ARE REALLY DOING THIS? HERE? NOW?
WHAT'S GOIN' ON?
THEY USED TO DATE.
OHHH.
WAIT. REWIND.
SOMEONE HIRED YOU FOR THIS? WHO'D DO THAT?!
THE THING.
BEN?!
YEAH. AND HE'S ALSO DROPPING THE CHARGES FOR BREAKING AND ENTERING. THINK ABOUT IT.
HOW WOULD A COUPLE OF YANCY STREET KIDS GET THAT FLARE GUN IN THE FIRST PLACE?

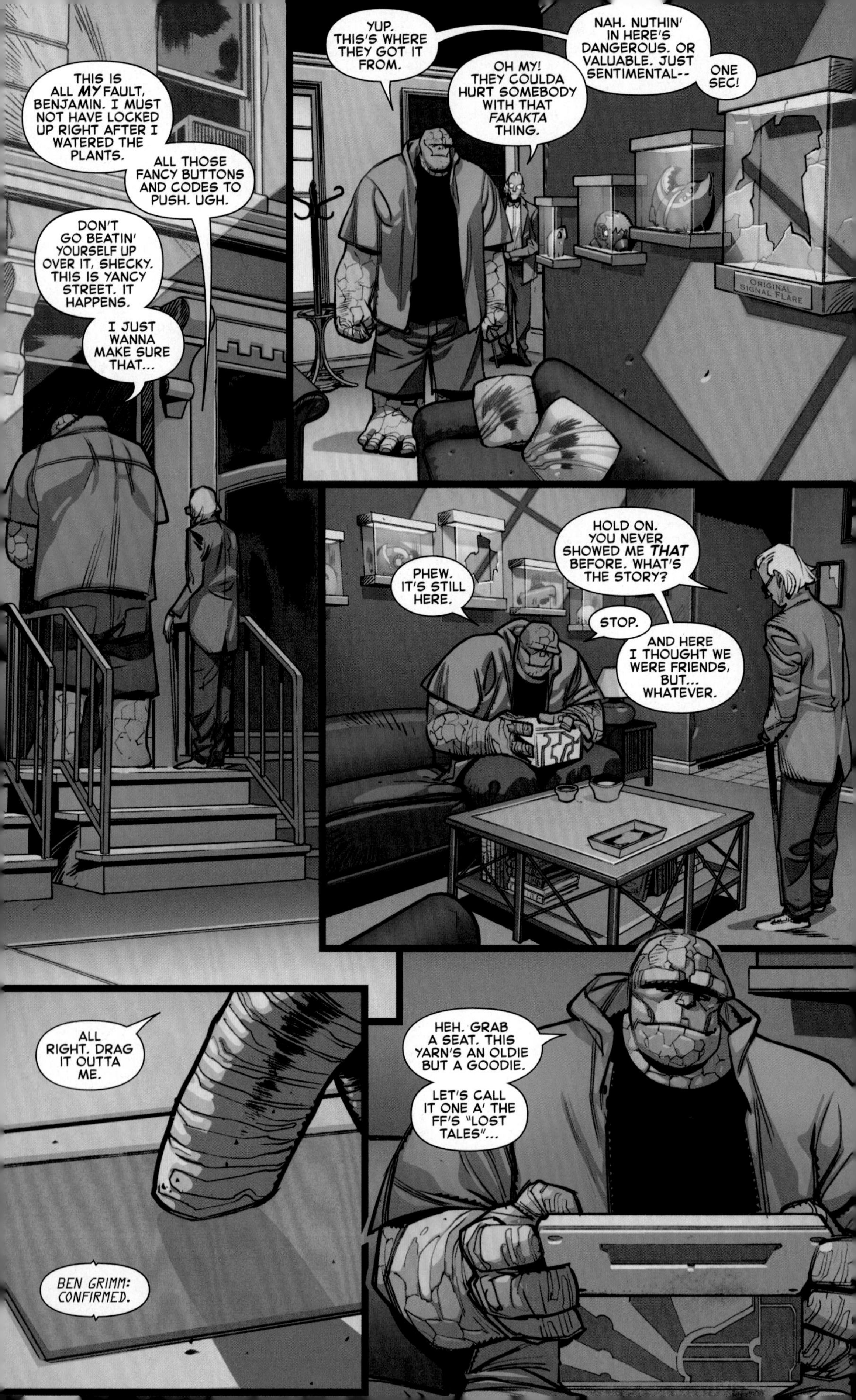
THIS IS ALL *MY* FAULT, BENJAMIN. I MUST NOT HAVE LOCKED UP RIGHT AFTER I WATERED THE PLANTS.
ALL THOSE FANCY BUTTONS AND CODES TO PUSH. UGH.
DON'T GO BEATIN' YOURSELF UP OVER IT, SHECKY. THIS IS YANCY STREET. IT HAPPENS.
I JUST WANNA MAKE SURE THAT...
YUP. THIS'S WHERE THEY GOT IT FROM.
OH MY! THEY COULDA HURT SOMEBODY WITH THAT *FAKAKTA* THING.
NAH. NUTHIN' IN HERE'S DANGEROUS. OR VALUABLE. JUST SENTIMENTAL--
ONE SEC!
ORIGINAL SIGNAL FLARE
PHEW. IT'S STILL HERE.
HOLD ON. YOU NEVER SHOWED ME *THAT* BEFORE. WHAT'S THE STORY?
STOP.
AND HERE I THOUGHT WE WERE FRIENDS, BUT... WHATEVER.
ALL RIGHT. DRAG IT OUTTA ME.
BEN GRIMM: CONFIRMED.
HEH. GRAB A SEAT. THIS YARN'S AN OLDIE BUT A GOODIE.
LET'S CALL IT ONE A' THE FF'S "LOST TALES"...

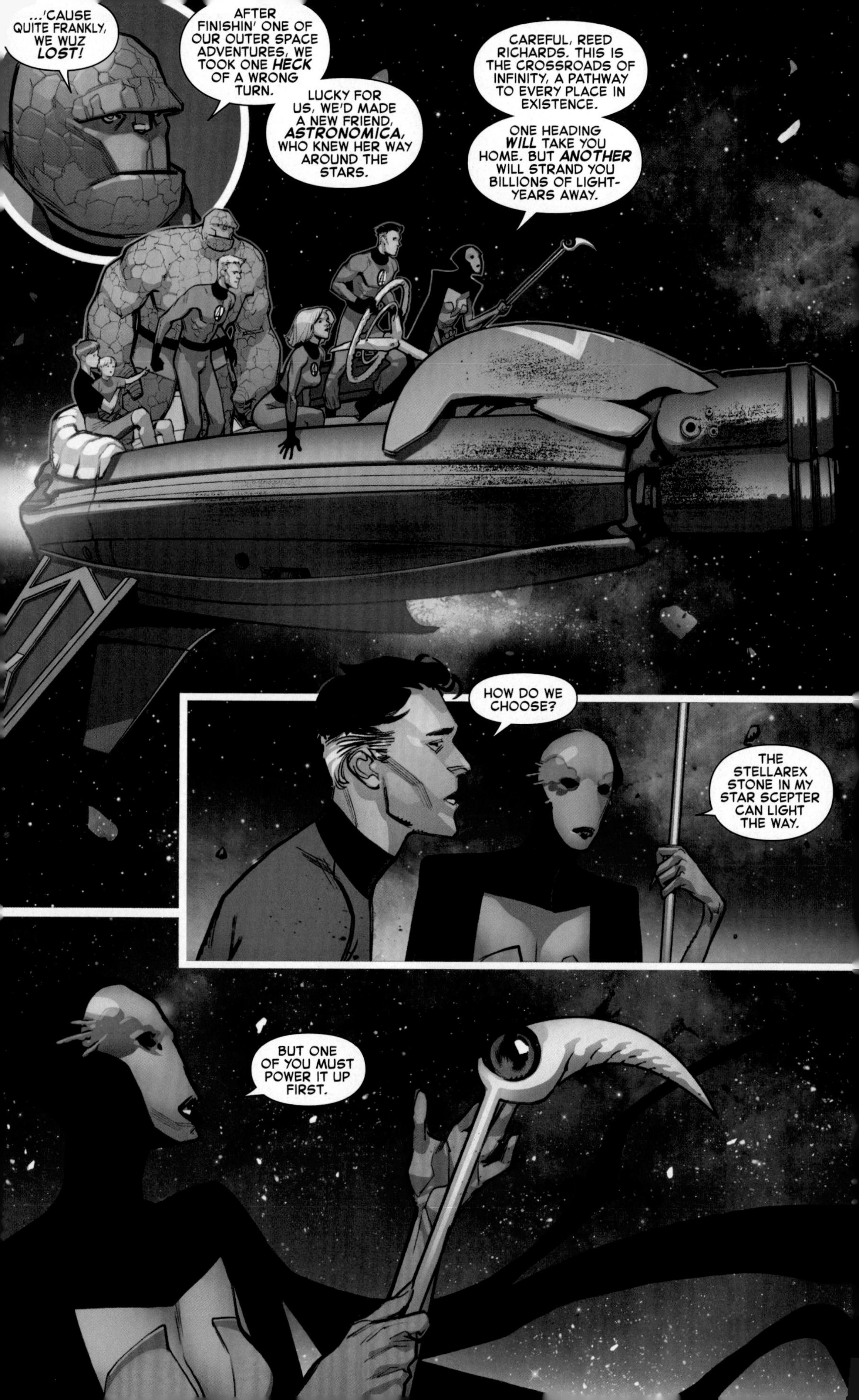
...'CAUSE QUITE FRANKLY, WE WUZ LOST!
AFTER FINISHIN' ONE OF OUR OUTER SPACE ADVENTURES, WE TOOK ONE HECK OF A WRONG TURN.
LUCKY FOR US, WE'D MADE A NEW FRIEND, ASTRONOMICA, WHO KNEW HER WAY AROUND THE STARS.
CAREFUL, REED RICHARDS. THIS IS THE CROSSROADS OF INFINITY, A PATHWAY TO EVERY PLACE IN EXISTENCE.
ONE HEADING WILL TAKE YOU HOME. BUT ANOTHER WILL STRAND YOU BILLIONS OF LIGHT-YEARS AWAY.
HOW DO WE CHOOSE?
THE STELLAREX STONE IN MY STAR SCEPTER CAN LIGHT THE WAY.
BUT ONE OF YOU MUST POWER IT UP FIRST.

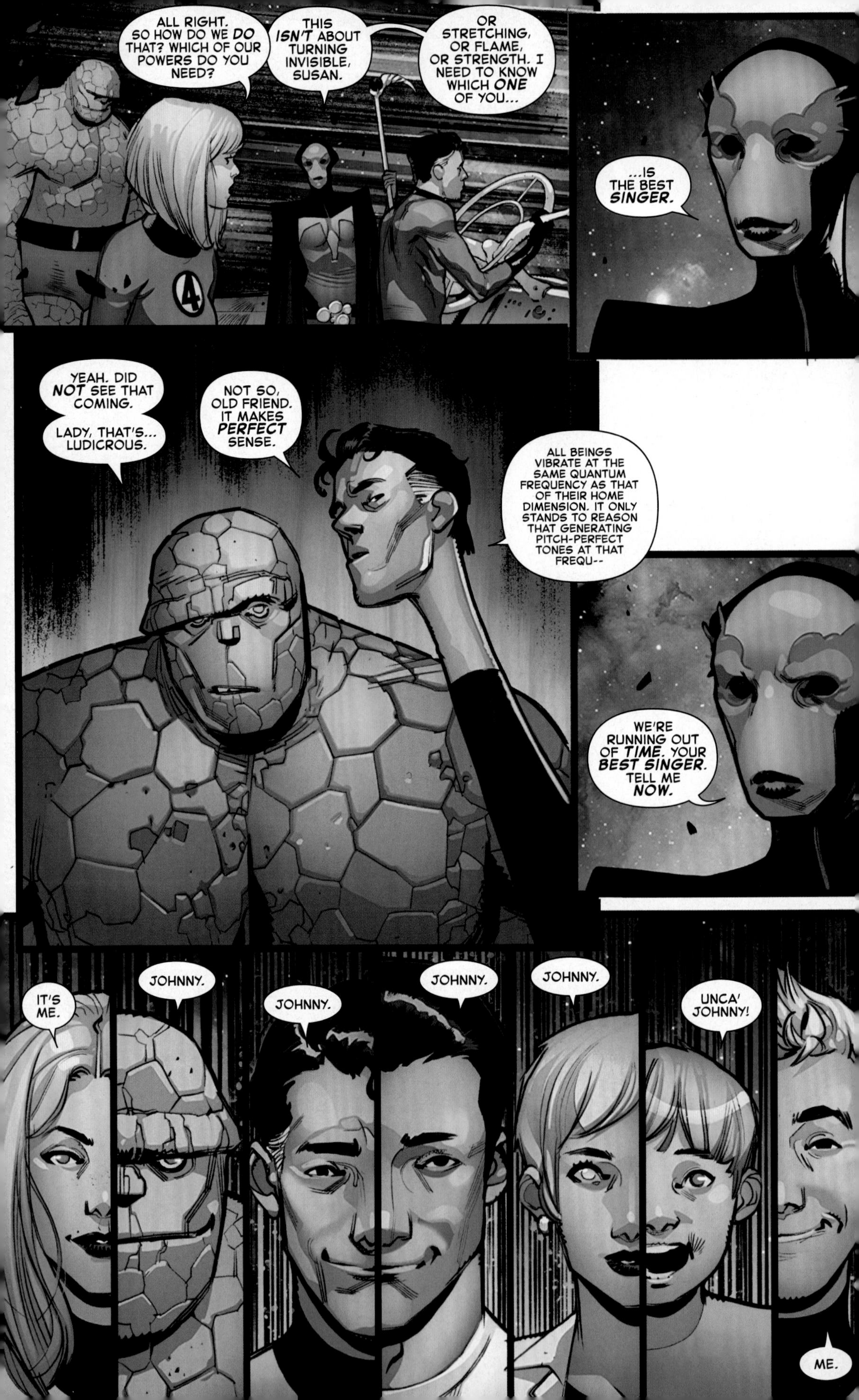

ALL RIGHT. SO HOW DO WE DO THAT? WHICH OF OUR POWERS DO YOU NEED?
THIS ISN'T ABOUT TURNING INVISIBLE, SUSAN.
OR STRETCHING, OR FLAME, OR STRENGTH. I NEED TO KNOW WHICH ONE OF YOU...
...IS THE BEST SINGER.
YEAH. DID NOT SEE THAT COMING.
LADY, THAT'S... LUDICROUS.
NOT SO, OLD FRIEND. IT MAKES PERFECT SENSE.
ALL BEINGS VIBRATE AT THE SAME QUANTUM FREQUENCY AS THAT OF THEIR HOME DIMENSION. IT ONLY STANDS TO REASON THAT GENERATING PITCH-PERFECT TONES AT THAT FREQU--
WE'RE RUNNING OUT OF TIME. YOUR BEST SINGER. TELL ME NOW.
IT'S ME.
JOHNNY.
JOHNNY.
JOHNNY.
JOHNNY.
UNCA' JOHNNY!
ME.

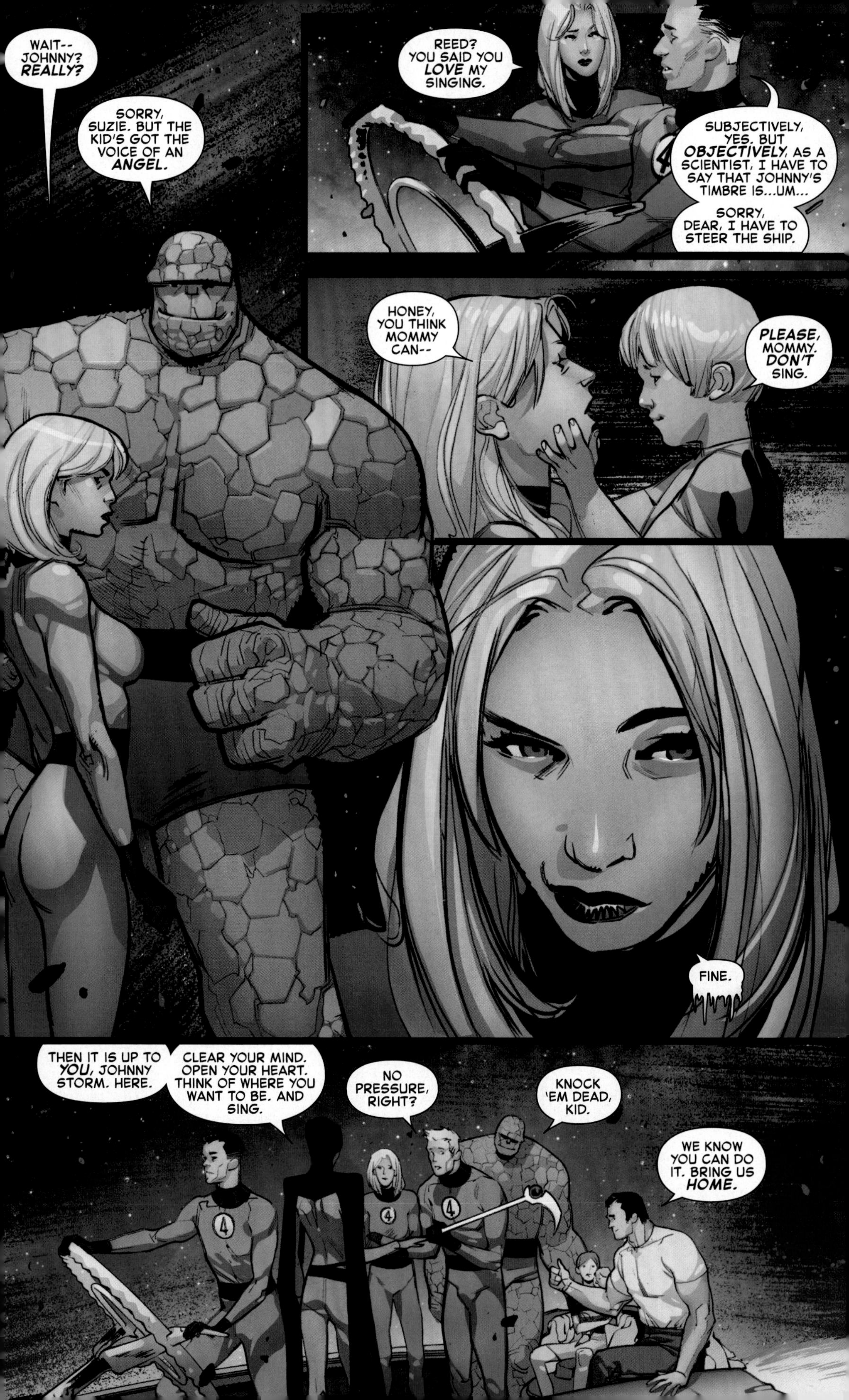
WAIT-- JOHNNY? REALLY?
SORRY, SUZIE. BUT THE KID'S GOT THE VOICE OF AN ANGEL.
REED? YOU SAID YOU LOVE MY SINGING.
SUBJECTIVELY, YES. BUT OBJECTIVELY, AS A SCIENTIST, I HAVE TO SAY THAT JOHNNY'S TIMBRE IS...UM...
SORRY, DEAR, I HAVE TO STEER THE SHIP.
HONEY, YOU THINK MOMMY CAN--
PLEASE, MOMMY. DON'T SING.
FINE.
THEN IT IS UP TO YOU, JOHNNY STORM. HERE.
CLEAR YOUR MIND. OPEN YOUR HEART. THINK OF WHERE YOU WANT TO BE. AND SING.
NO PRESSURE, RIGHT?
KNOCK 'EM DEAD, KID.
WE KNOW YOU CAN DO IT. BRING US HOME.

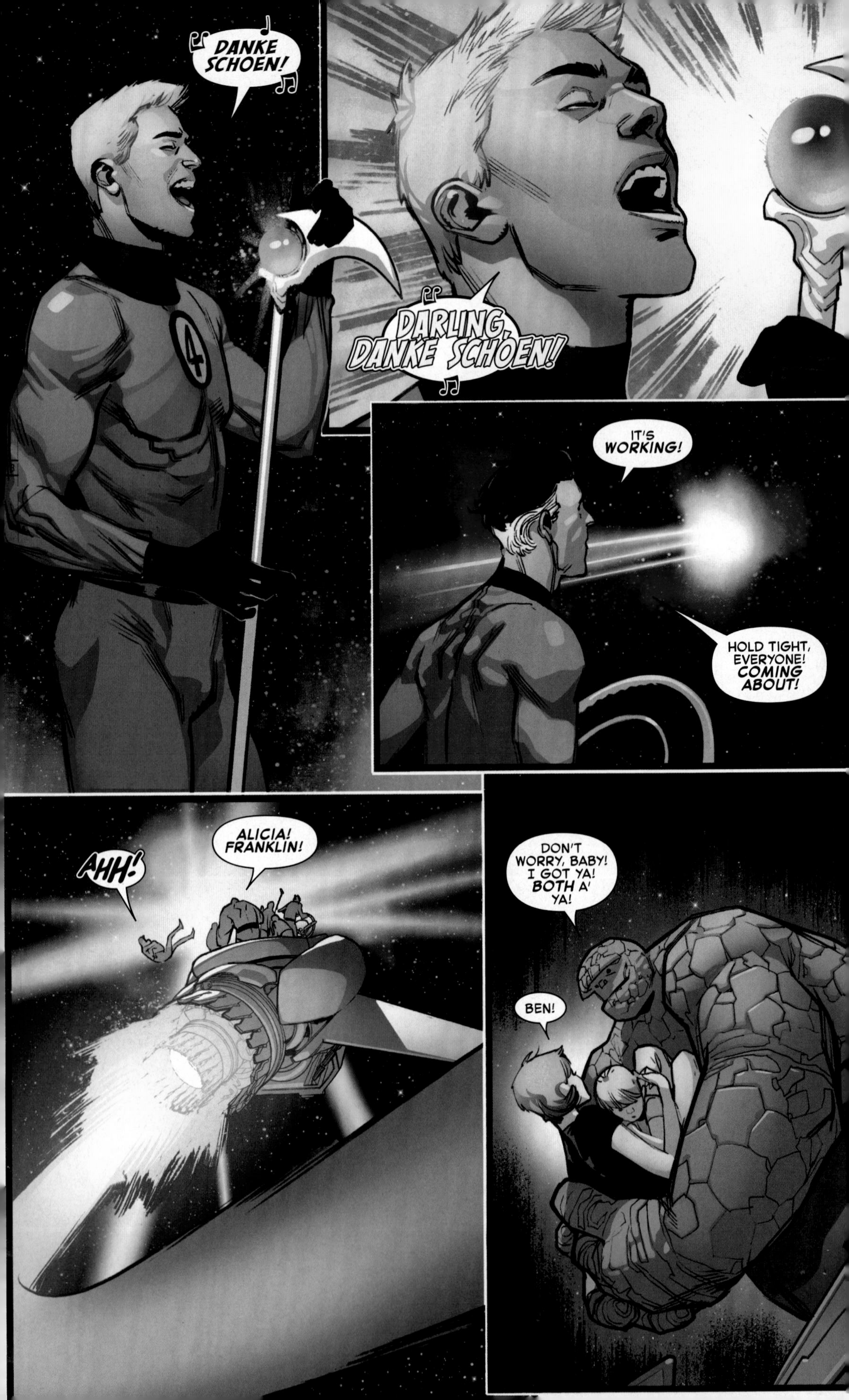
DANKE SCHOEN!
DARLING, DANKE SCHOEN!
IT'S WORKING!
HOLD TIGHT, EVERYONE! COMING ABOUT!
AHH!
ALICIA! FRANKLIN!
DON'T WORRY, BABY! I GOT YA! BOTH A' YA!
BEN!

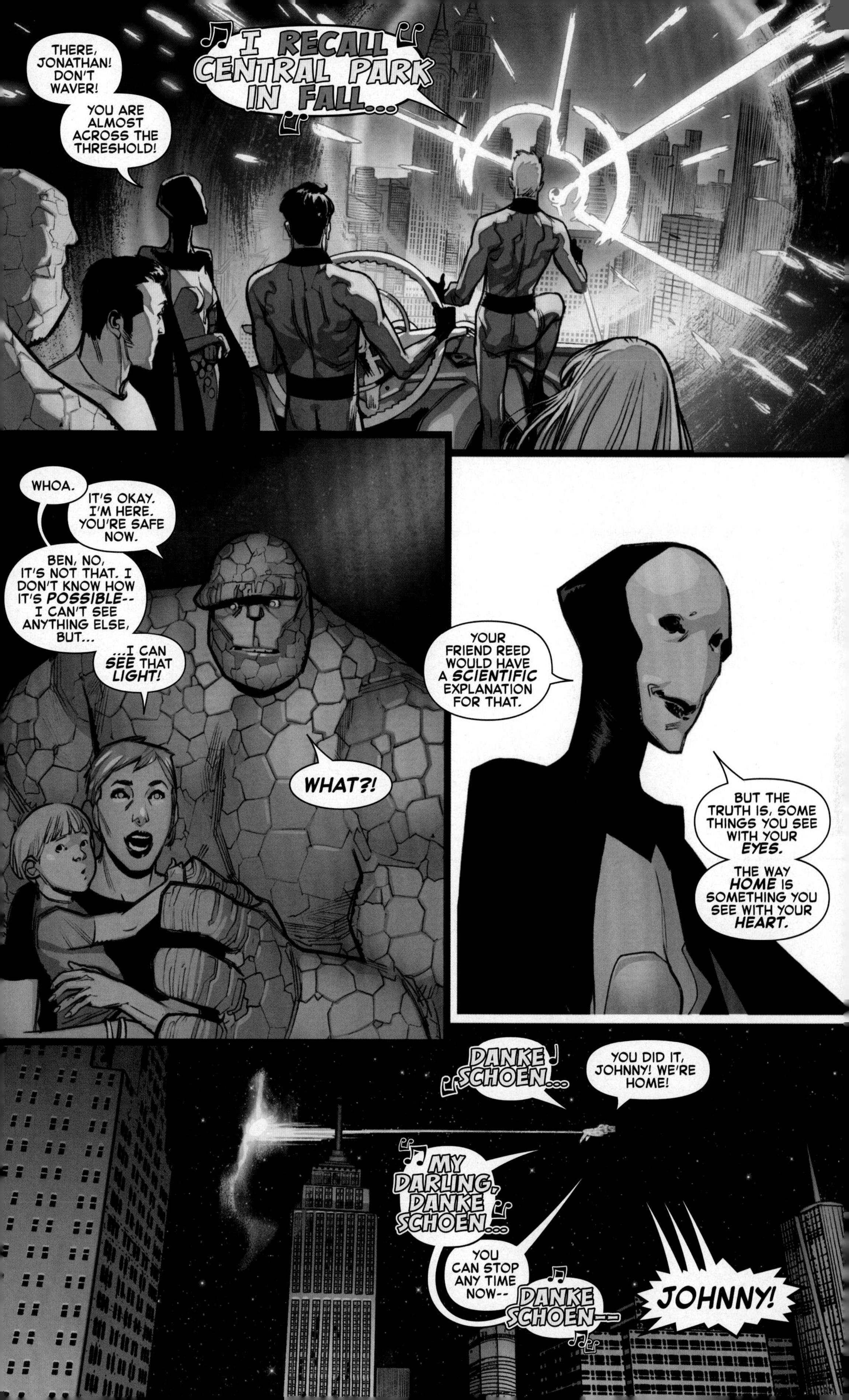
THERE, JONATHAN! DON'T WAVER!
YOU ARE ALMOST ACROSS THE THRESHOLD!
I RECALL CENTRAL PARK IN FALL...
WHOA.
IT'S OKAY. I'M HERE. YOU'RE SAFE NOW.
BEN, NO, IT'S NOT THAT. I DON'T KNOW HOW IT'S POSSIBLE-- I CAN'T SEE ANYTHING ELSE, BUT...
...I CAN SEE THAT LIGHT!
WHAT?!
YOUR FRIEND REED WOULD HAVE A SCIENTIFIC EXPLANATION FOR THAT.
BUT THE TRUTH IS, SOME THINGS YOU SEE WITH YOUR EYES.
THE WAY HOME IS SOMETHING YOU SEE WITH YOUR HEART.
DANKE SCHOEN...
YOU DID IT, JOHNNY! WE'RE HOME!
MY DARLING, DANKE SCHOEN...
YOU CAN STOP ANY TIME NOW--
DANKE SCHOEN--
JOHNNY!

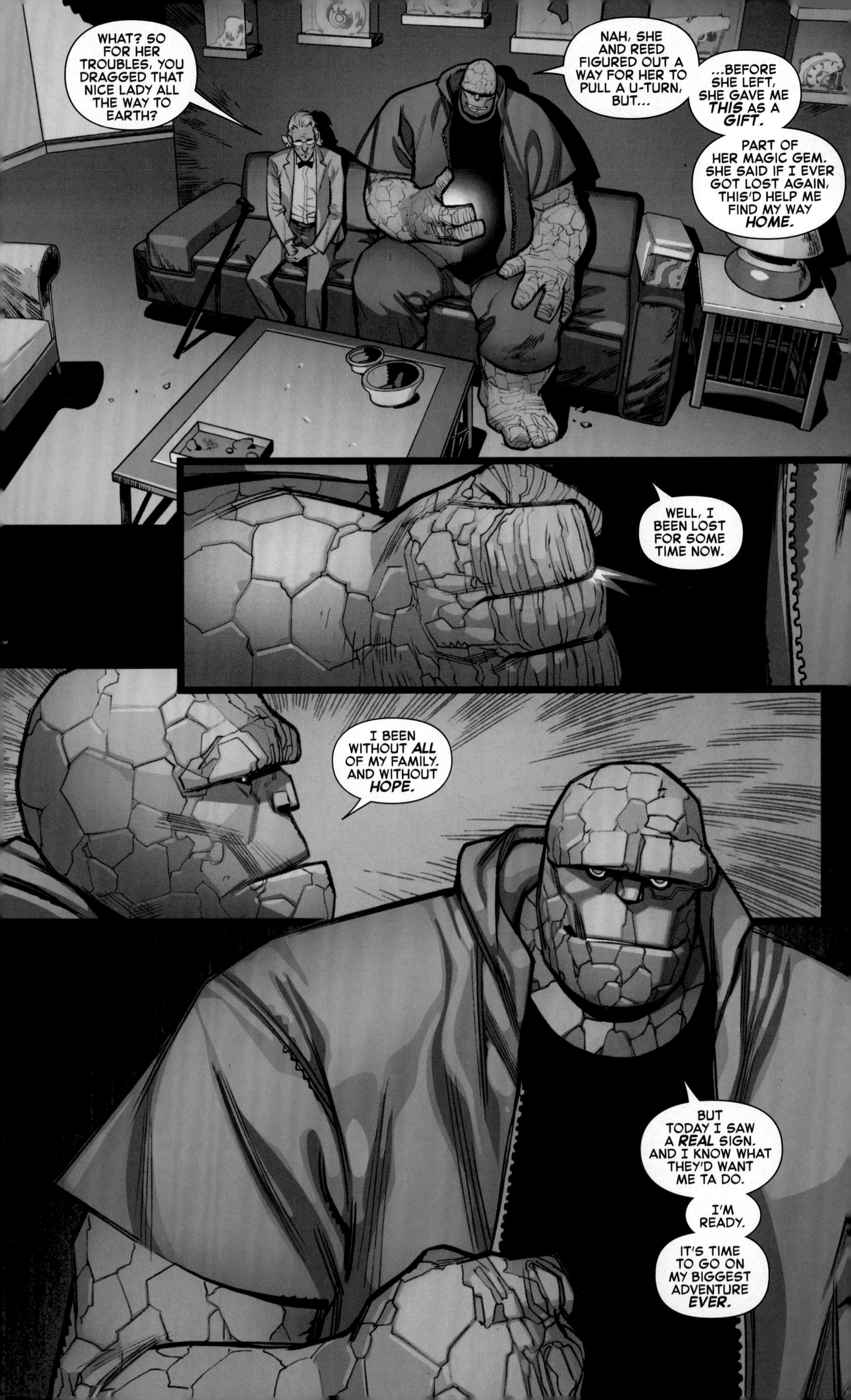
WHAT? SO FOR HER TROUBLES, YOU DRAGGED THAT NICE LADY ALL THE WAY TO EARTH?
NAH, SHE AND REED FIGURED OUT A WAY FOR HER TO PULL A U-TURN, BUT...
...BEFORE SHE LEFT, SHE GAVE ME *THIS* AS A *GIFT.*
PART OF HER MAGIC GEM. SHE SAID IF I EVER GOT LOST AGAIN, THIS'D HELP ME FIND MY WAY *HOME.*
WELL, I BEEN LOST FOR SOME TIME NOW.
I BEEN WITHOUT *ALL* OF MY FAMILY. AND WITHOUT *HOPE.*
BUT TODAY I SAW A *REAL* SIGN. AND I KNOW WHAT THEY'D WANT ME TA DO.
I'M READY.
IT'S TIME TO GO ON MY BIGGEST ADVENTURE *EVER.*

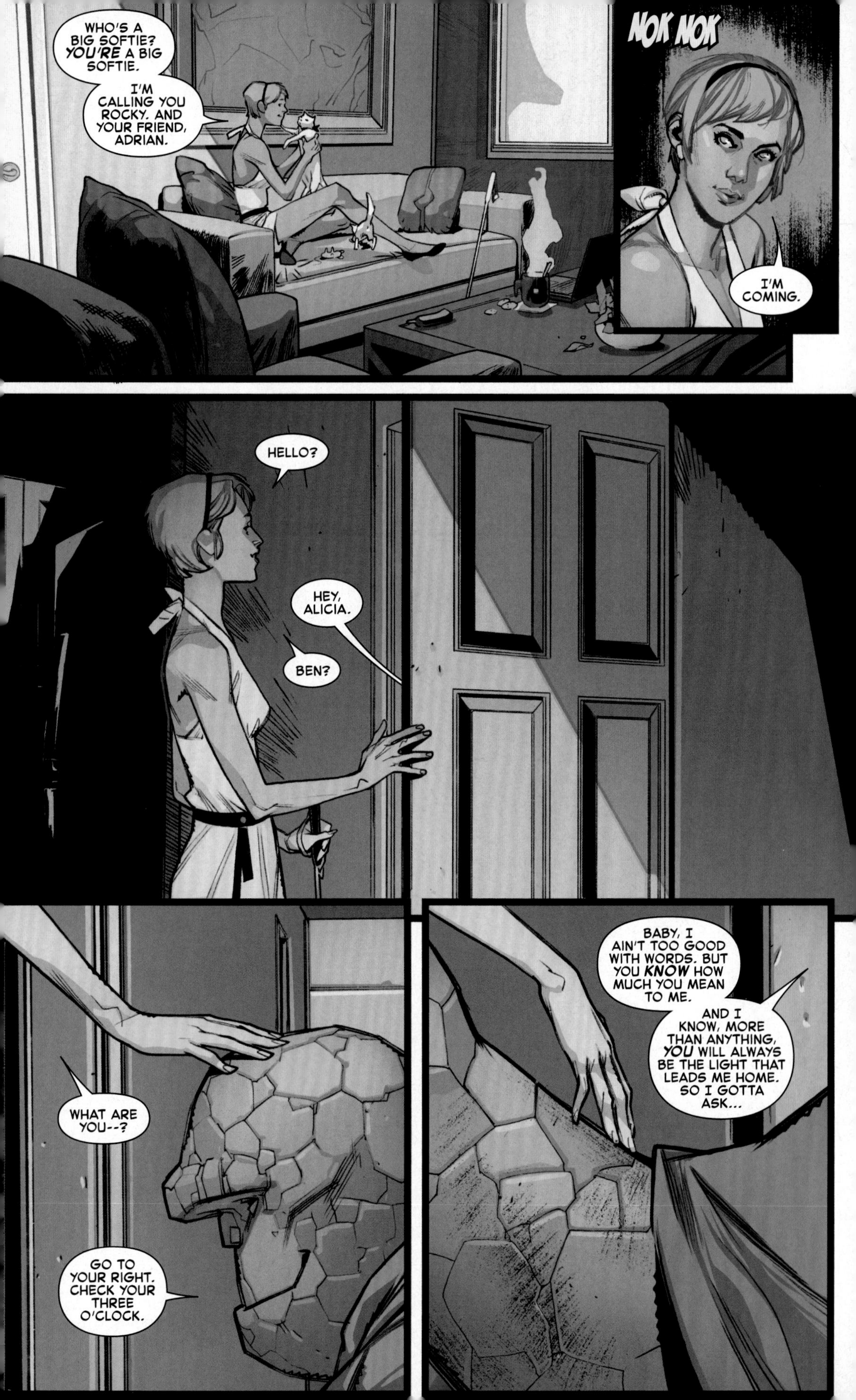
WHO'S A BIG SOFTIE? *YOU'RE* A BIG SOFTIE.
I'M CALLING YOU ROCKY. AND YOUR FRIEND, ADRIAN.
NOK NOK
I'M COMING.
HELLO?
HEY, ALICIA.
BEN?
WHAT ARE YOU--?
GO TO YOUR RIGHT. CHECK YOUR THREE O'CLOCK.
BABY, I AIN'T TOO GOOD WITH WORDS. BUT YOU *KNOW* HOW MUCH YOU MEAN TO ME.
AND I KNOW, MORE THAN ANYTHING, *YOU* WILL ALWAYS BE THE LIGHT THAT LEADS ME HOME. SO I GOTTA ASK...

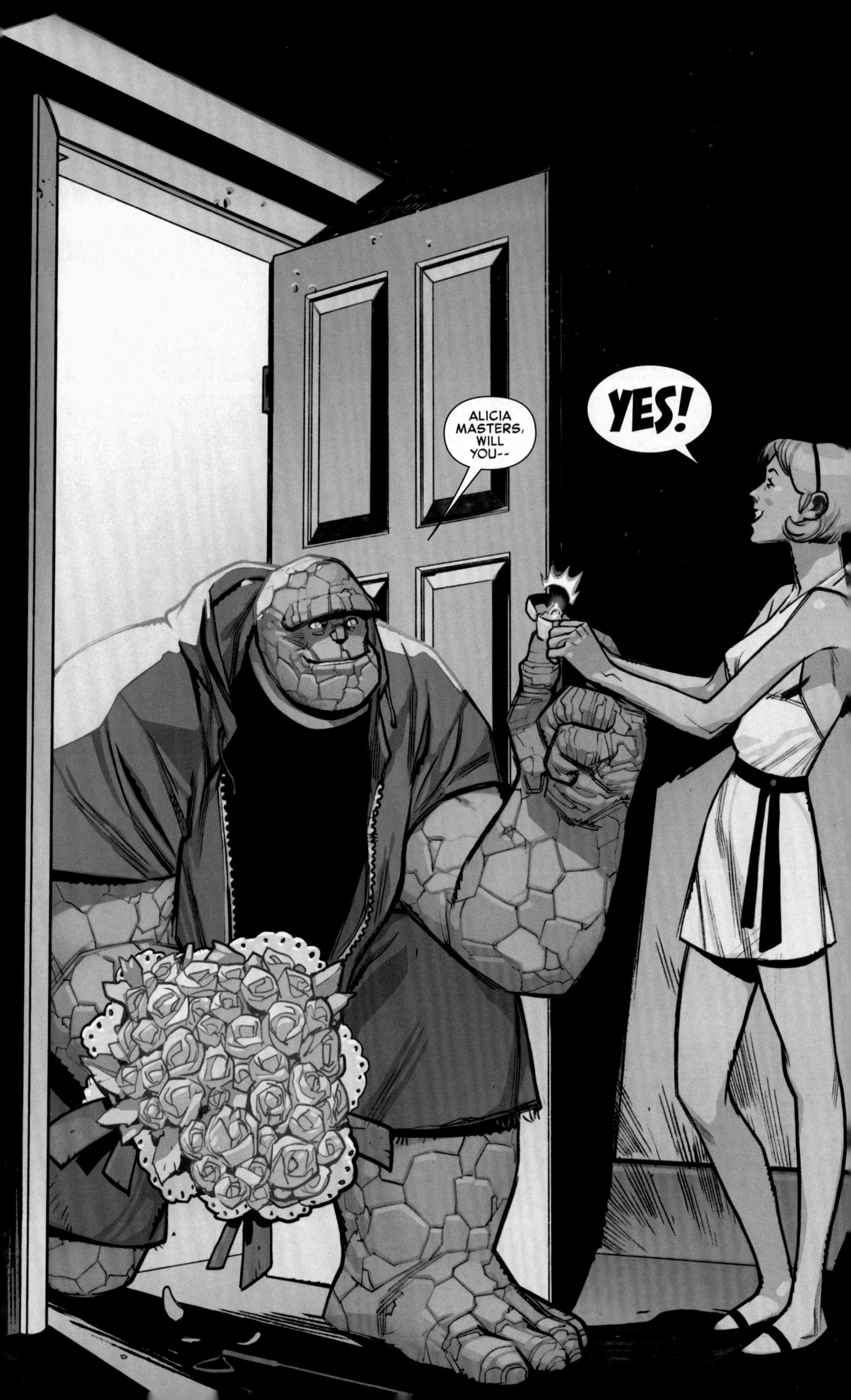
ALICIA MASTERS, WILL YOU--
YES!

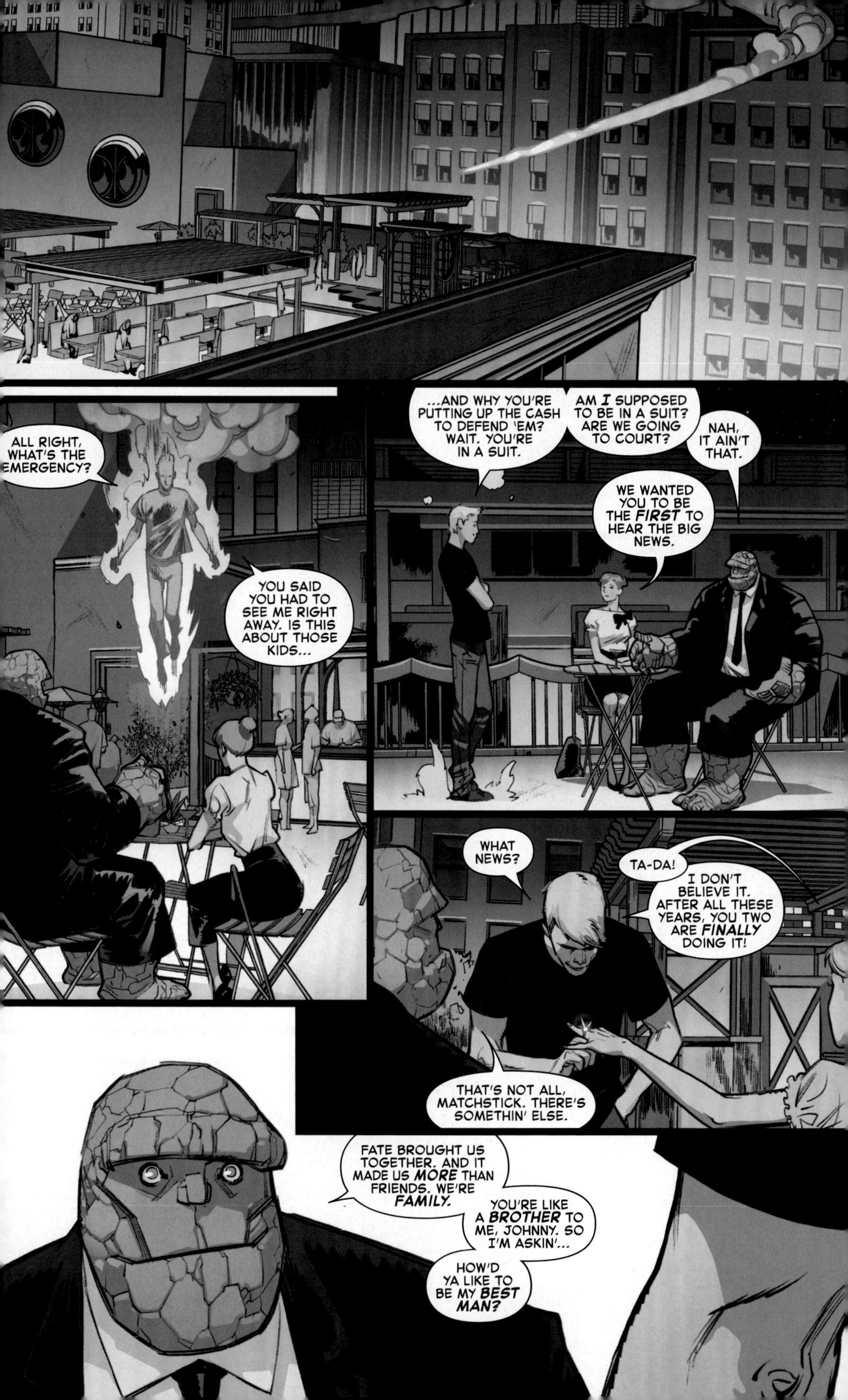
ALL RIGHT, WHAT'S THE EMERGENCY?
YOU SAID YOU HAD TO SEE ME RIGHT AWAY. IS THIS ABOUT THOSE KIDS...
...AND WHY YOU'RE PUTTING UP THE CASH TO DEFEND 'EM? WAIT. YOU'RE IN A SUIT.
AM *I* SUPPOSED TO BE IN A SUIT? ARE WE GOING TO COURT?
NAH, IT AIN'T THAT.
WE WANTED YOU TO BE THE *FIRST* TO HEAR THE BIG NEWS.
WHAT NEWS?
TA-DA!
I DON'T BELIEVE IT. AFTER ALL THESE YEARS, YOU TWO ARE *FINALLY* DOING IT!
THAT'S NOT ALL, MATCHSTICK. THERE'S SOMETHIN' ELSE.
FATE BROUGHT US TOGETHER. AND IT MADE US *MORE* THAN FRIENDS. WE'RE *FAMILY.*
YOU'RE LIKE A *BROTHER* TO ME, JOHNNY. SO I'M ASKIN'...
HOW'D YA LIKE TO BE MY *BEST MAN?*

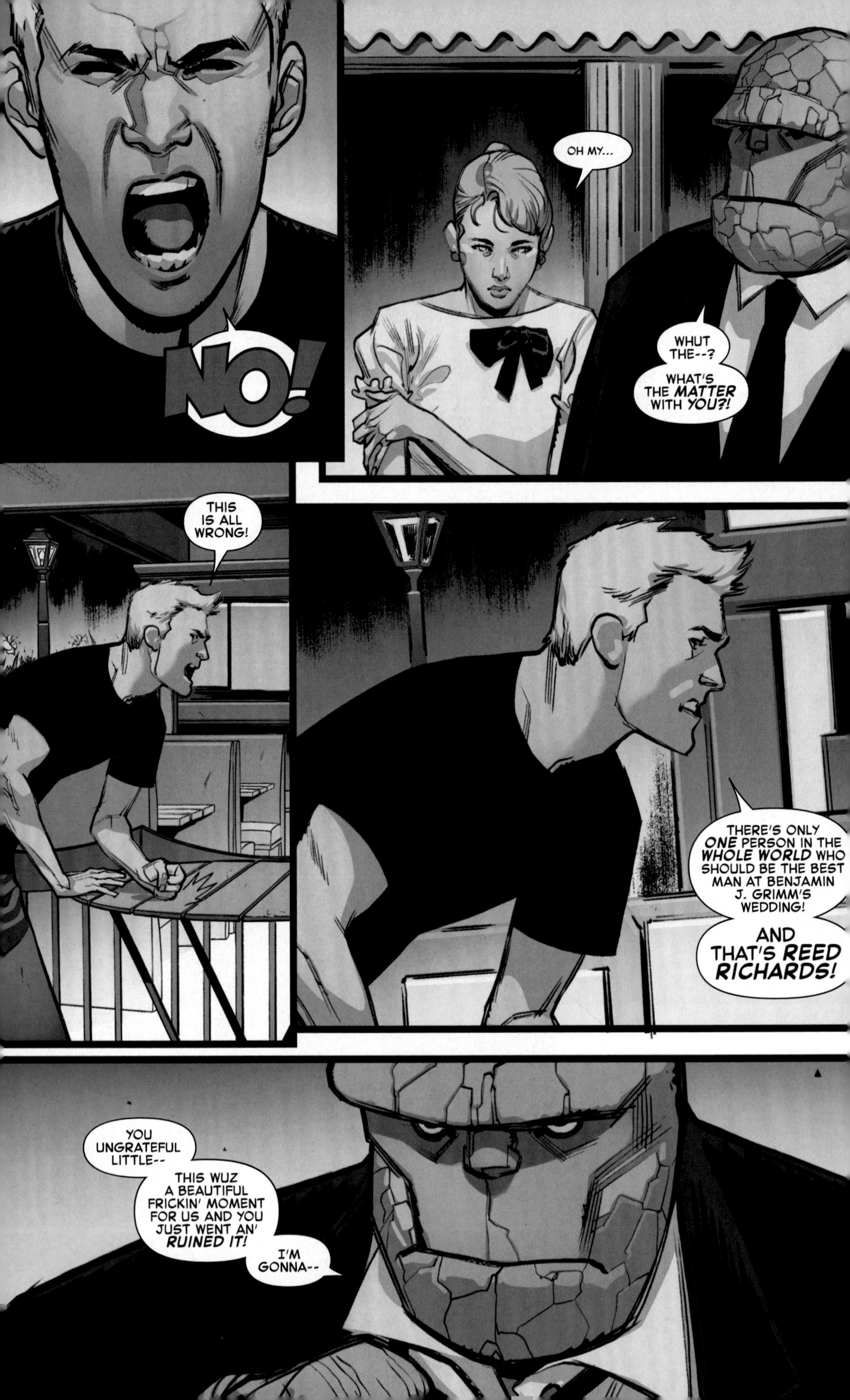
NO!
OH MY...
WHUT THE--?
WHAT'S THE MATTER WITH YOU?!
THIS IS ALL WRONG!
THERE'S ONLY ONE PERSON IN THE WHOLE WORLD WHO SHOULD BE THE BEST MAN AT BENJAMIN J. GRIMM'S WEDDING!
AND THAT'S REED RICHARDS!
YOU UNGRATEFUL LITTLE--
THIS WUZ A BEAUTIFUL FRICKIN' MOMENT FOR US AND YOU JUST WENT AN' RUINED IT!
I'M GONNA--

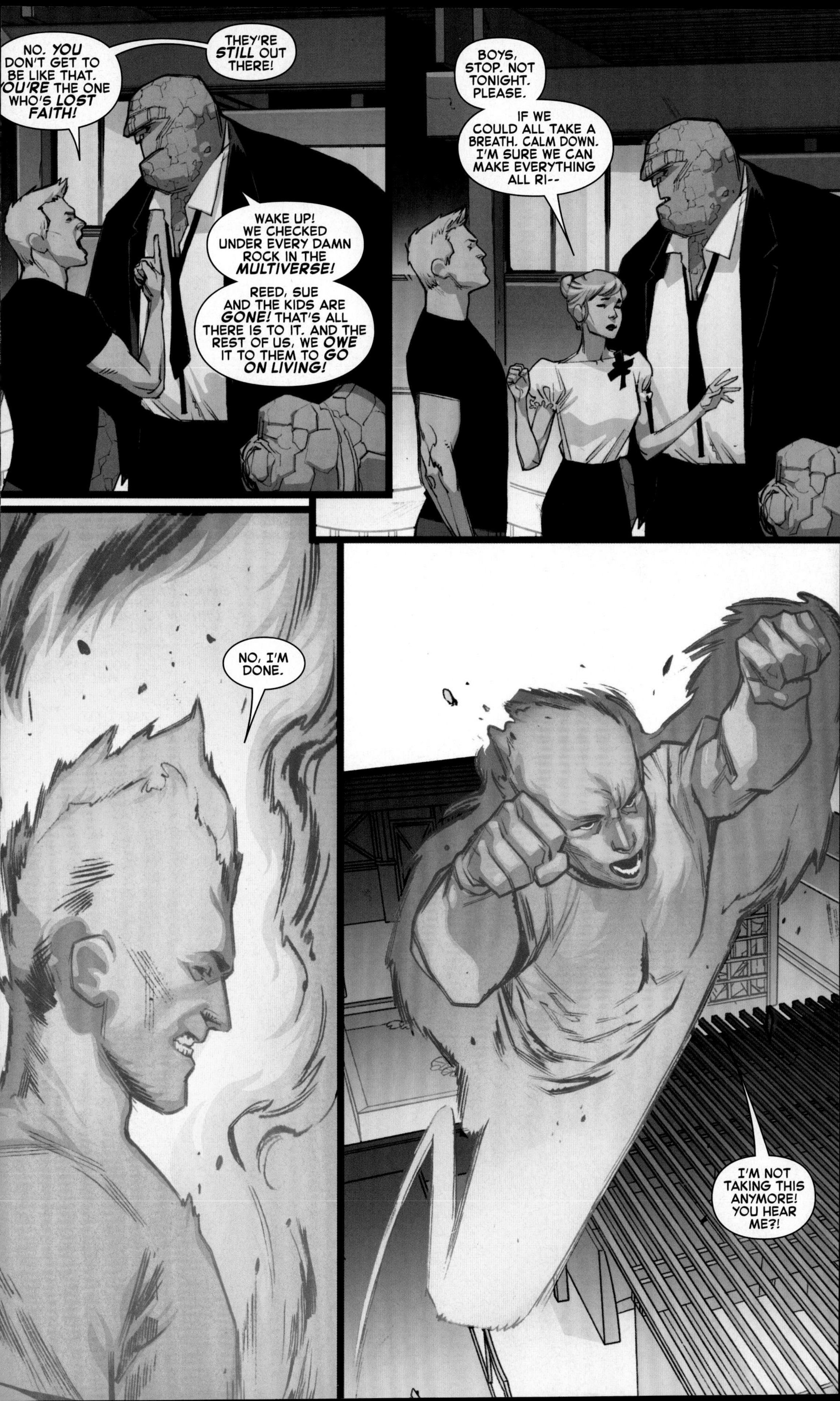

THEY'RE *STILL* OUT THERE!
NO. *YOU* DON'T GET TO BE LIKE THAT. *YOU'RE* THE ONE WHO'S *LOST FAITH!*
WAKE UP! WE CHECKED UNDER EVERY DAMN ROCK IN THE *MULTIVERSE!*
REED, SUE AND THE KIDS ARE *GONE!* THAT'S ALL THERE IS TO IT. AND THE REST OF US, WE *OWE* IT TO THEM TO *GO ON LIVING!*
BOYS, STOP. NOT TONIGHT. PLEASE.
IF WE COULD ALL TAKE A BREATH. CALM DOWN. I'M SURE WE CAN MAKE EVERYTHING ALL RI--
NO, I'M DONE.
I'M NOT TAKING THIS ANYMORE! YOU HEAR ME?!

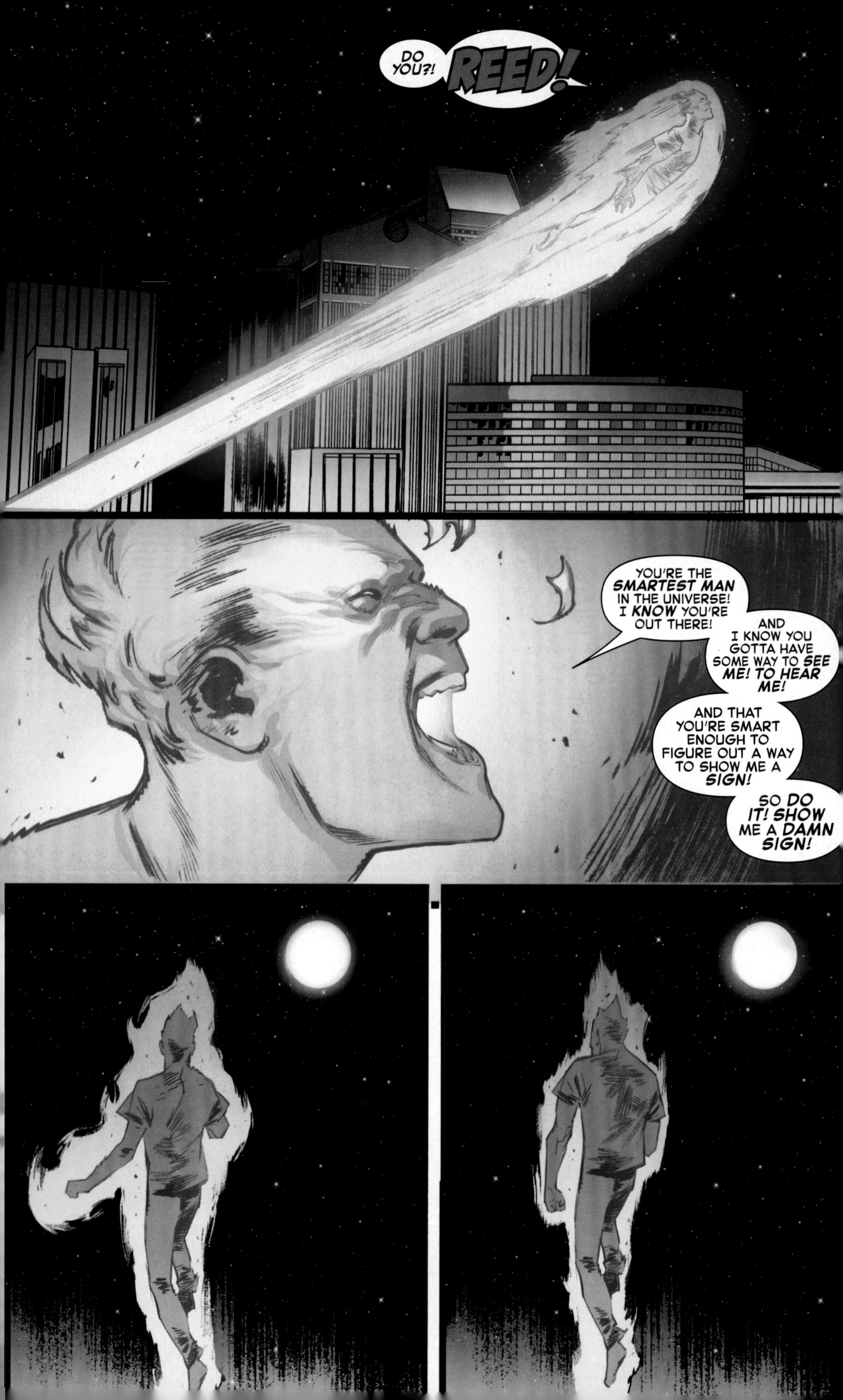
DO YOU?!
REED!
YOU'RE THE SMARTEST MAN IN THE UNIVERSE! I KNOW YOU'RE OUT THERE!
AND I KNOW YOU GOTTA HAVE SOME WAY TO SEE ME! TO HEAR ME!
AND THAT YOU'RE SMART ENOUGH TO FIGURE OUT A WAY TO SHOW ME A SIGN!
SO DO IT! SHOW ME A DAMN SIGN!

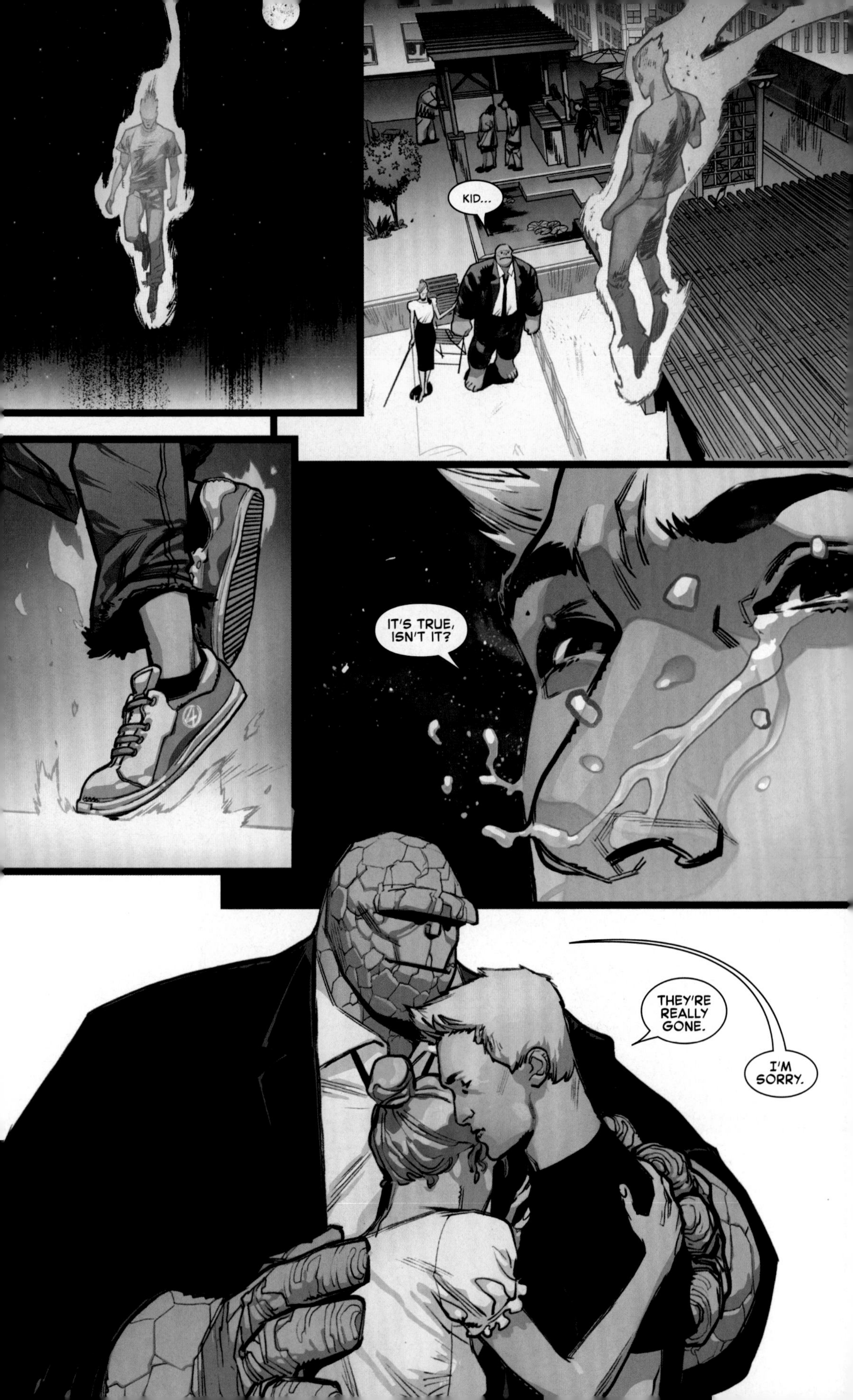
KID...
IT'S TRUE, ISN'T IT?
THEY'RE REALLY GONE.
I'M SORRY.

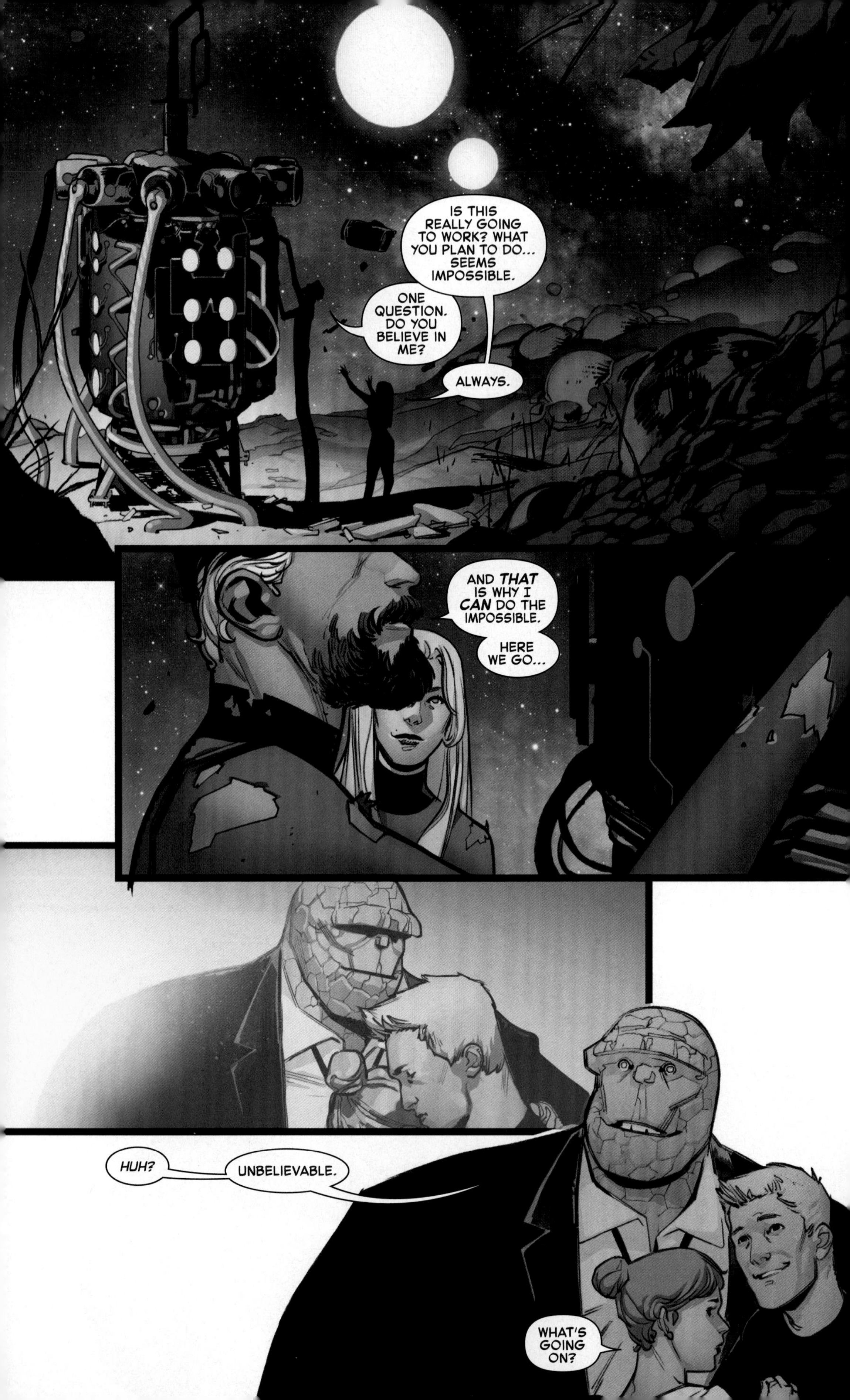
IS THIS REALLY GOING TO WORK? WHAT YOU PLAN TO DO... SEEMS IMPOSSIBLE.
ONE QUESTION. DO YOU BELIEVE IN ME?
ALWAYS.
AND THAT IS WHY I CAN DO THE IMPOSSIBLE.
HERE WE GO...
HUH?
UNBELIEVABLE.
WHAT'S GOING ON?

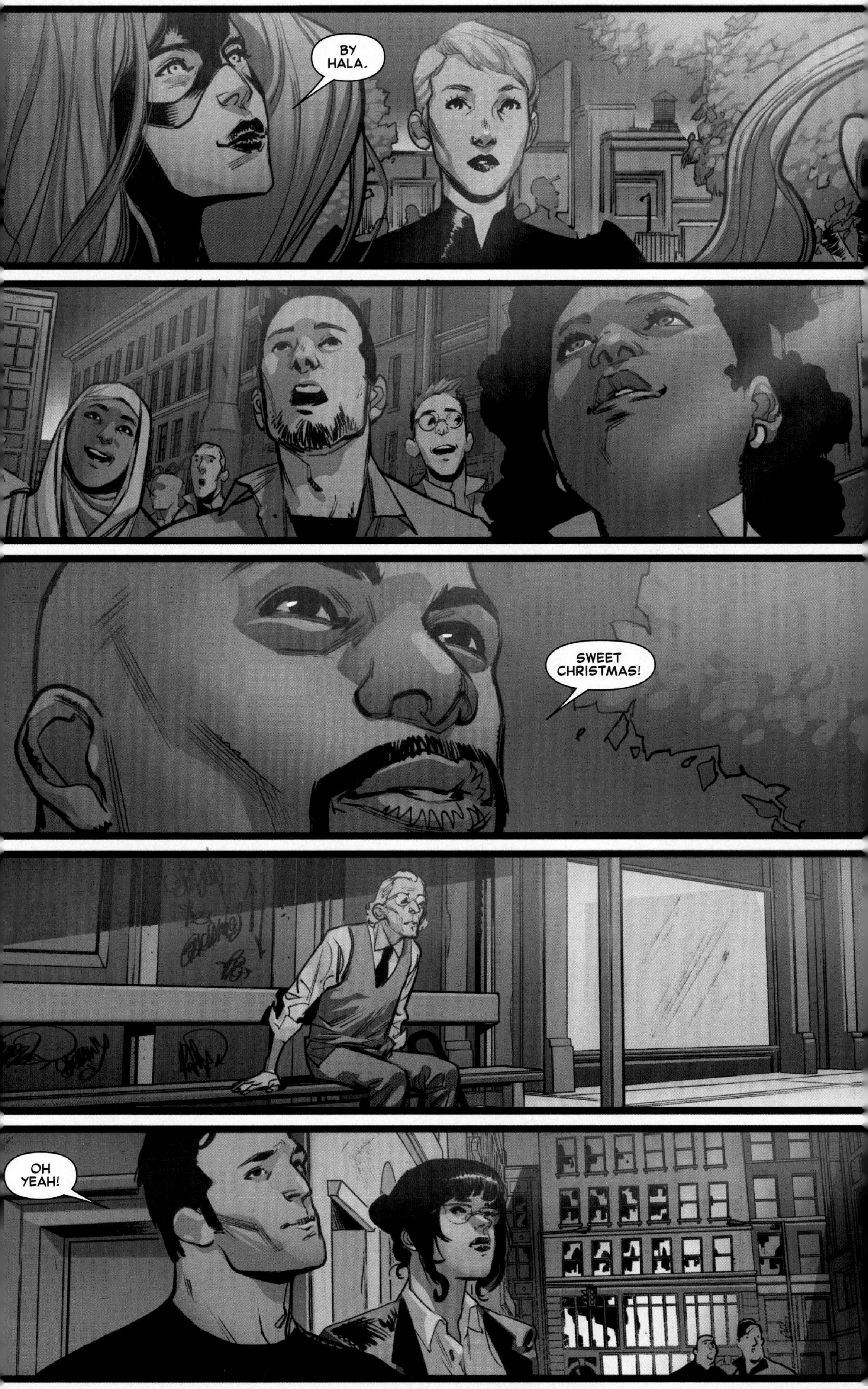
BY HALA.
SWEET CHRISTMAS!
OH YEAH!

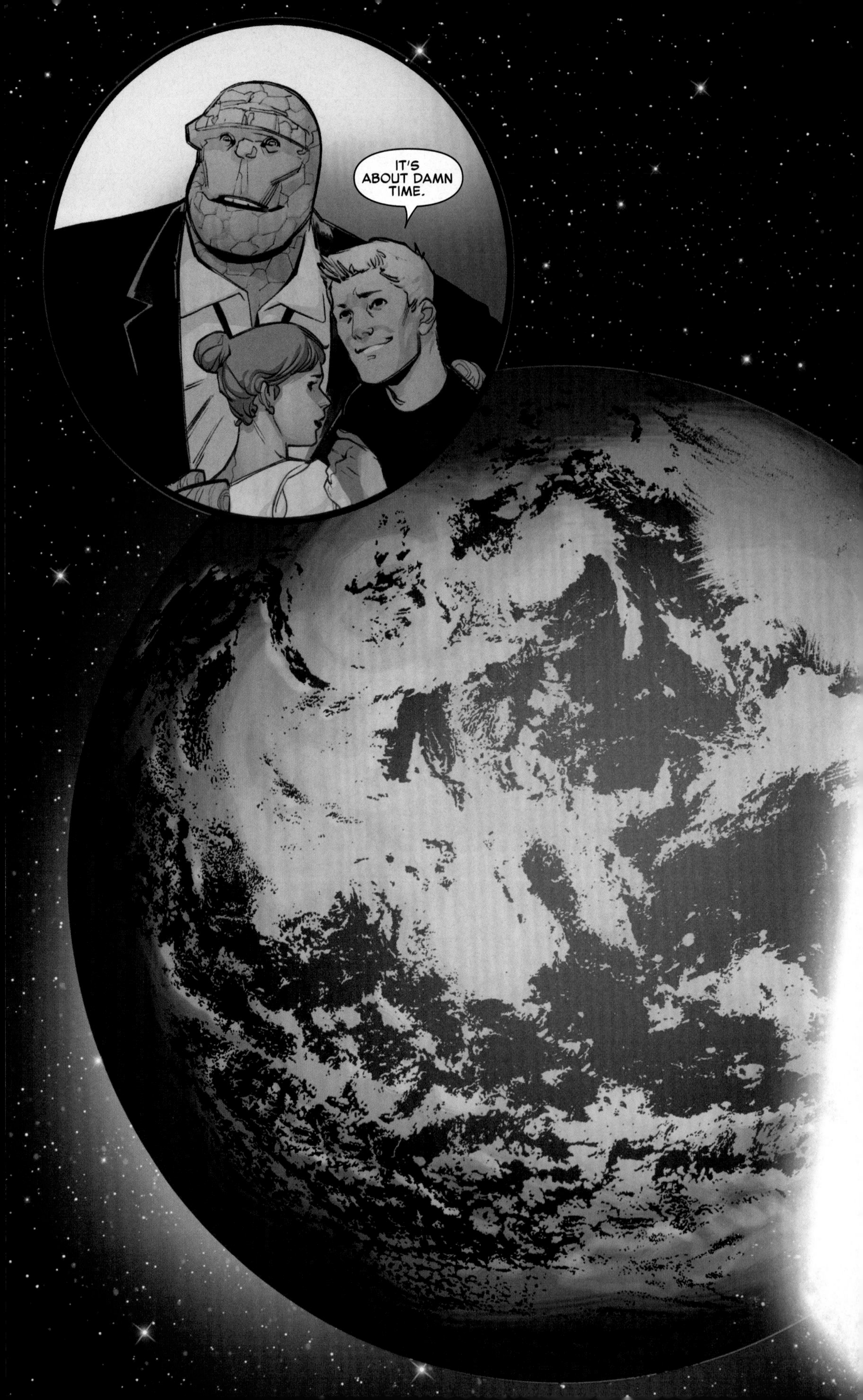
IT'S ABOUT DAMN TIME.

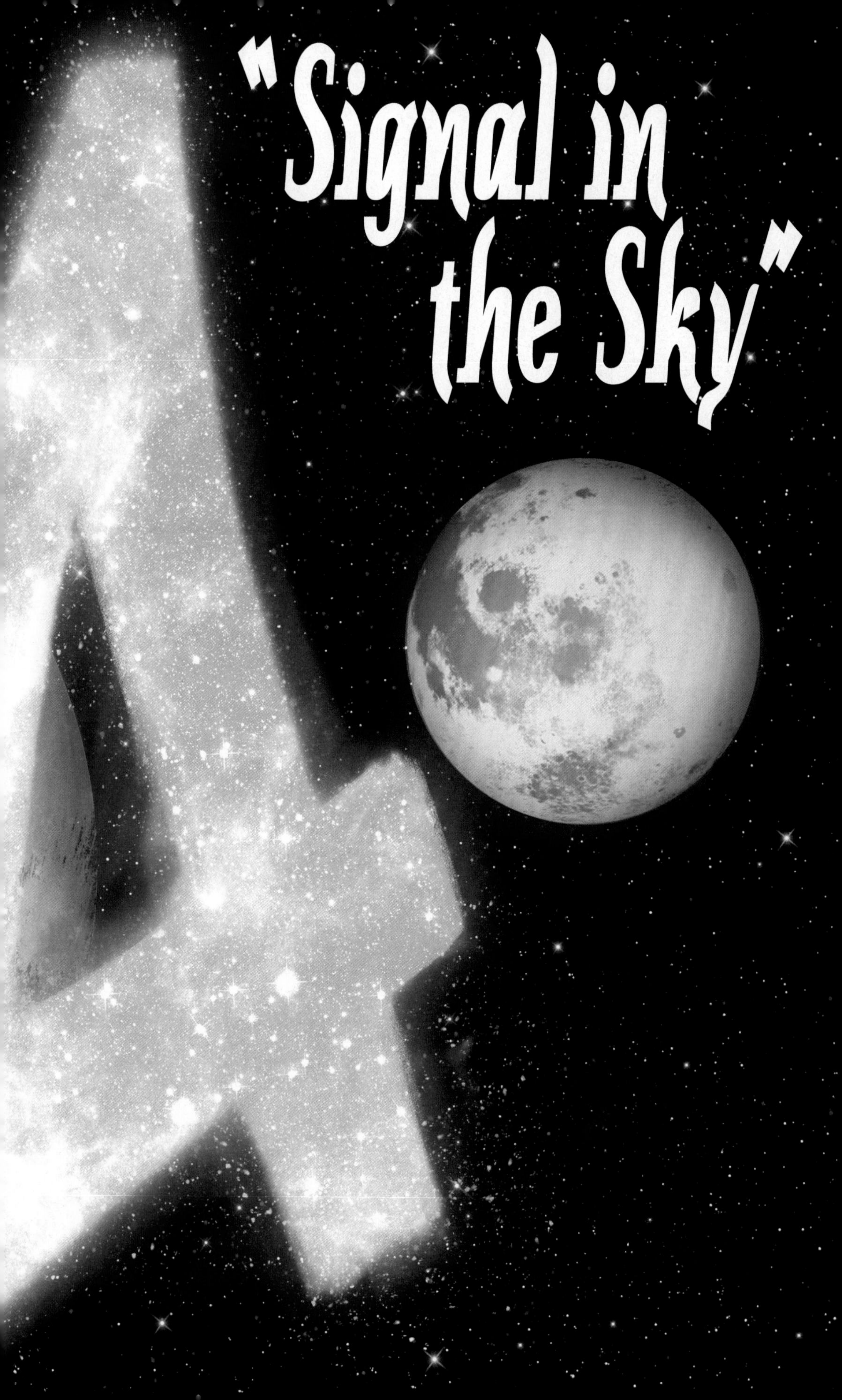
"Signal in the Sky"

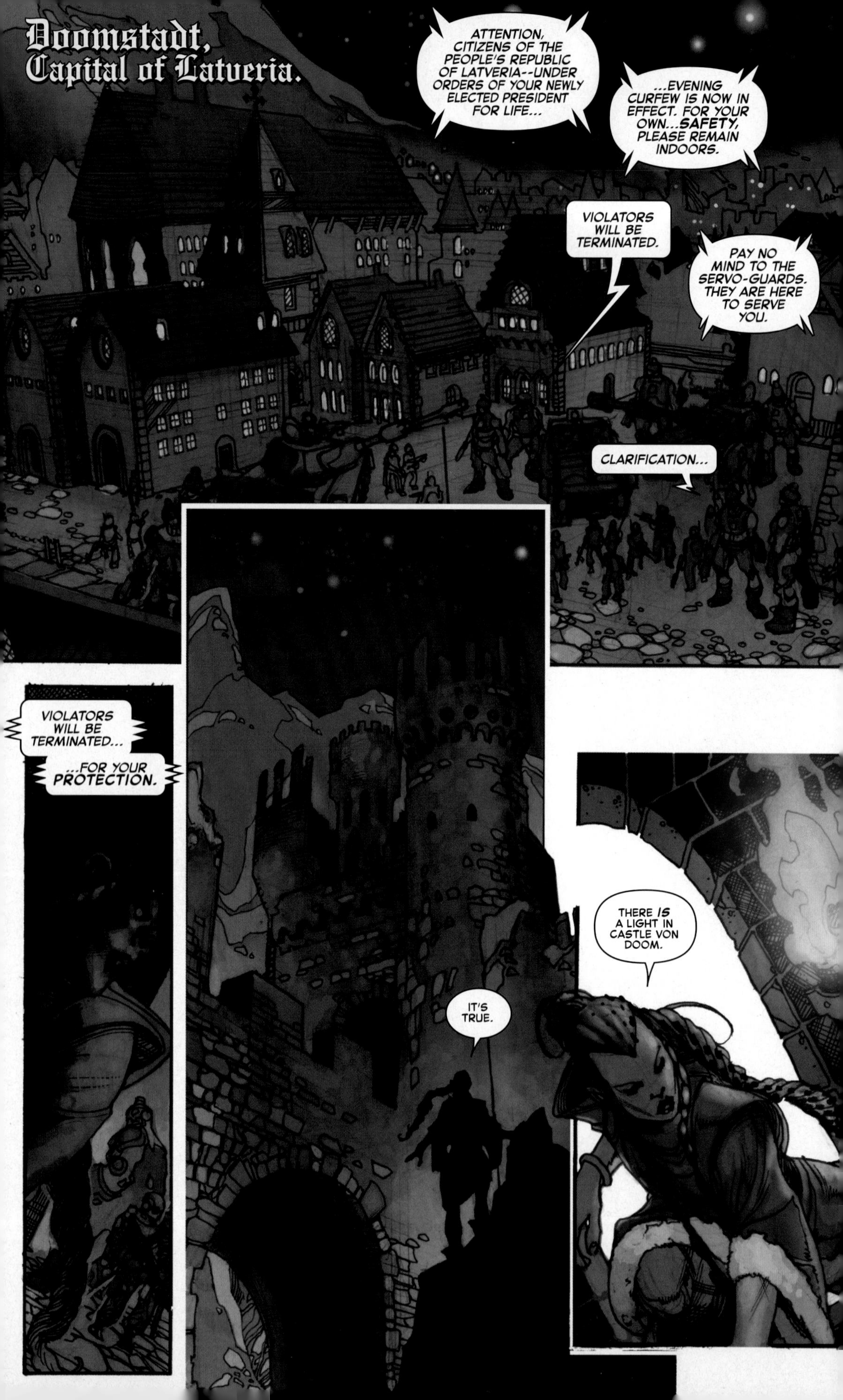
Doomstadt, Capital of Latveria.
ATTENTION, CITIZENS OF THE PEOPLE'S REPUBLIC OF LATVERIA--UNDER ORDERS OF YOUR NEWLY ELECTED PRESIDENT FOR LIFE...
...EVENING CURFEW IS NOW IN EFFECT. FOR YOUR OWN...SAFETY, PLEASE REMAIN INDOORS.
VIOLATORS WILL BE TERMINATED.
PAY NO MIND TO THE SERVO-GUARDS. THEY ARE HERE TO SERVE YOU.
CLARIFICATION...
VIOLATORS WILL BE TERMINATED...
...FOR YOUR PROTECTION.
IT'S TRUE.
THERE IS A LIGHT IN CASTLE VON DOOM.

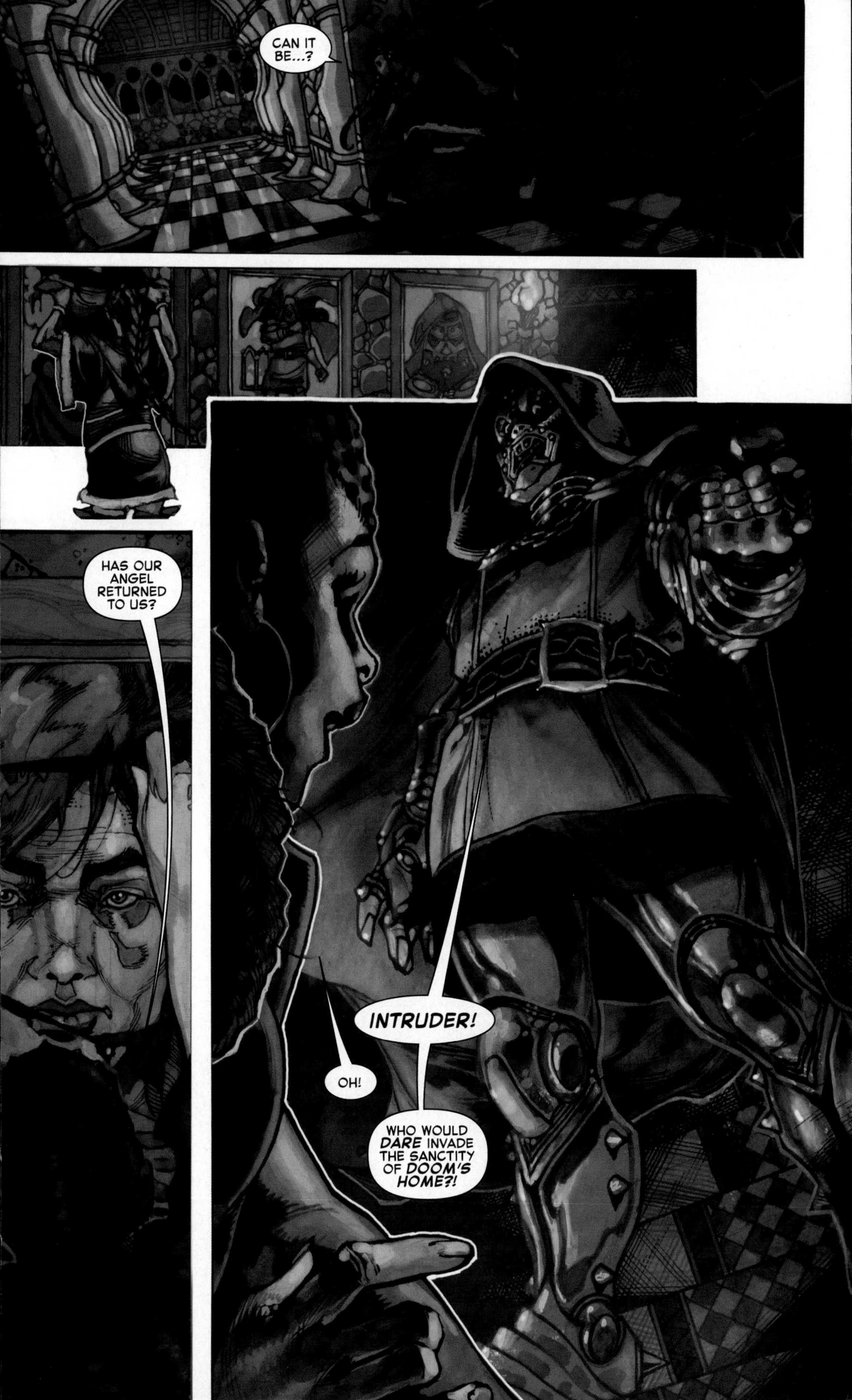

CAN IT BE...?
HAS OUR ANGEL RETURNED TO US?
INTRUDER!
OH!
WHO WOULD DARE INVADE THE SANCTITY OF DOOM'S HOME?!

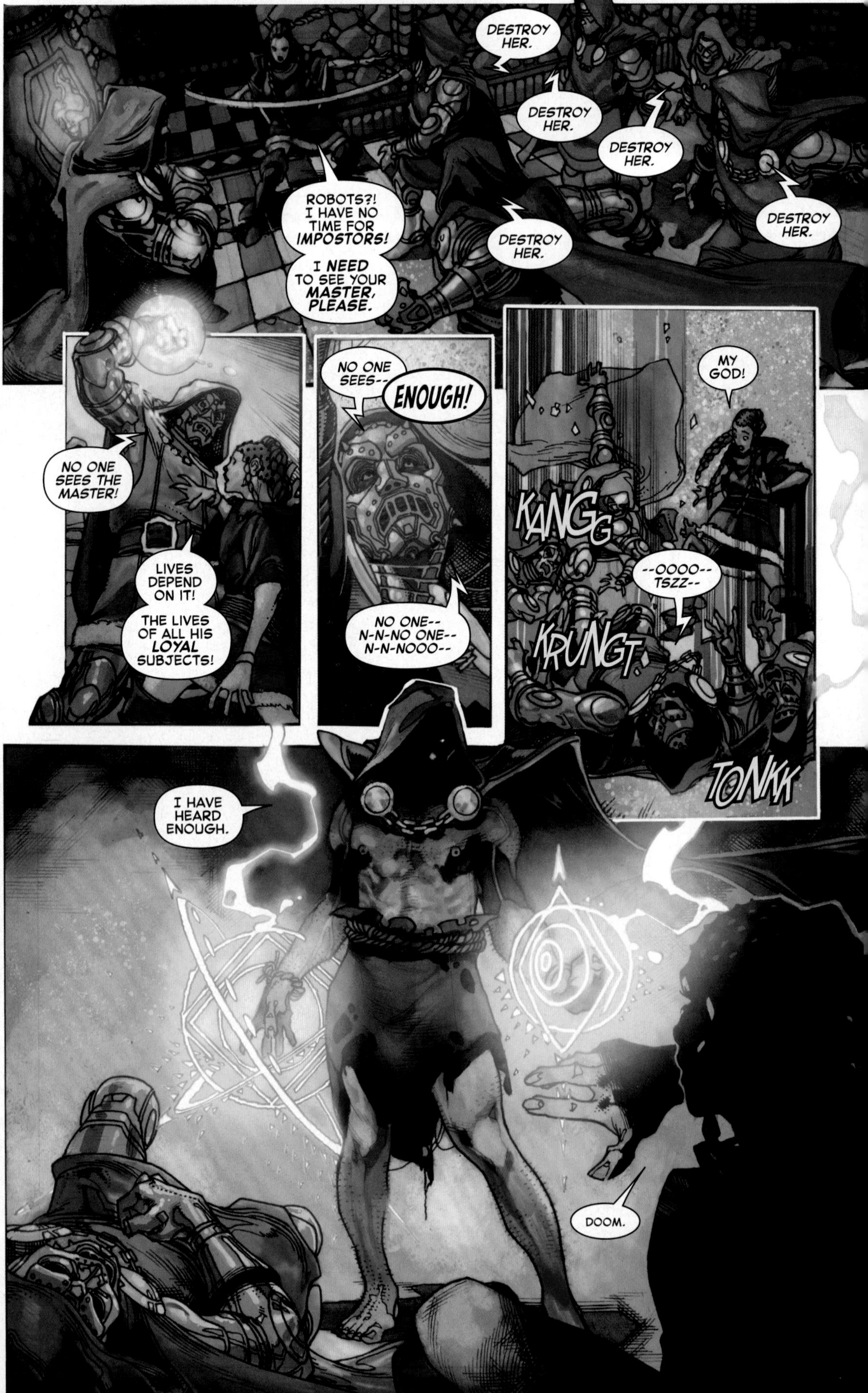
DESTROY HER.
DESTROY HER.
DESTROY HER.
ROBOTS?! I HAVE NO TIME FOR IMPOSTORS!
I NEED TO SEE YOUR MASTER, PLEASE.
DESTROY HER.
DESTROY HER.
NO ONE SEES THE MASTER!
LIVES DEPEND ON IT!
THE LIVES OF ALL HIS LOYAL SUBJECTS!
NO ONE SEES--
ENOUGH!
NO ONE-- N-N-NO ONE-- N-N-NOOO--
MY GOD!
KANGG
--OOOO-- TSZZ--
KRUNGT
TONKK
I HAVE HEARD ENOUGH.
DOOM.

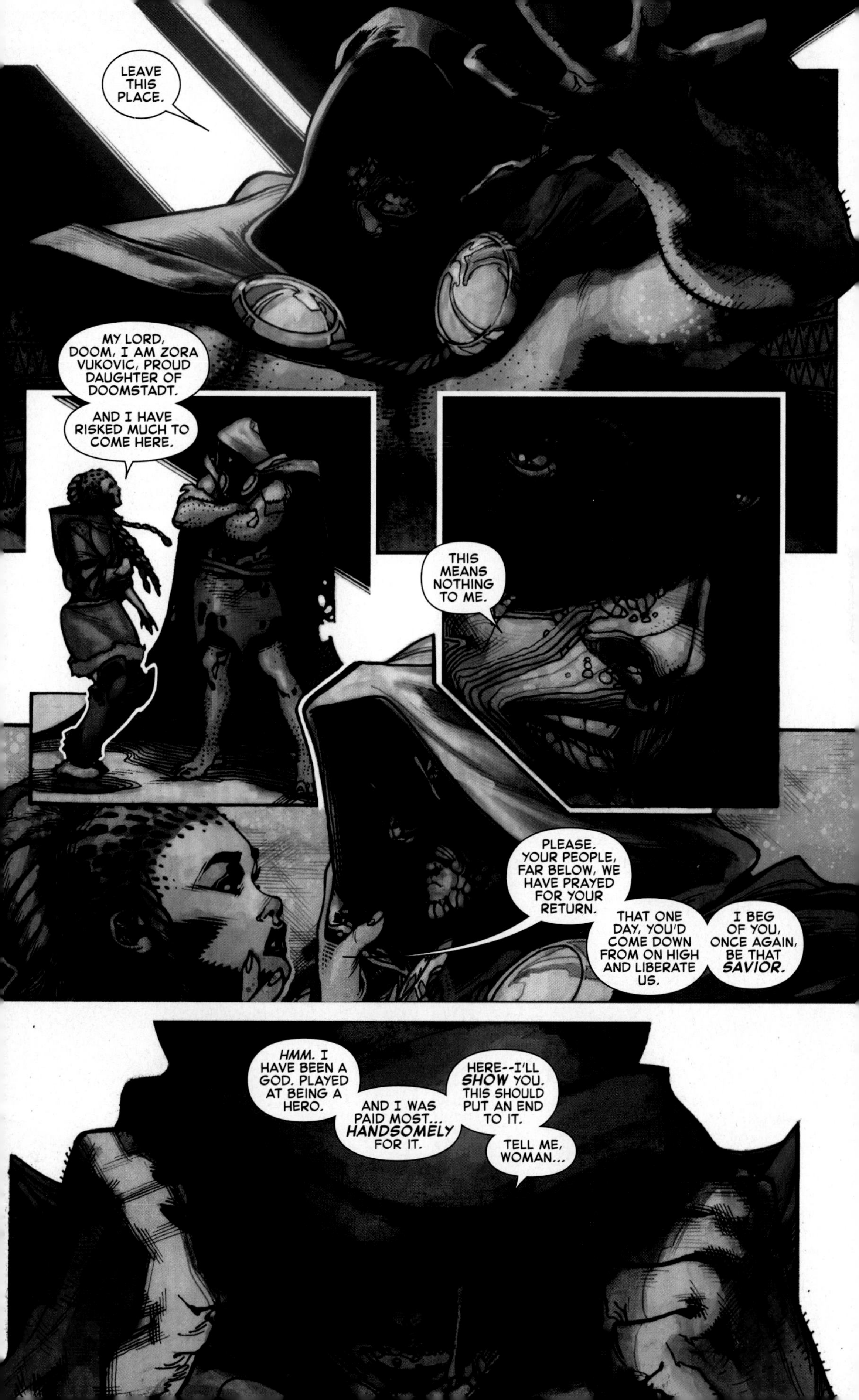
LEAVE THIS PLACE.
MY LORD, DOOM, I AM ZORA VUKOVIC, PROUD DAUGHTER OF DOOMSTADT.
AND I HAVE RISKED MUCH TO COME HERE.
THIS MEANS NOTHING TO ME.
PLEASE. YOUR PEOPLE, FAR BELOW, WE HAVE PRAYED FOR YOUR RETURN.
THAT ONE DAY, YOU'D COME DOWN FROM ON HIGH AND LIBERATE US.
I BEG OF YOU, ONCE AGAIN, BE THAT SAVIOR.
HMM. I HAVE BEEN A GOD. PLAYED AT BEING A HERO.
AND I WAS PAID MOST... HANDSOMELY FOR IT.
HERE--I'LL SHOW YOU. THIS SHOULD PUT AN END TO IT.
TELL ME, WOMAN...

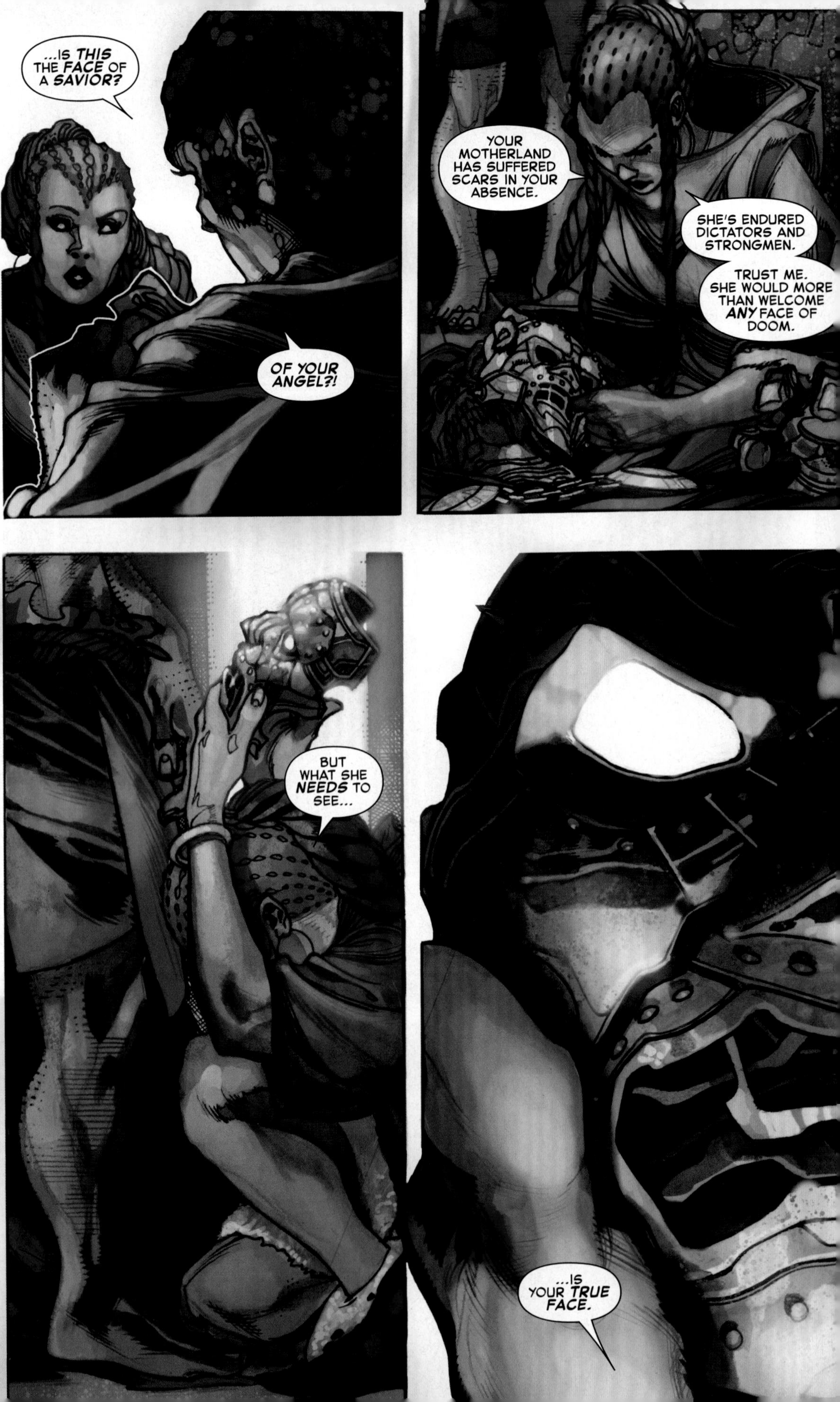
...IS THIS THE FACE OF A SAVIOR?
OF YOUR ANGEL?!
YOUR MOTHERLAND HAS SUFFERED SCARS IN YOUR ABSENCE.
SHE'S ENDURED DICTATORS AND STRONGMEN.
TRUST ME. SHE WOULD MORE THAN WELCOME ANY FACE OF DOOM.
BUT WHAT SHE NEEDS TO SEE...
...IS YOUR TRUE FACE.

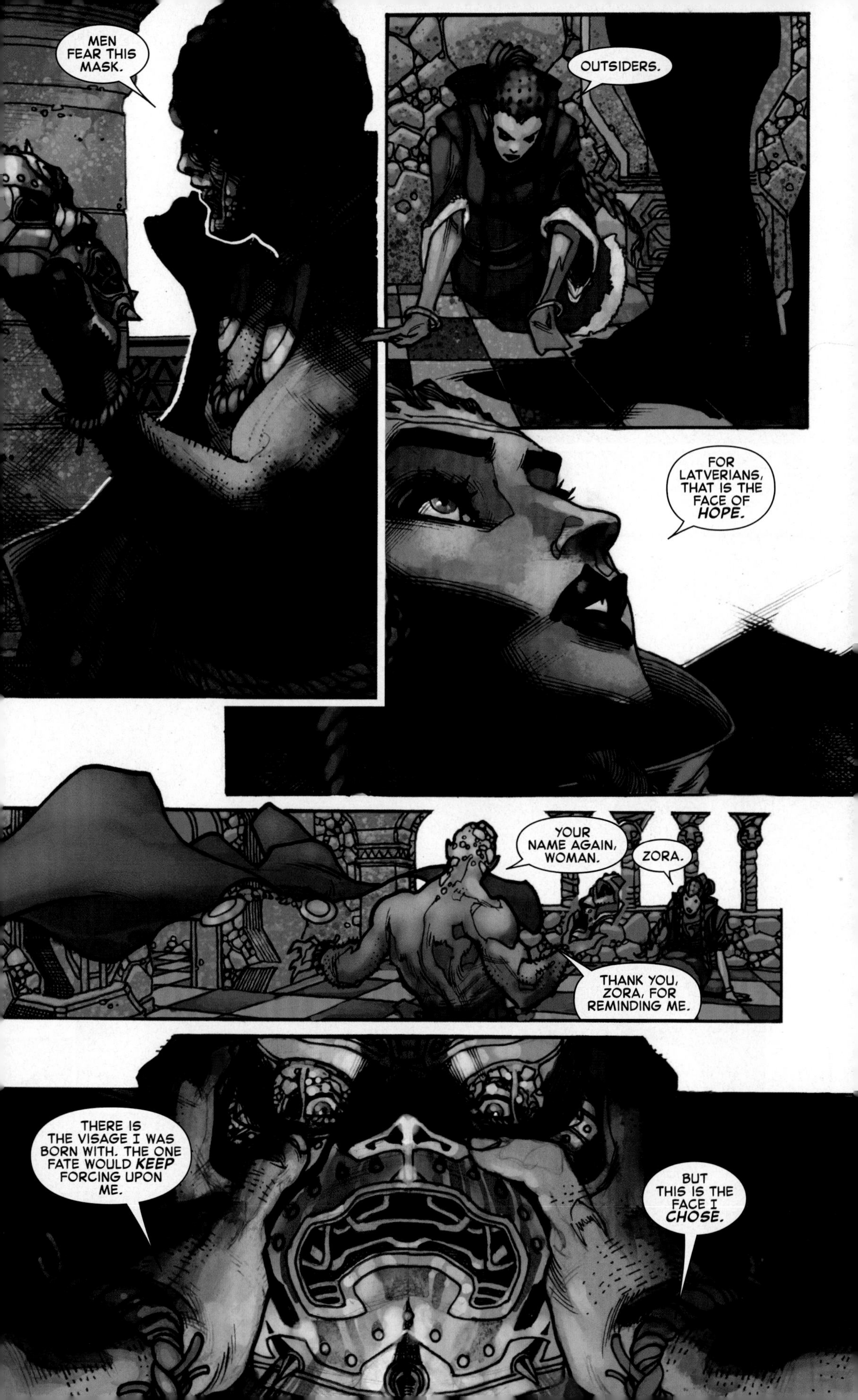
MEN FEAR THIS MASK.
OUTSIDERS.
FOR LATVERIANS, THAT IS THE FACE OF HOPE.
YOUR NAME AGAIN, WOMAN.
ZORA.
THANK YOU, ZORA, FOR REMINDING ME.
THERE IS THE VISAGE I WAS BORN WITH. THE ONE FATE WOULD KEEP FORCING UPON ME.
BUT THIS IS THE FACE I CHOSE.

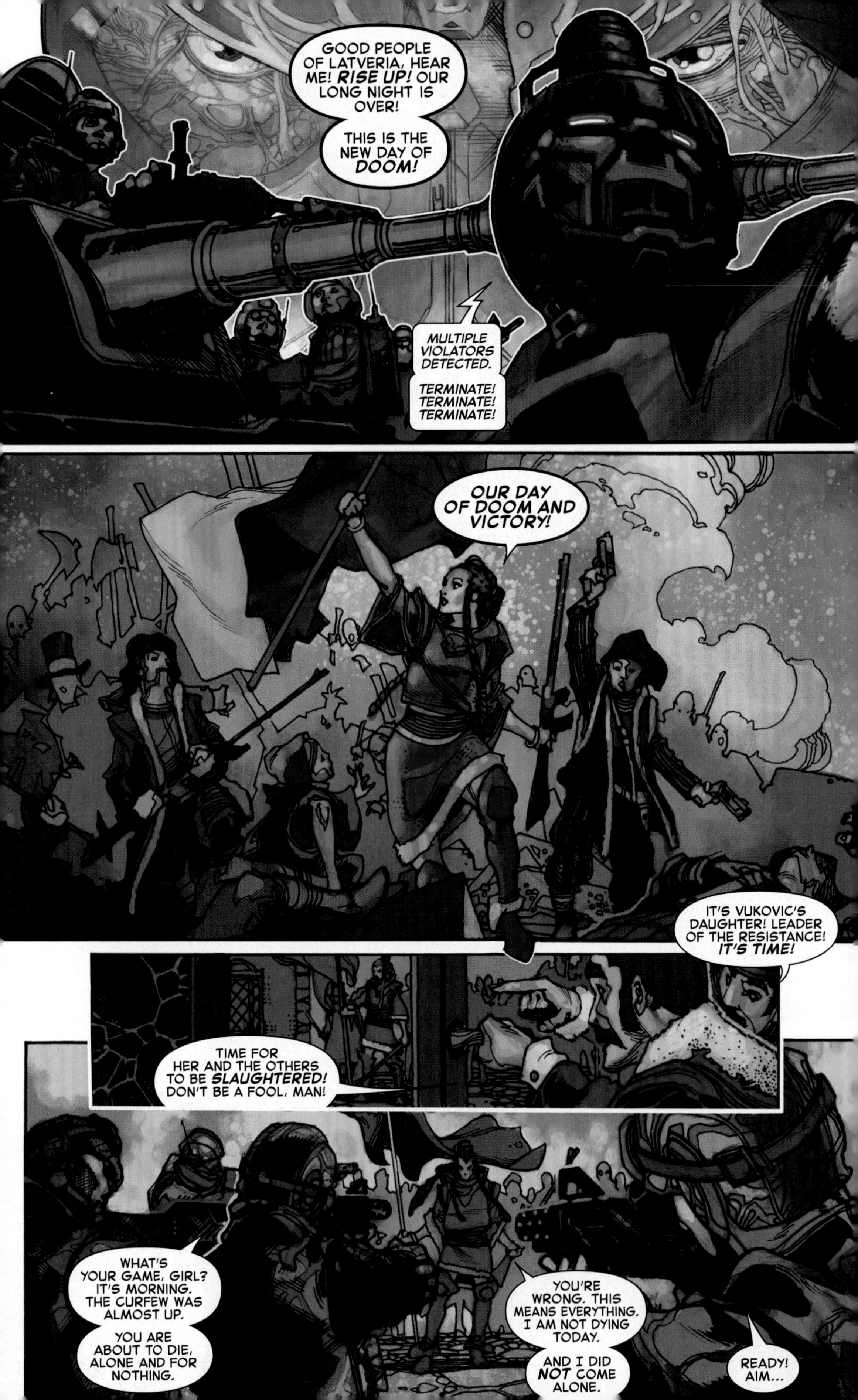
GOOD PEOPLE OF LATVERIA, HEAR ME! RISE UP! OUR LONG NIGHT IS OVER!
THIS IS THE NEW DAY OF DOOM!
MULTIPLE VIOLATORS DETECTED.
TERMINATE! TERMINATE! TERMINATE!
OUR DAY OF DOOM AND VICTORY!
IT'S VUKOVIC'S DAUGHTER! LEADER OF THE RESISTANCE! IT'S TIME!
TIME FOR HER AND THE OTHERS TO BE SLAUGHTERED! DON'T BE A FOOL, MAN!
WHAT'S YOUR GAME, GIRL? IT'S MORNING. THE CURFEW WAS ALMOST UP.
YOU ARE ABOUT TO DIE, ALONE AND FOR NOTHING.
YOU'RE WRONG. THIS MEANS EVERYTHING. I AM NOT DYING TODAY.
AND I DID NOT COME ALONE.
READY! AIM...

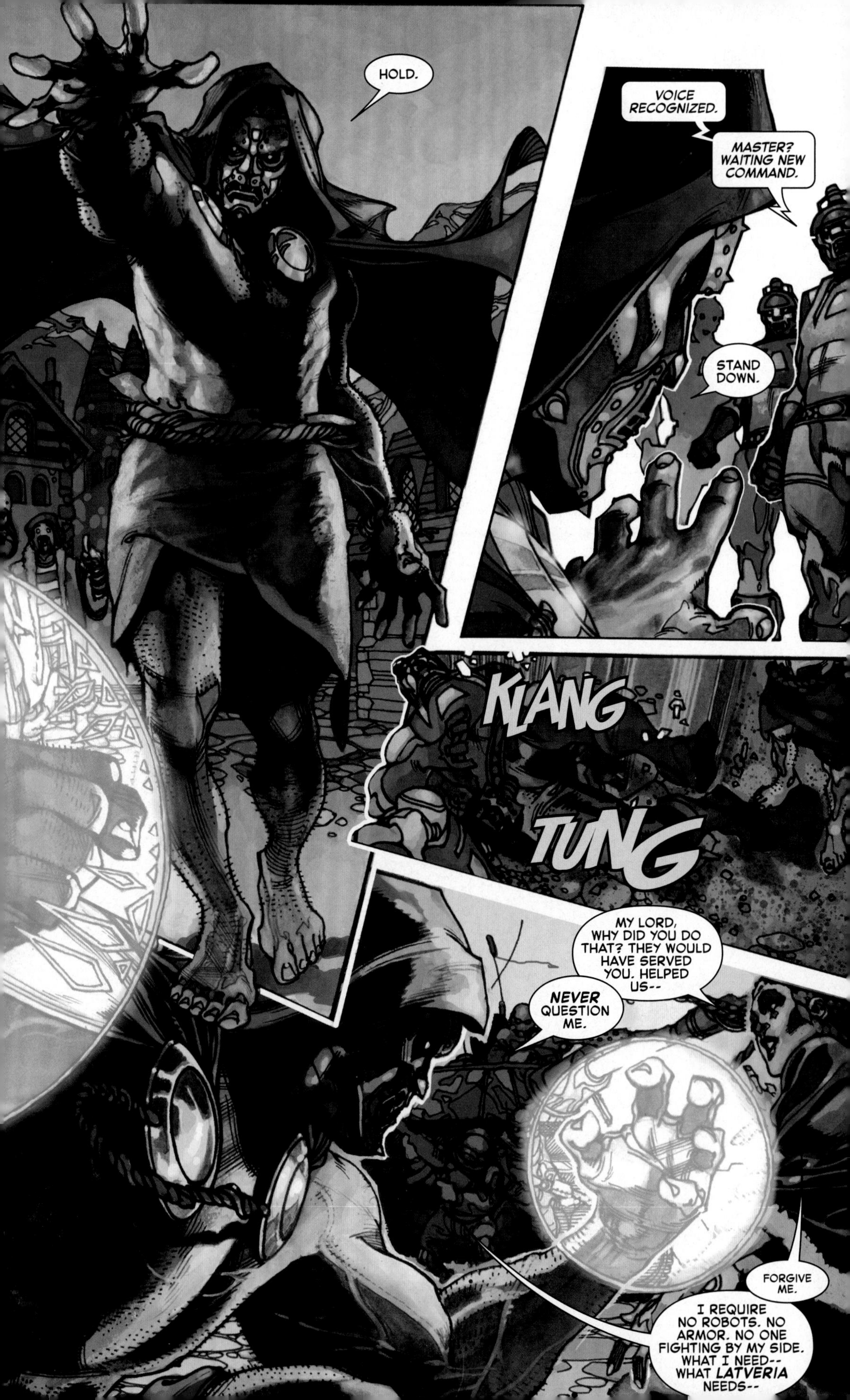
HOLD.
VOICE RECOGNIZED.
MASTER? WAITING NEW COMMAND.
STAND DOWN.
KLANG
TUNG
MY LORD, WHY DID YOU DO THAT? THEY WOULD HAVE SERVED YOU. HELPED US--
NEVER QUESTION ME.
FORGIVE ME.
I REQUIRE NO ROBOTS. NO ARMOR. NO ONE FIGHTING BY MY SIDE. WHAT I NEED-- WHAT LATVERIA NEEDS--

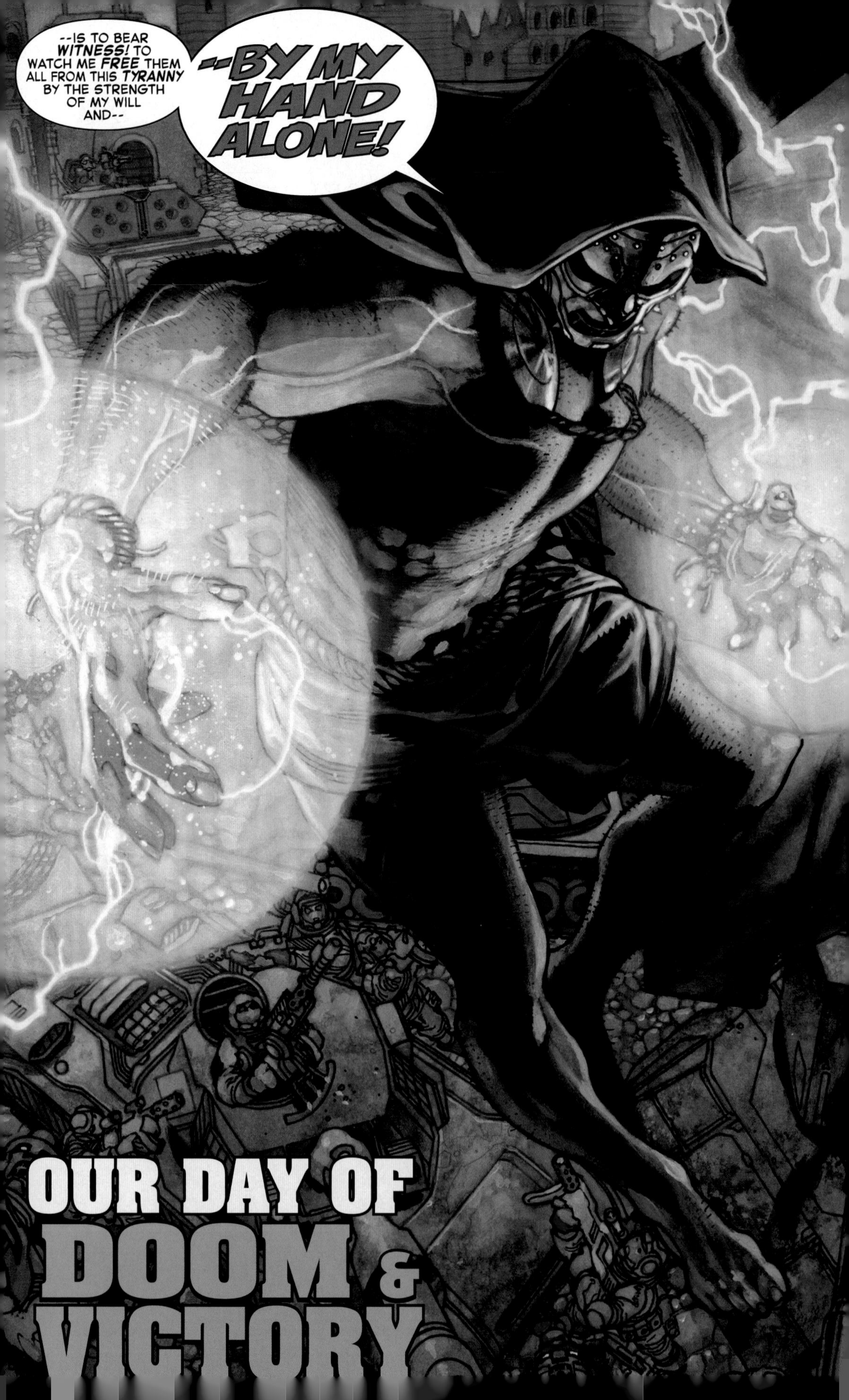
--IS TO BEAR WITNESS! TO WATCH ME FREE THEM ALL FROM THIS TYRANNY BY THE STRENGTH OF MY WILL AND--
--BY MY HAND ALONE!
OUR DAY OF DOOM & VICTORY

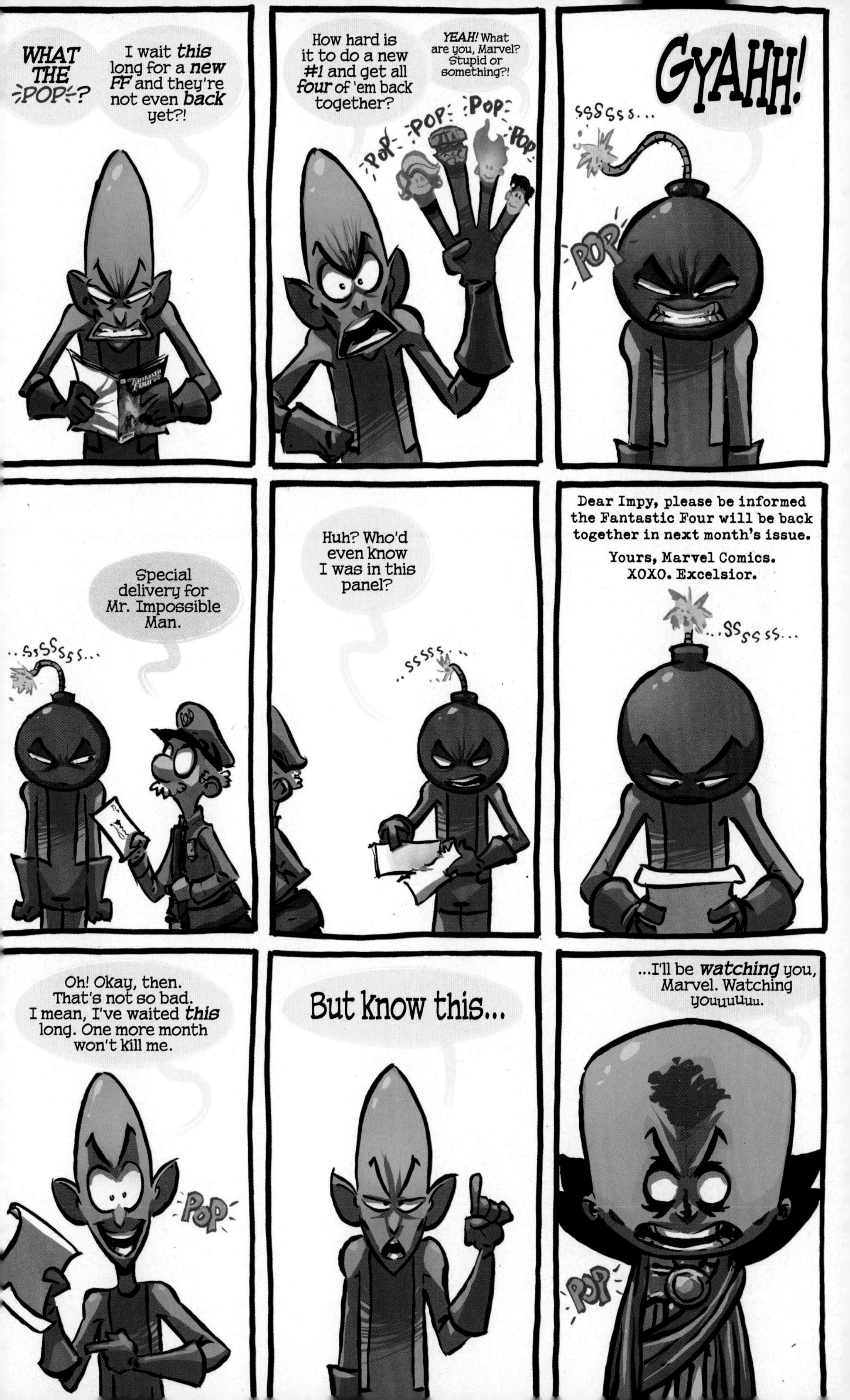
WHAT THE POP?
I wait this long for a new FF and they're not even back yet?!
How hard is it to do a new #1 and get all four of 'em back together?
YEAH! What are you, Marvel? Stupid or something?!
POP POP POP POP
GYAHH!
SSSSSS...
POP
Special delivery for Mr. Impossible Man.
...SSSSSSS...
Huh? Who'd even know I was in this panel?
..SSSSS..
Dear Impy, please be informed the Fantastic Four will be back together in next month's issue.
Yours, Marvel Comics. XOXO. Excelsior.
...SSSSSS...
Oh! Okay, then. That's not so bad. I mean, I've waited this long. One more month won't kill me.
POP
But know this...
...I'll be watching you, Marvel. Watching youuuuuu.
POP

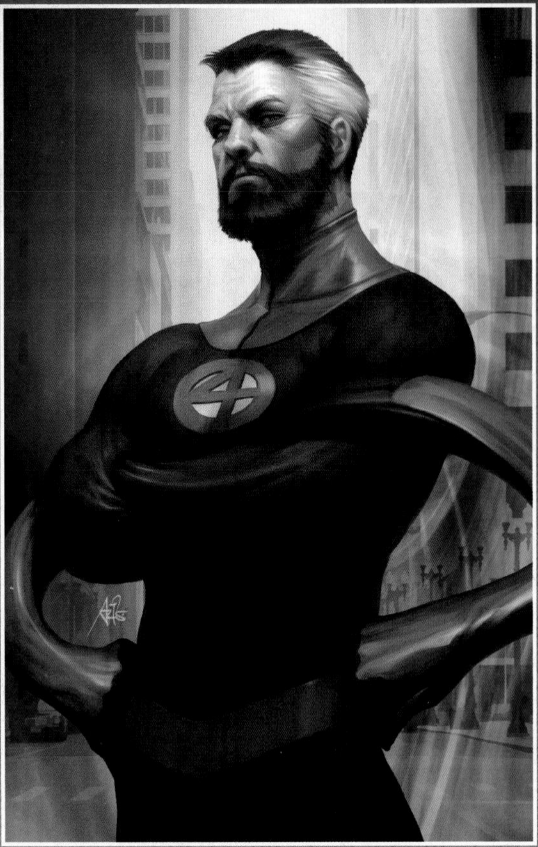
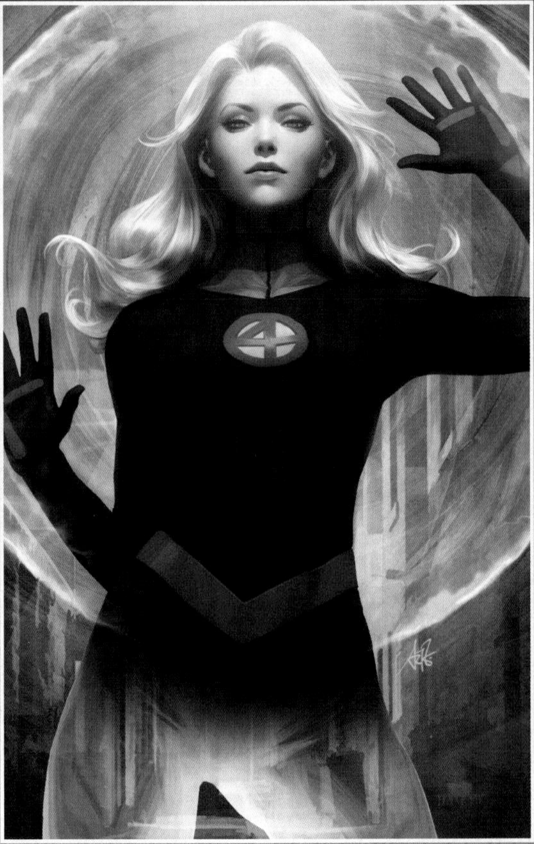
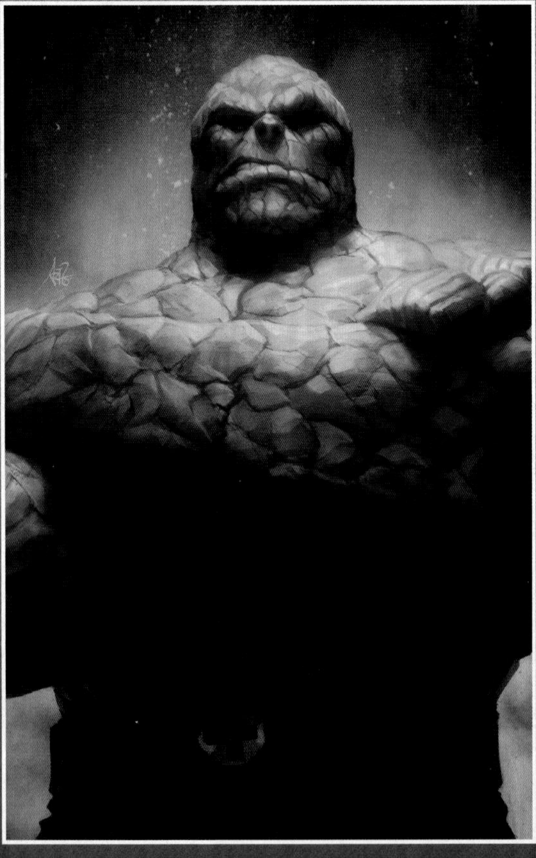
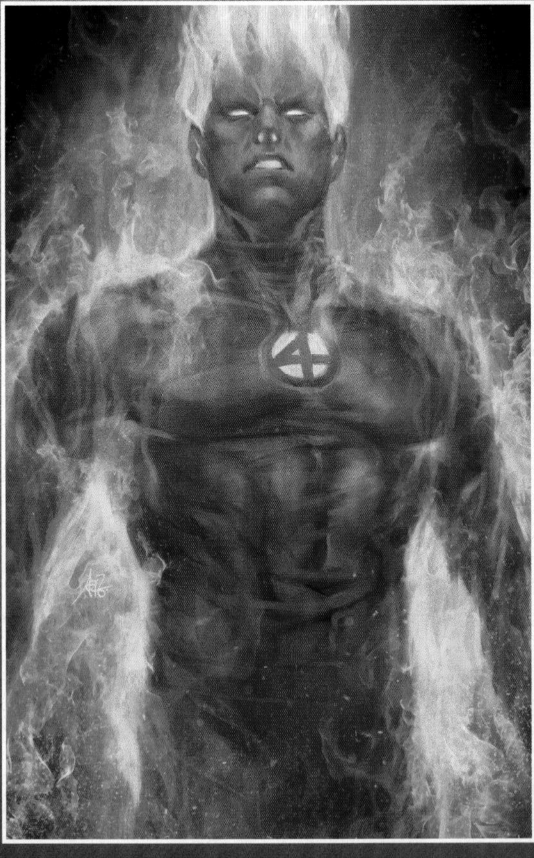

#1 variants by **Artgerm**

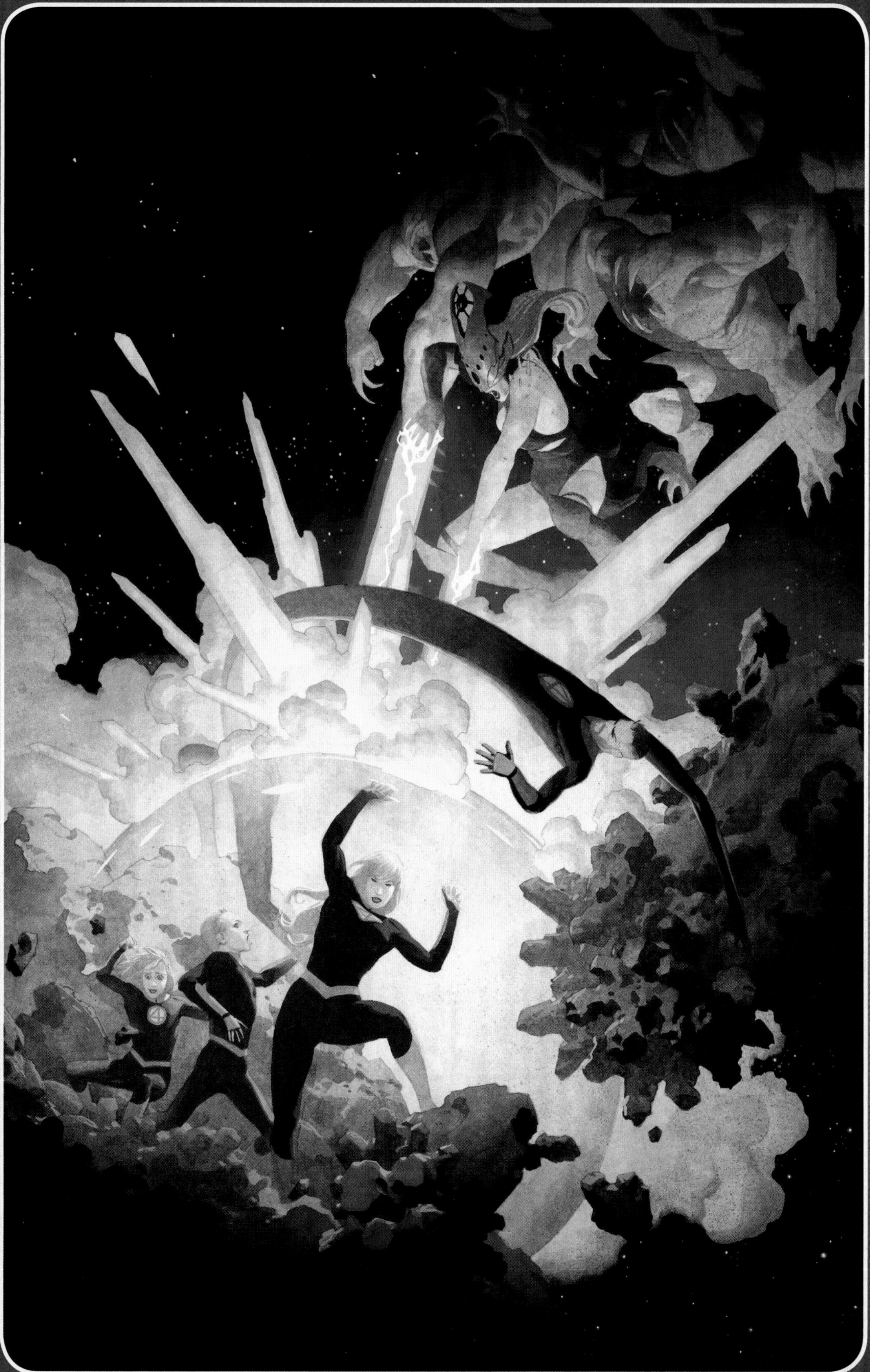

2

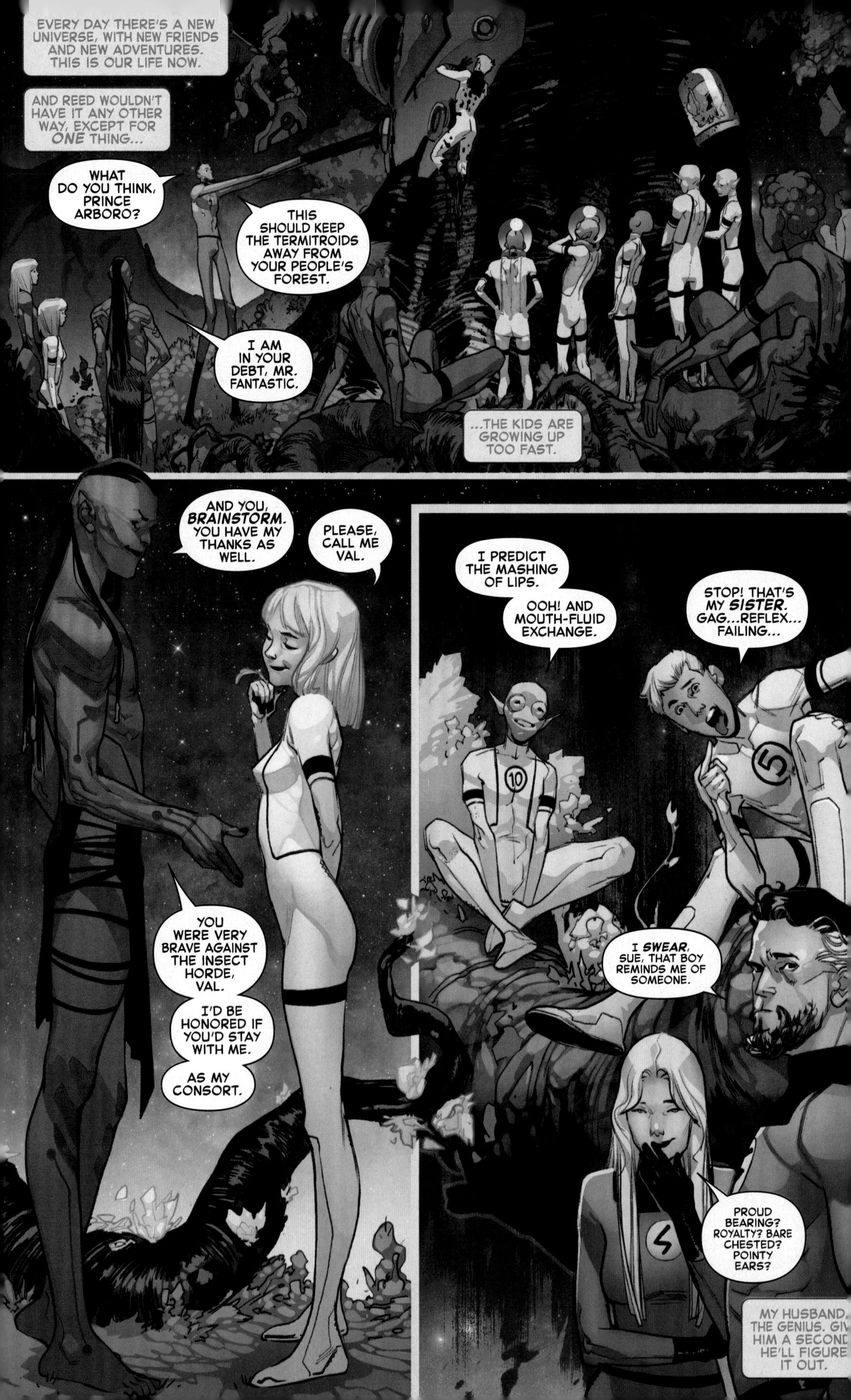
EVERY DAY THERE'S A NEW UNIVERSE, WITH NEW FRIENDS AND NEW ADVENTURES. THIS IS OUR LIFE NOW.
AND REED WOULDN'T HAVE IT ANY OTHER WAY, EXCEPT FOR ONE THING...
WHAT DO YOU THINK, PRINCE ARBORO?
THIS SHOULD KEEP THE TERMITROIDS AWAY FROM YOUR PEOPLE'S FOREST.
I AM IN YOUR DEBT, MR. FANTASTIC.
...THE KIDS ARE GROWING UP TOO FAST.
AND YOU, BRAINSTORM. YOU HAVE MY THANKS AS WELL.
PLEASE, CALL ME VAL.
YOU WERE VERY BRAVE AGAINST THE INSECT HORDE, VAL.
I'D BE HONORED IF YOU'D STAY WITH ME.
AS MY CONSORT.
I PREDICT THE MASHING OF LIPS.
OOH! AND MOUTH-FLUID EXCHANGE.
STOP! THAT'S MY SISTER. GAG...REFLEX... FAILING...
I SWEAR, SUE, THAT BOY REMINDS ME OF SOMEONE.
PROUD BEARING? ROYALTY? BARE CHESTED? POINTY EARS?
MY HUSBAND, THE GENIUS. GIV HIM A SECONE HE'LL FIGURE IT OUT.

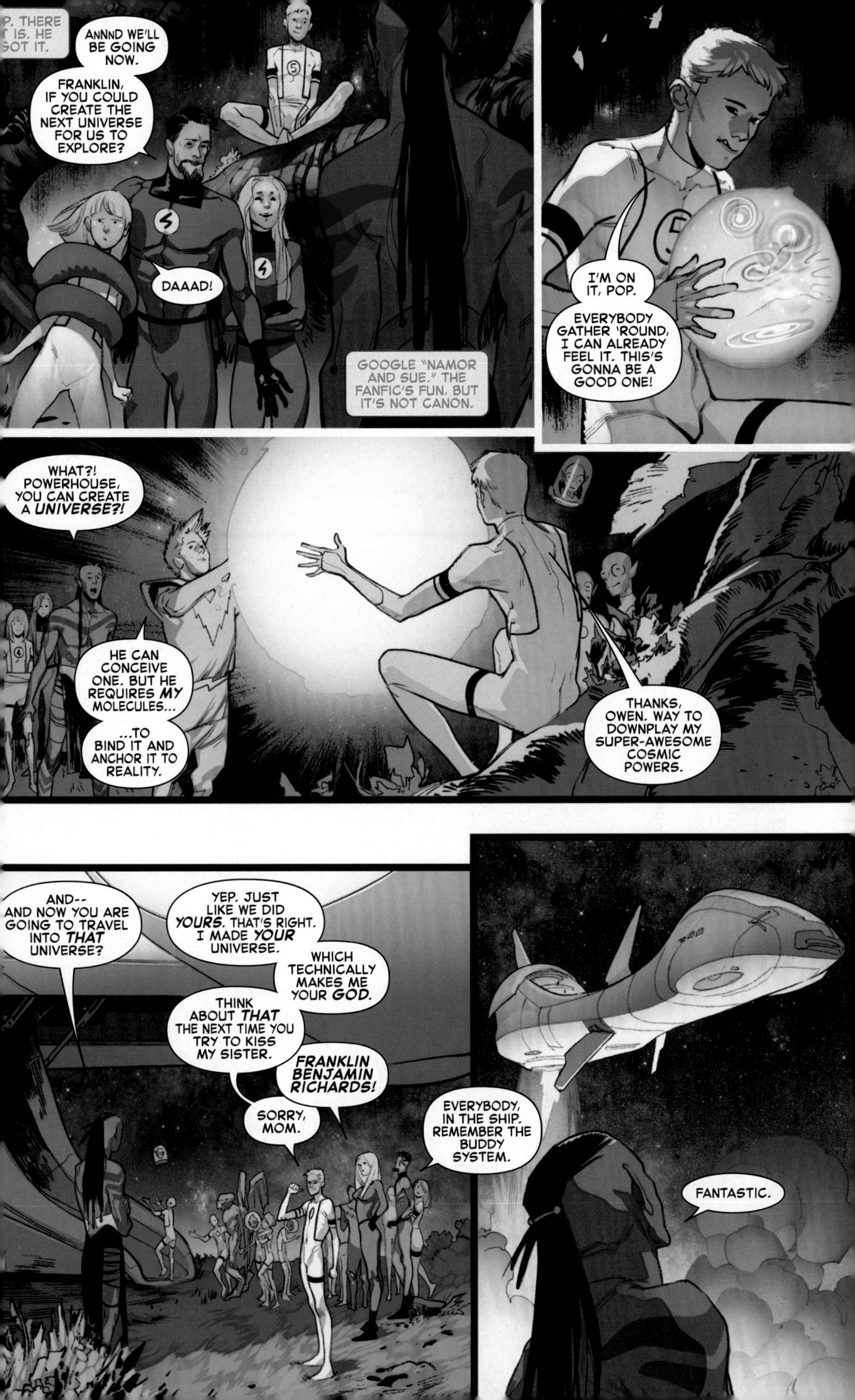
P. THERE
T IS. HE
GOT IT.
ANNND WE'LL BE GOING NOW.
FRANKLIN, IF YOU COULD CREATE THE NEXT UNIVERSE FOR US TO EXPLORE?
DAAAD!
GOOGLE "NAMOR AND SUE." THE FANFIC'S FUN, BUT IT'S NOT CANON.
I'M ON IT, POP.
EVERYBODY GATHER 'ROUND, I CAN ALREADY FEEL IT. THIS'S GONNA BE A GOOD ONE!
WHAT?! POWERHOUSE, YOU CAN CREATE A *UNIVERSE?!*
HE CAN CONCEIVE ONE. BUT HE REQUIRES *MY* MOLECULES...
...TO BIND IT AND ANCHOR IT TO REALITY.
THANKS, OWEN. WAY TO DOWNPLAY MY SUPER-AWESOME COSMIC POWERS.
AND-- AND NOW YOU ARE GOING TO TRAVEL INTO *THAT* UNIVERSE?
YEP. JUST LIKE WE DID *YOURS*. THAT'S RIGHT. I MADE *YOUR* UNIVERSE.
WHICH TECHNICALLY MAKES ME YOUR *GOD*.
THINK ABOUT *THAT* THE NEXT TIME YOU TRY TO KISS MY SISTER.
FRANKLIN BENJAMIN RICHARDS!
SORRY, MOM.
EVERYBODY, IN THE SHIP. REMEMBER THE BUDDY SYSTEM.
FANTASTIC.

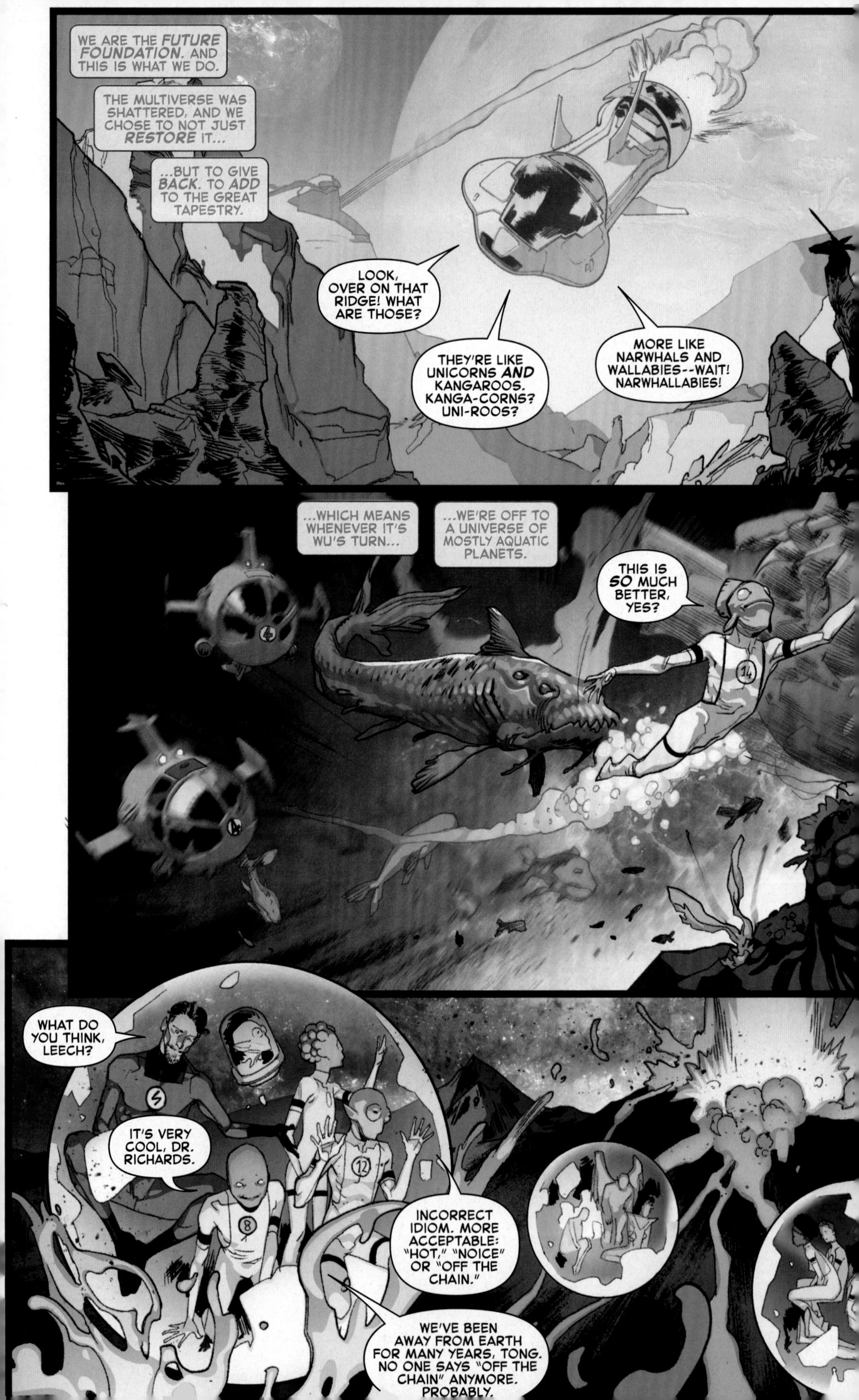
WE ARE THE *FUTURE FOUNDATION*. AND THIS IS WHAT WE DO.
THE MULTIVERSE WAS SHATTERED, AND WE CHOSE TO NOT JUST *RESTORE* IT...
...BUT TO GIVE *BACK*. TO *ADD* TO THE GREAT TAPESTRY.
LOOK, OVER ON THAT RIDGE! WHAT ARE THOSE?
THEY'RE LIKE UNICORNS *AND* KANGAROOS. KANGA-CORNS? UNI-ROOS?
MORE LIKE NARWHALS AND WALLABIES--WAIT! NARWHALLABIES!
...WHICH MEANS WHENEVER IT'S WU'S TURN...
...WE'RE OFF TO A UNIVERSE OF MOSTLY AQUATIC PLANETS.
THIS IS *SO* MUCH BETTER, YES?
WHAT DO YOU THINK, LEECH?
IT'S VERY COOL, DR. RICHARDS.
INCORRECT IDIOM. MORE ACCEPTABLE: "HOT," "NOICE" OR "OFF THE CHAIN."
WE'VE BEEN AWAY FROM EARTH FOR MANY YEARS, TONG. NO ONE SAYS "OFF THE CHAIN" ANYMORE. PROBABLY.

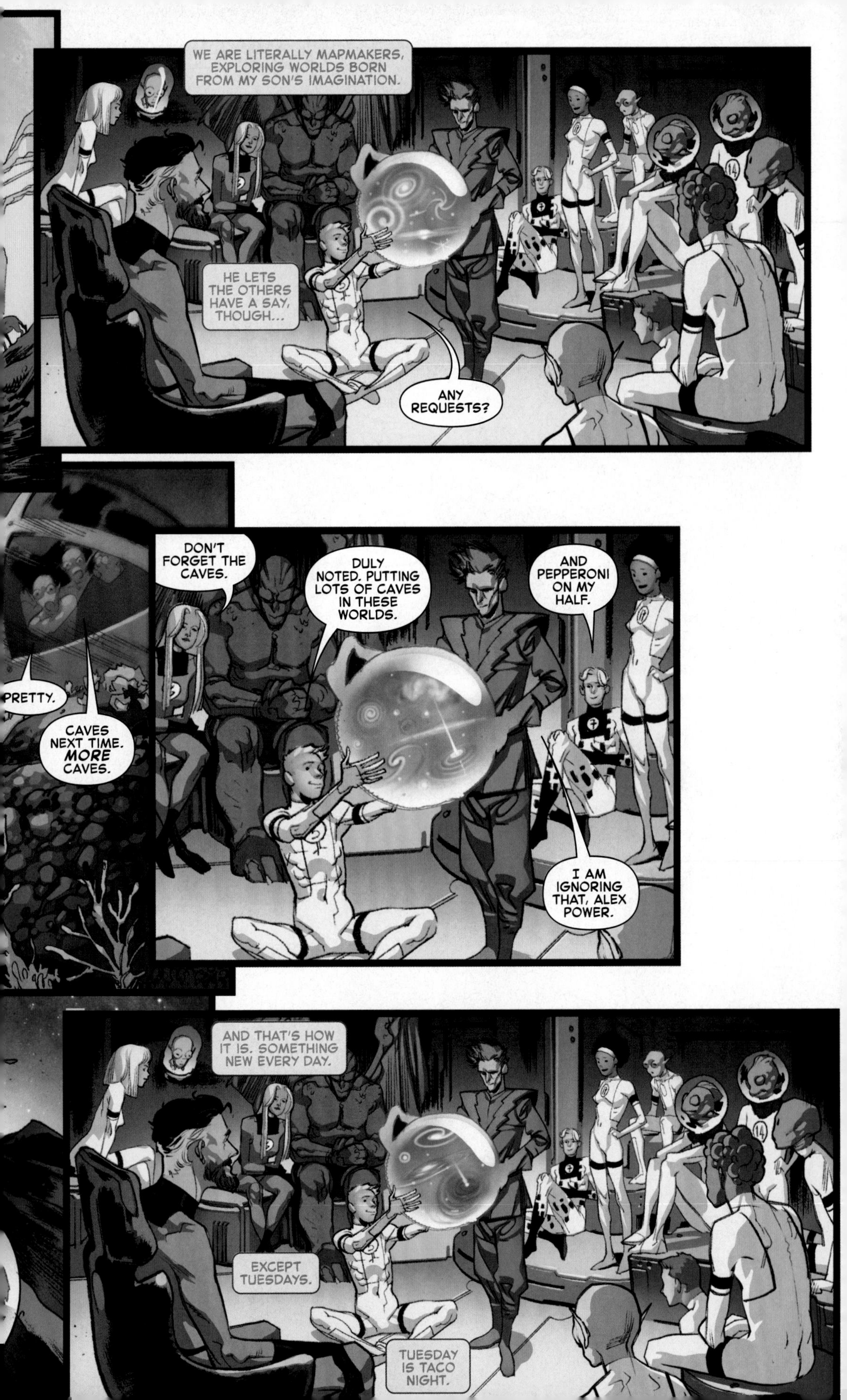
WE ARE LITERALLY MAPMAKERS, EXPLORING WORLDS BORN FROM MY SON'S IMAGINATION.
HE LETS THE OTHERS HAVE A SAY, THOUGH...
ANY REQUESTS?
PRETTY.
CAVES NEXT TIME. *MORE* CAVES.
DON'T FORGET THE CAVES.
DULY NOTED. PUTTING LOTS OF CAVES IN THESE WORLDS.
AND PEPPERONI ON MY HALF.
I AM IGNORING THAT, ALEX POWER.
AND THAT'S HOW IT IS. SOMETHING NEW EVERY DAY.
EXCEPT TUESDAYS.
TUESDAY IS TACO NIGHT.

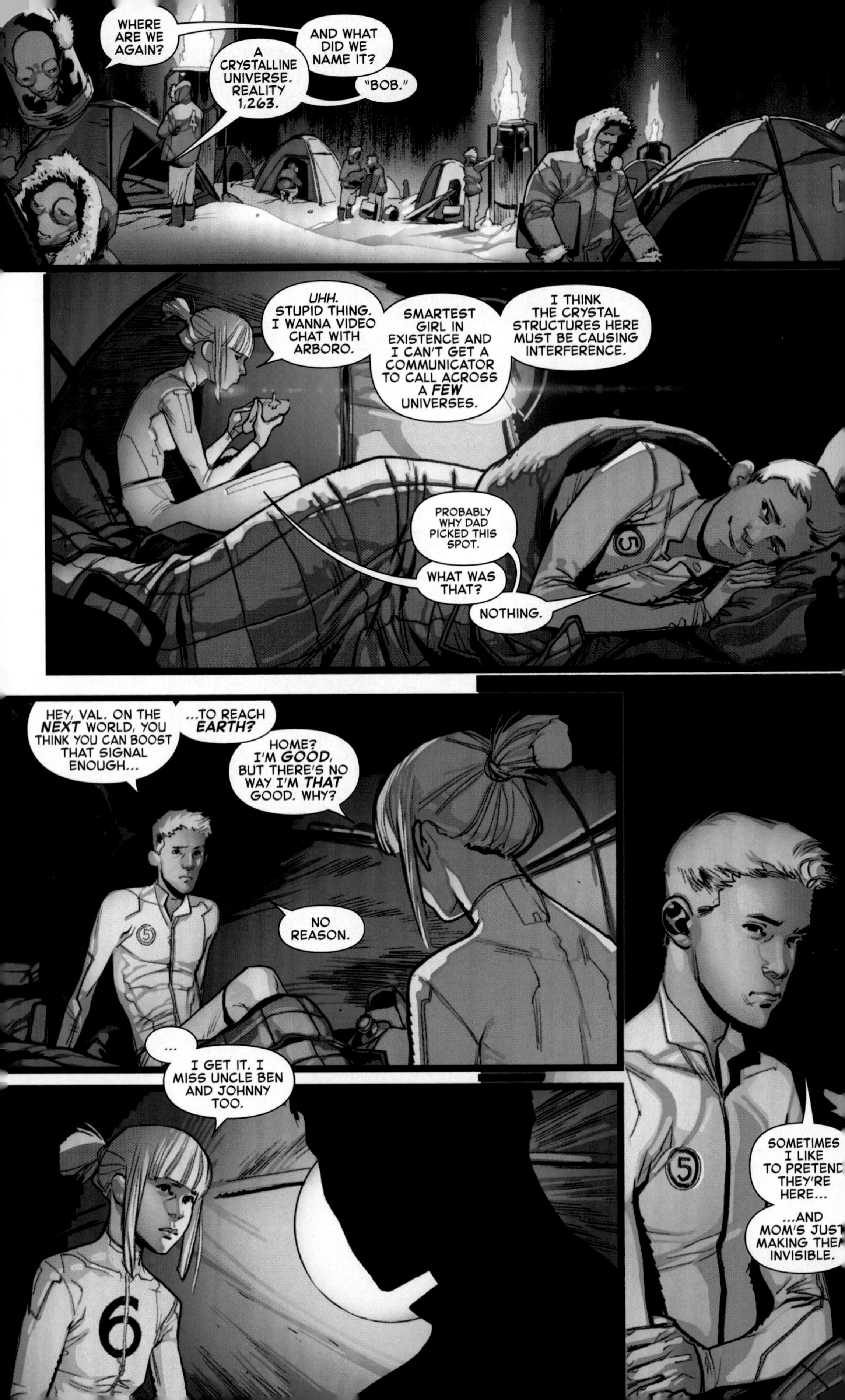
WHERE ARE WE AGAIN?
A CRYSTALLINE UNIVERSE. REALITY 1,263.
AND WHAT DID WE NAME IT?
"BOB."
UHH. STUPID THING. I WANNA VIDEO CHAT WITH ARBORO.
SMARTEST GIRL IN EXISTENCE AND I CAN'T GET A COMMUNICATOR TO CALL ACROSS A FEW UNIVERSES.
I THINK THE CRYSTAL STRUCTURES HERE MUST BE CAUSING INTERFERENCE.
PROBABLY WHY DAD PICKED THIS SPOT.
WHAT WAS THAT?
NOTHING.
HEY, VAL. ON THE NEXT WORLD, YOU THINK YOU CAN BOOST THAT SIGNAL ENOUGH...
...TO REACH EARTH?
HOME? I'M GOOD, BUT THERE'S NO WAY I'M THAT GOOD. WHY?
NO REASON.
...
I GET IT. I MISS UNCLE BEN AND JOHNNY TOO.
SOMETIMES I LIKE TO PRETEND THEY'RE HERE...
...AND MOM'S JUST MAKING THEM INVISIBLE.

KIDS ASLEEP?

PROBABLY.

YOU DIDN'T CHECK?

I WAS WITH OWEN.

GOT HIM TO CHANGE THE MOLECULES OF OUR COLOMBIAN BLEND...

...INTO SUMATRA.

OHHH. GOD, I LOVE THAT MAN.

SORRY, DEAR. YOU'RE STUCK WITH ME.

AND OUR WONDERFUL KIDS. EXPLORING UNIVERSES OF OUR OWN MAKING.

IS THERE A SCIENTIFIC TERM FOR THAT?

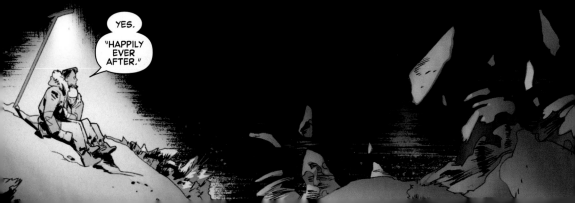

YES. "HAPPILY EVER AFTER."

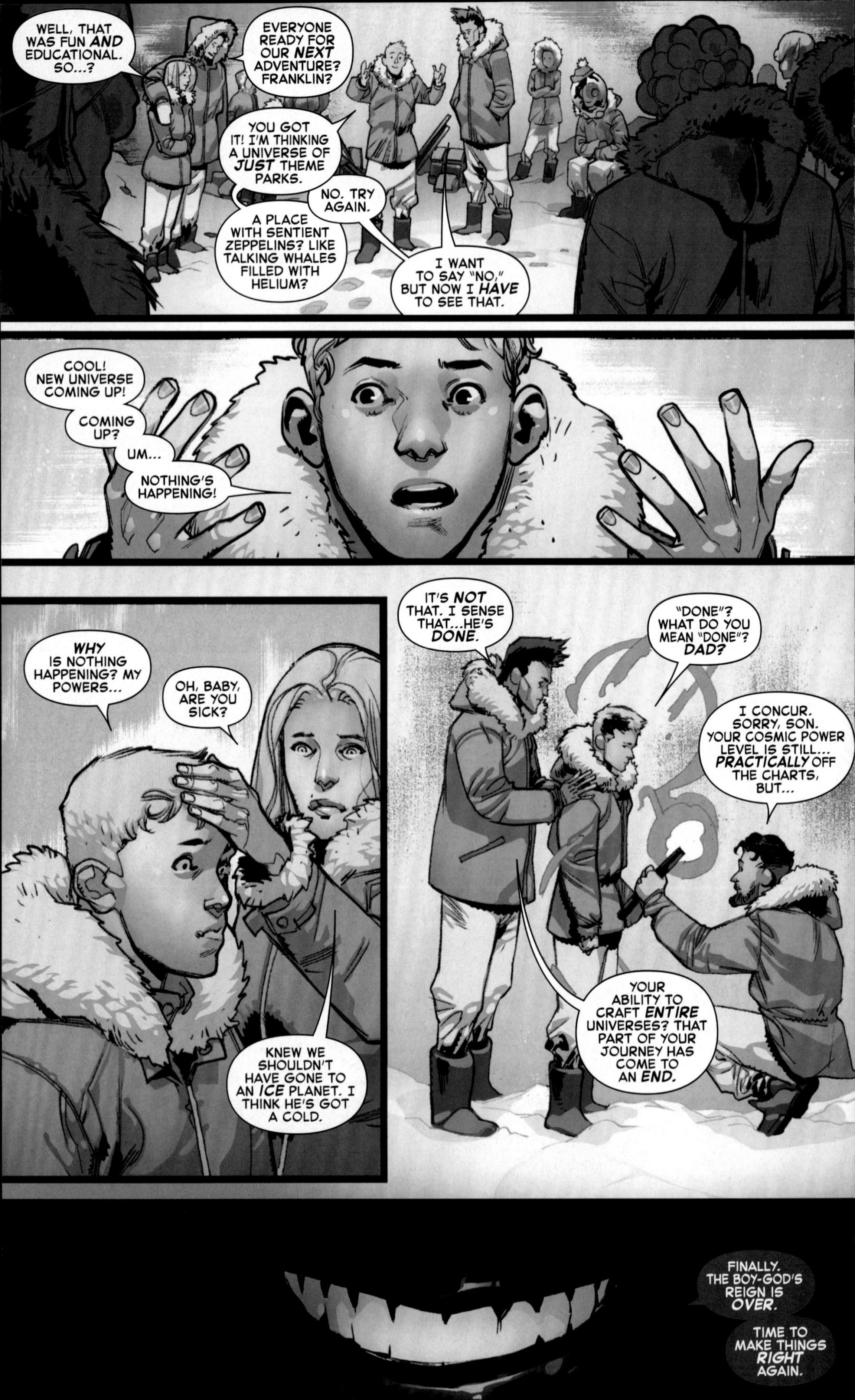

WELL, THAT WAS FUN AND EDUCATIONAL. SO...?
EVERYONE READY FOR OUR NEXT ADVENTURE? FRANKLIN?
YOU GOT IT! I'M THINKING A UNIVERSE OF JUST THEME PARKS.
NO. TRY AGAIN.
A PLACE WITH SENTIENT ZEPPELINS? LIKE TALKING WHALES FILLED WITH HELIUM?
I WANT TO SAY "NO," BUT NOW I HAVE TO SEE THAT.
COOL! NEW UNIVERSE COMING UP!
COMING UP?
UM...
NOTHING'S HAPPENING!
WHY IS NOTHING HAPPENING? MY POWERS...
OH, BABY, ARE YOU SICK?
KNEW WE SHOULDN'T HAVE GONE TO AN ICE PLANET. I THINK HE'S GOT A COLD.
IT'S NOT THAT. I SENSE THAT...HE'S DONE.
"DONE"? WHAT DO YOU MEAN "DONE"? DAD?
I CONCUR. SORRY, SON. YOUR COSMIC POWER LEVEL IS STILL... PRACTICALLY OFF THE CHARTS, BUT...
YOUR ABILITY TO CRAFT ENTIRE UNIVERSES? THAT PART OF YOUR JOURNEY HAS COME TO AN END.
FINALLY. THE BOY-GOD'S REIGN IS OVER.
TIME TO MAKE THINGS RIGHT AGAIN.

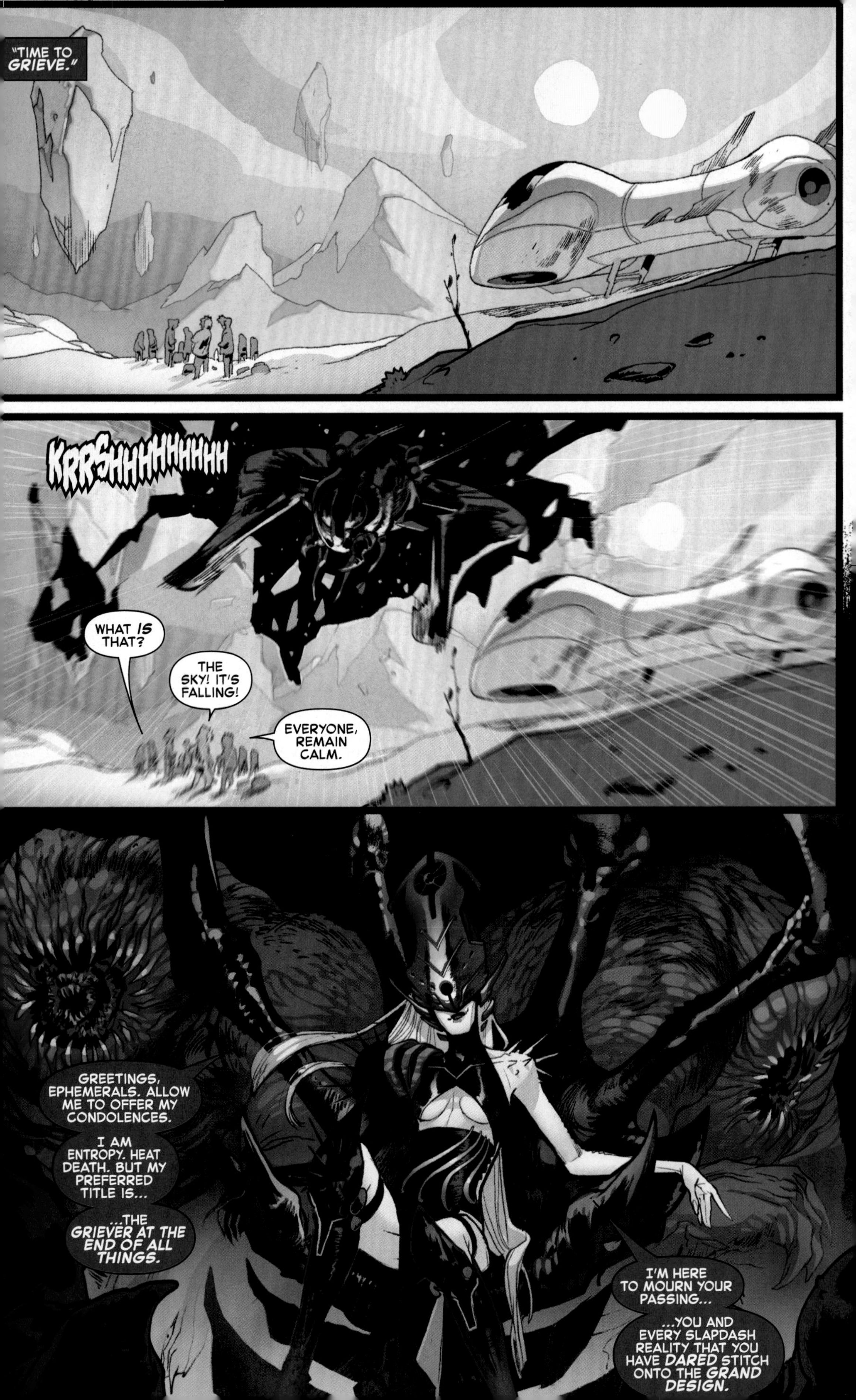

"TIME TO GRIEVE."
KRRSHHHHHHHH
WHAT IS THAT?
THE SKY! IT'S FALLING!
EVERYONE, REMAIN CALM.
GREETINGS, EPHEMERALS. ALLOW ME TO OFFER MY CONDOLENCES.
I AM ENTROPY. HEAT DEATH. BUT MY PREFERRED TITLE IS...
...THE GRIEVER AT THE END OF ALL THINGS.
I'M HERE TO MOURN YOUR PASSING...
...YOU AND EVERY SLAPDASH REALITY THAT YOU HAVE DARED STITCH ONTO THE GRAND DESIGN.

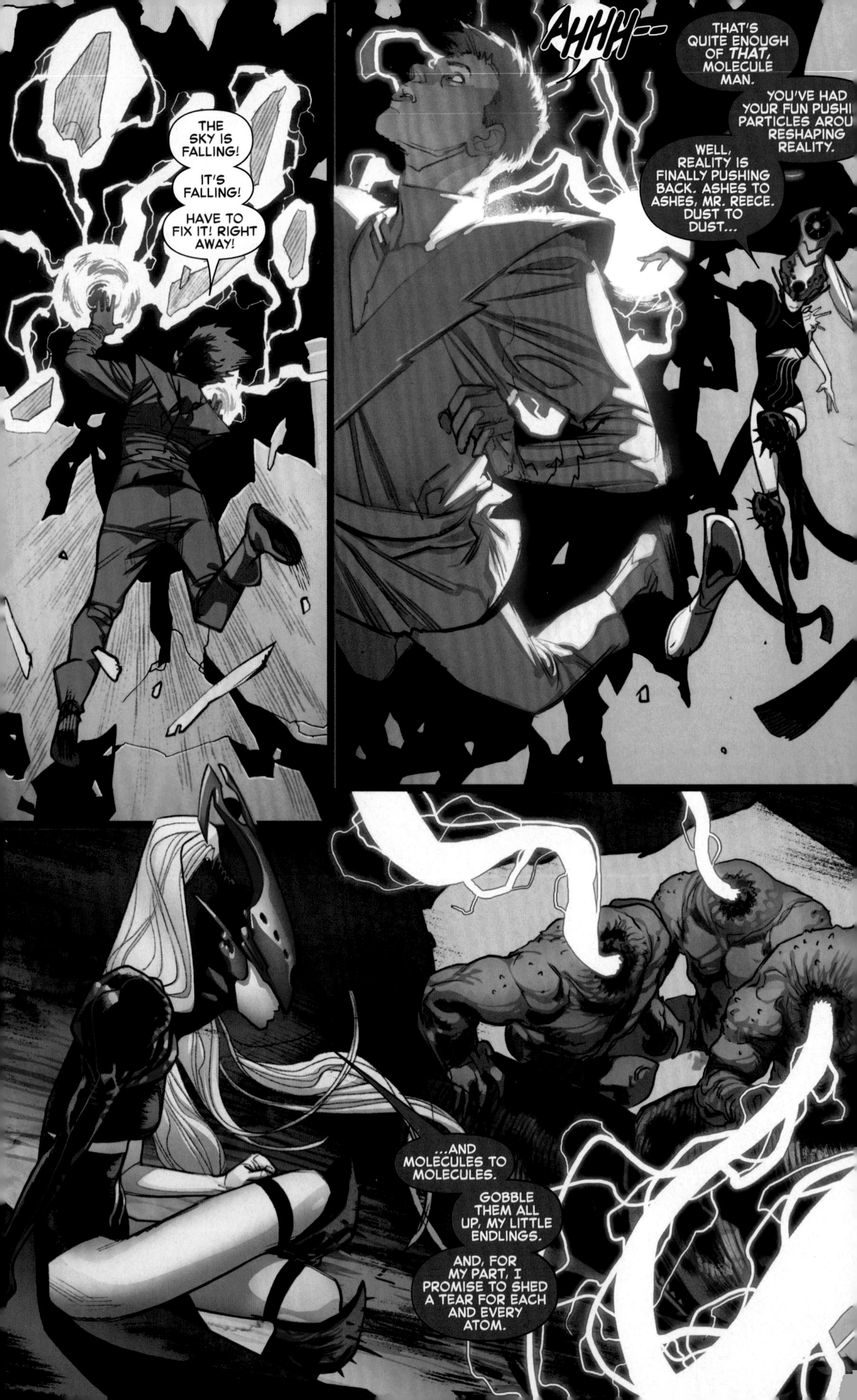
THE SKY IS FALLING!
IT'S FALLING!
HAVE TO FIX IT! RIGHT AWAY!
AHHH--
THAT'S QUITE ENOUGH OF THAT, MOLECULE MAN.
YOU'VE HAD YOUR FUN PUSHI PARTICLES AROU RESHAPING REALITY.
WELL, REALITY IS FINALLY PUSHING BACK. ASHES TO ASHES, MR. REECE. DUST TO DUST...
...AND MOLECULES TO MOLECULES.
GOBBLE THEM ALL UP, MY LITTLE ENDLINGS.
AND, FOR MY PART, I PROMISE TO SHED A TEAR FOR EACH AND EVERY ATOM.

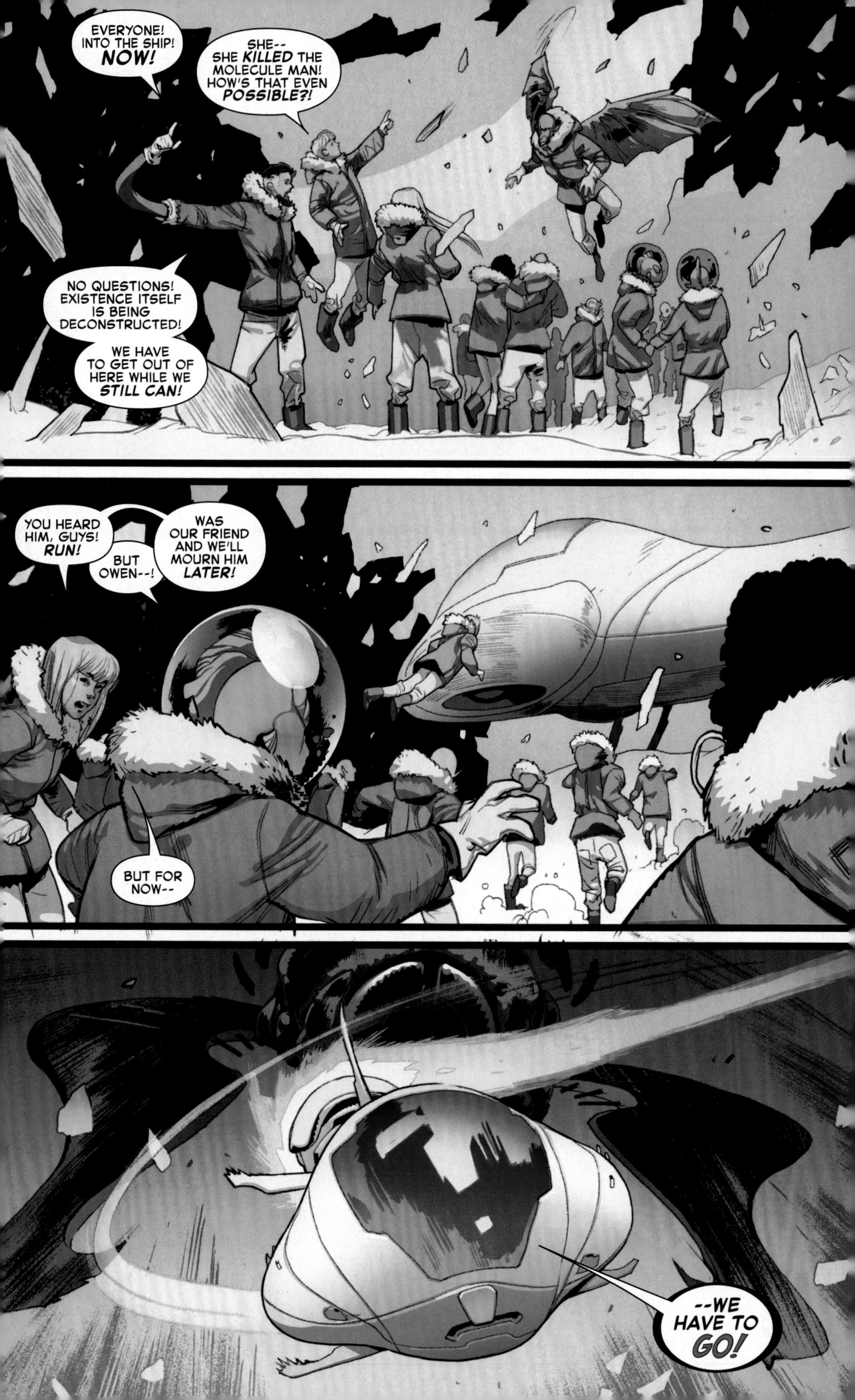
EVERYONE! INTO THE SHIP! NOW!
SHE-- SHE KILLED THE MOLECULE MAN! HOW'S THAT EVEN POSSIBLE?!
NO QUESTIONS! EXISTENCE ITSELF IS BEING DECONSTRUCTED!
WE HAVE TO GET OUT OF HERE WHILE WE STILL CAN!
YOU HEARD HIM, GUYS! RUN!
BUT OWEN--!
WAS OUR FRIEND AND WE'LL MOURN HIM LATER!
BUT FOR NOW--
--WE HAVE TO GO!

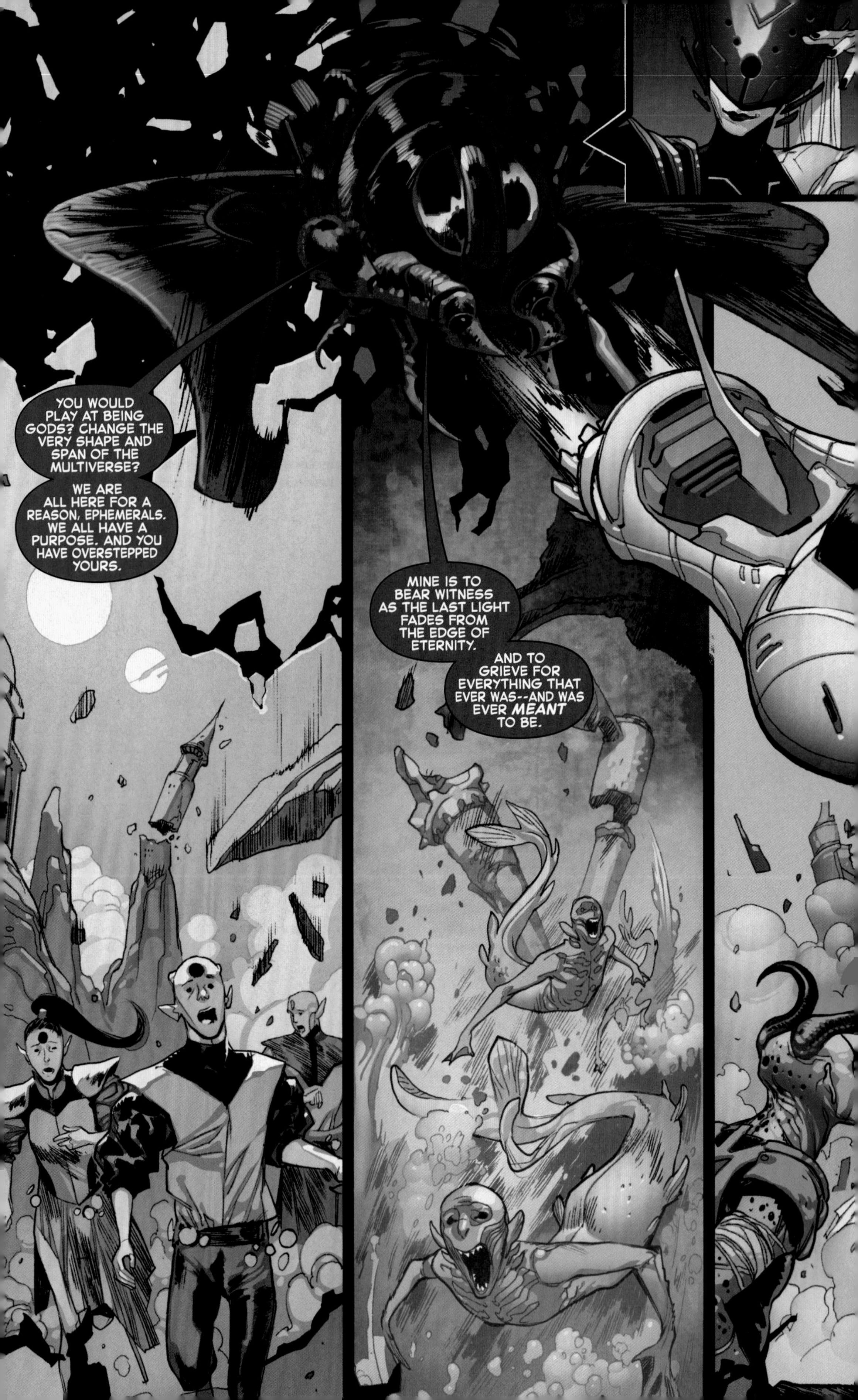
YOU WOULD PLAY AT BEING GODS? CHANGE THE VERY SHAPE AND SPAN OF THE MULTIVERSE?
WE ARE ALL HERE FOR A REASON, EPHEMERALS. WE ALL HAVE A PURPOSE. AND YOU HAVE OVERSTEPPED YOURS.
MINE IS TO BEAR WITNESS AS THE LAST LIGHT FADES FROM THE EDGE OF ETERNITY.
AND TO GRIEVE FOR EVERYTHING THAT EVER WAS--AND WAS EVER MEANT TO BE.

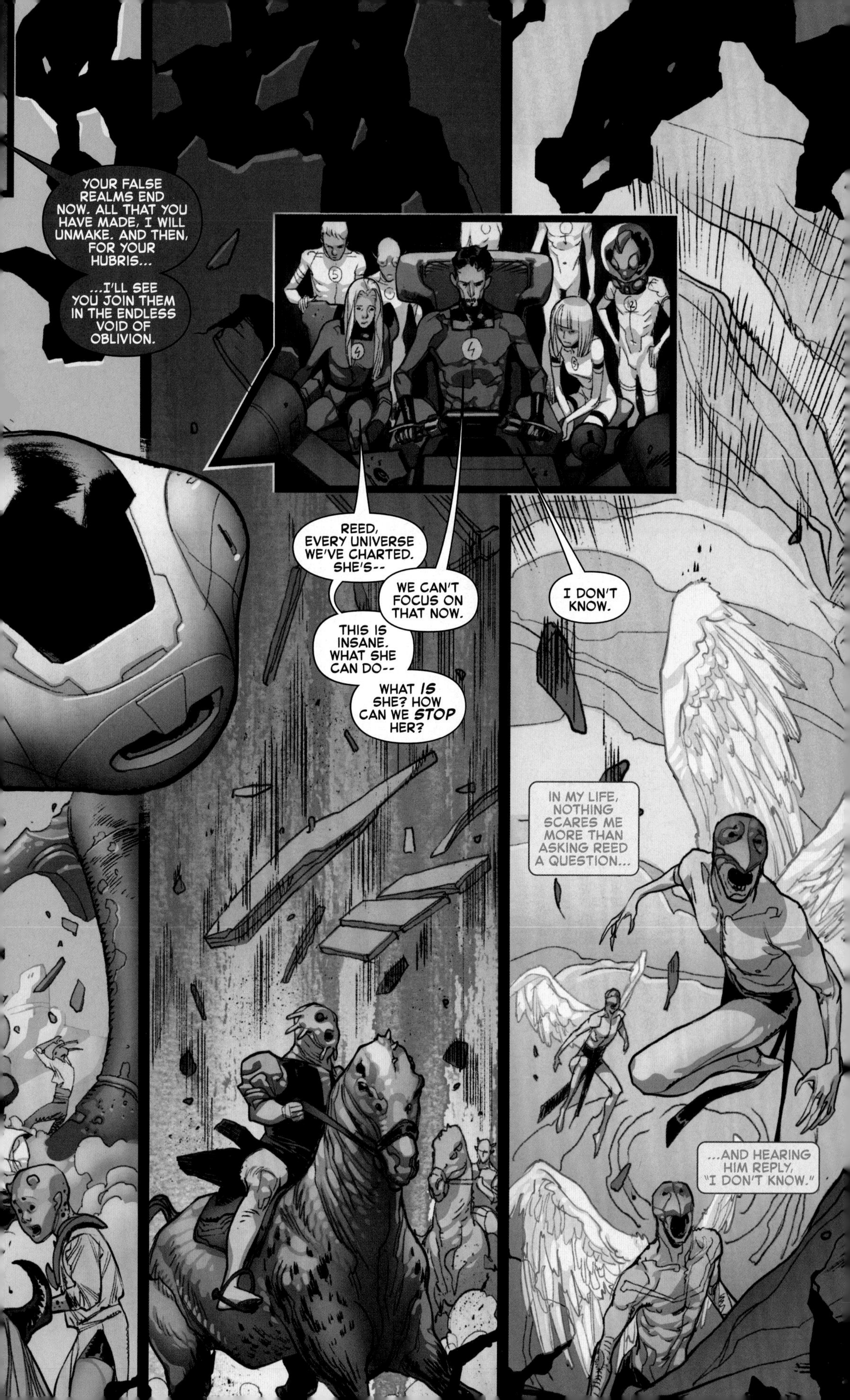
YOUR FALSE REALMS END NOW. ALL THAT YOU HAVE MADE, I WILL UNMAKE. AND THEN, FOR YOUR HUBRIS...
...I'LL SEE YOU JOIN THEM IN THE ENDLESS VOID OF OBLIVION.
REED, EVERY UNIVERSE WE'VE CHARTED. SHE'S--
WE CAN'T FOCUS ON THAT NOW.
THIS IS INSANE. WHAT SHE CAN DO--
WHAT *IS* SHE? HOW CAN WE *STOP* HER?
I DON'T KNOW.
IN MY LIFE, NOTHING SCARES ME MORE THAN ASKING REED A QUESTION...
...AND HEARING HIM REPLY, "I DON'T KNOW."

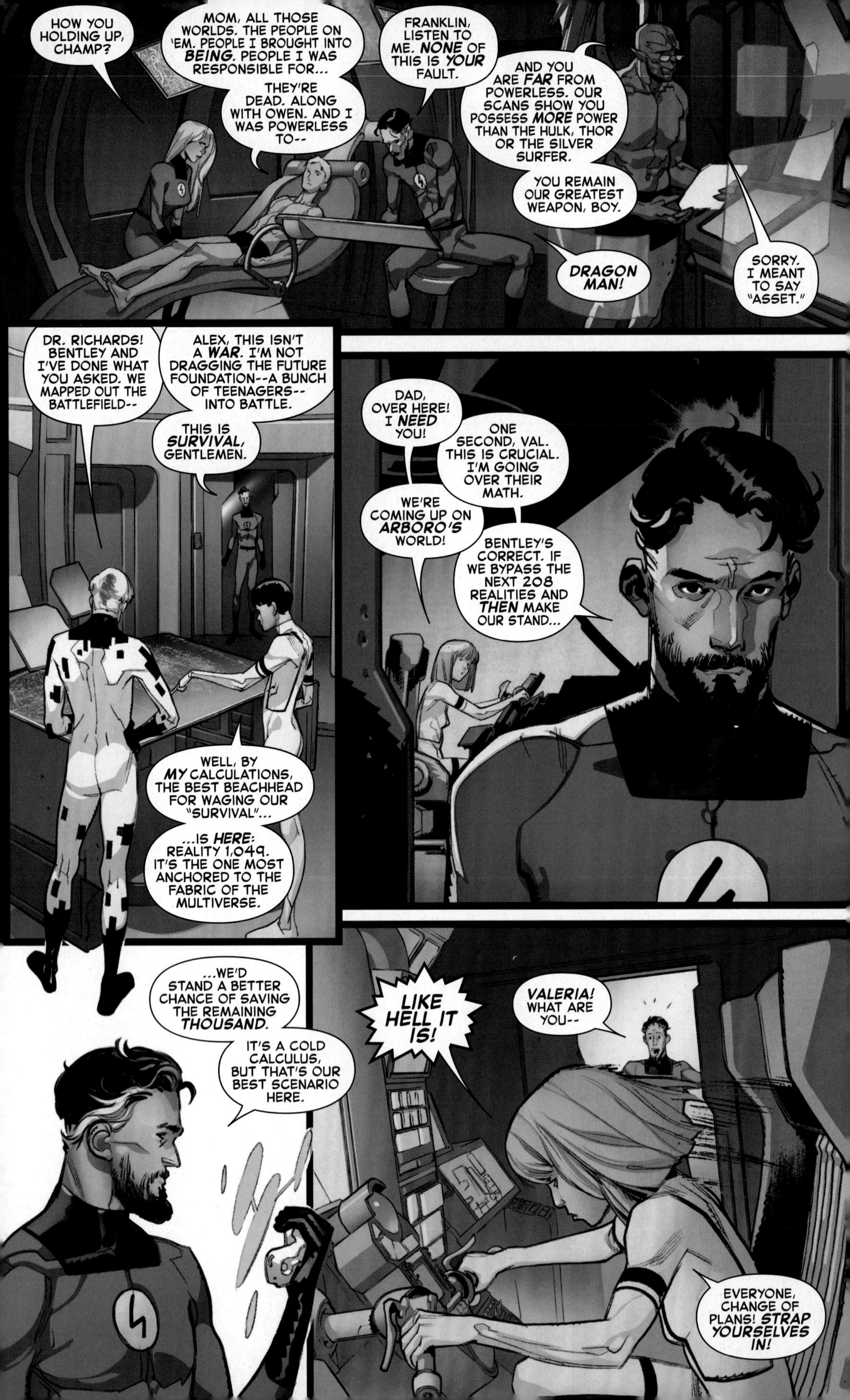

HOW YOU HOLDING UP, CHAMP?
MOM, ALL THOSE WORLDS. THE PEOPLE ON 'EM. PEOPLE I BROUGHT INTO BEING. PEOPLE I WAS RESPONSIBLE FOR...
THEY'RE DEAD. ALONG WITH OWEN. AND I WAS POWERLESS TO--
FRANKLIN, LISTEN TO ME. NONE OF THIS IS YOUR FAULT.
AND YOU ARE FAR FROM POWERLESS. OUR SCANS SHOW YOU POSSESS MORE POWER THAN THE HULK, THOR OR THE SILVER SURFER.
YOU REMAIN OUR GREATEST WEAPON, BOY.
DRAGON MAN!
SORRY. I MEANT TO SAY "ASSET."
DR. RICHARDS! BENTLEY AND I'VE DONE WHAT YOU ASKED. WE MAPPED OUT THE BATTLEFIELD--
ALEX, THIS ISN'T A WAR. I'M NOT DRAGGING THE FUTURE FOUNDATION--A BUNCH OF TEENAGERS--INTO BATTLE.
THIS IS SURVIVAL, GENTLEMEN.
WELL, BY MY CALCULATIONS, THE BEST BEACHHEAD FOR WAGING OUR "SURVIVAL"...
...IS HERE: REALITY 1,049. IT'S THE ONE MOST ANCHORED TO THE FABRIC OF THE MULTIVERSE.
DAD, OVER HERE! I NEED YOU!
ONE SECOND, VAL. THIS IS CRUCIAL. I'M GOING OVER THEIR MATH.
WE'RE COMING UP ON ARBORO'S WORLD!
BENTLEY'S CORRECT. IF WE BYPASS THE NEXT 208 REALITIES AND THEN MAKE OUR STAND...
...WE'D STAND A BETTER CHANCE OF SAVING THE REMAINING THOUSAND.
IT'S A COLD CALCULUS, BUT THAT'S OUR BEST SCENARIO HERE.
LIKE HELL IT IS!
VALERIA! WHAT ARE YOU--
EVERYONE, CHANGE OF PLANS! STRAP YOURSELVES IN!

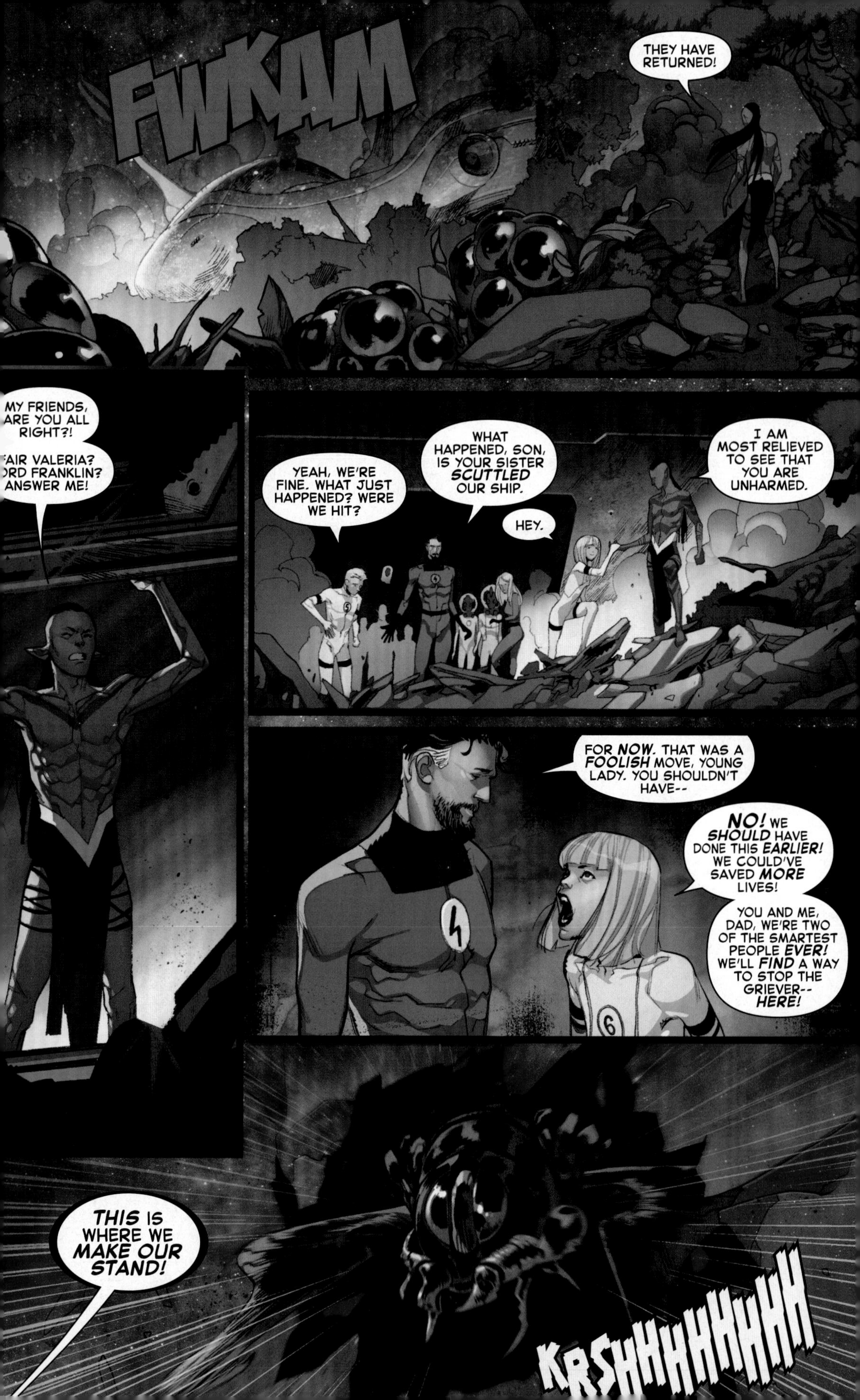
FWKAM
THEY HAVE RETURNED!
MY FRIENDS, ARE YOU ALL RIGHT?!
FAIR VALERIA? LORD FRANKLIN? ANSWER ME!
YEAH, WE'RE FINE. WHAT JUST HAPPENED? WERE WE HIT?
WHAT HAPPENED, SON, IS YOUR SISTER SCUTTLED OUR SHIP.
HEY.
I AM MOST RELIEVED TO SEE THAT YOU ARE UNHARMED.
FOR NOW. THAT WAS A FOOLISH MOVE, YOUNG LADY. YOU SHOULDN'T HAVE--
NO! WE SHOULD HAVE DONE THIS EARLIER! WE COULD'VE SAVED MORE LIVES!
YOU AND ME, DAD, WE'RE TWO OF THE SMARTEST PEOPLE EVER! WE'LL FIND A WAY TO STOP THE GRIEVER-- HERE!
THIS IS WHERE WE MAKE OUR STAND!
KRSHHHHHHHH

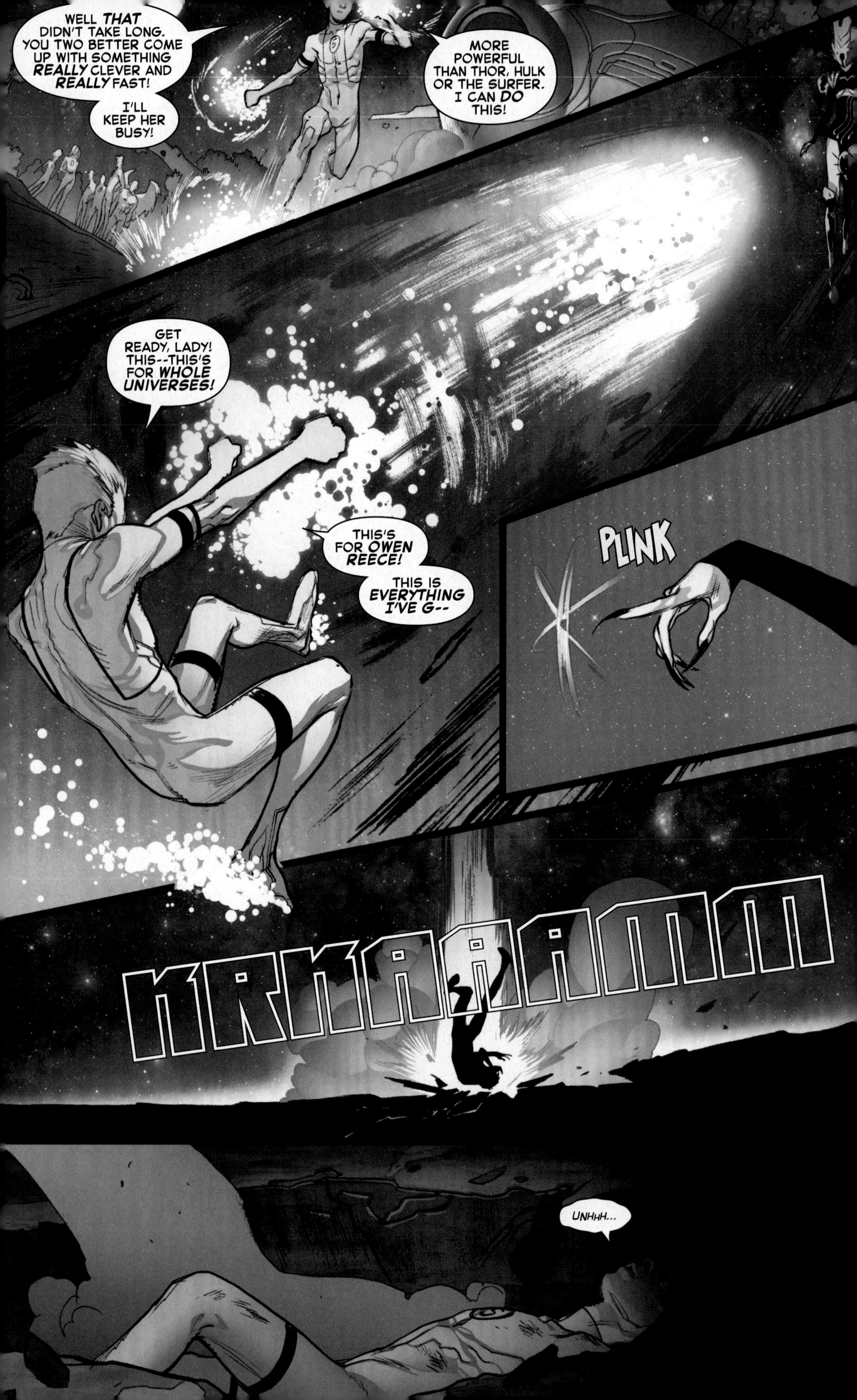
WELL THAT DIDN'T TAKE LONG. YOU TWO BETTER COME UP WITH SOMETHING REALLY CLEVER AND REALLY FAST!
I'LL KEEP HER BUSY!
MORE POWERFUL THAN THOR, HULK OR THE SURFER. I CAN DO THIS!
GET READY, LADY! THIS--THIS'S FOR WHOLE UNIVERSES!
THIS'S FOR OWEN REECE!
THIS IS EVERYTHING I'VE G--
PLINK
KRKAAMM
UNHHH...

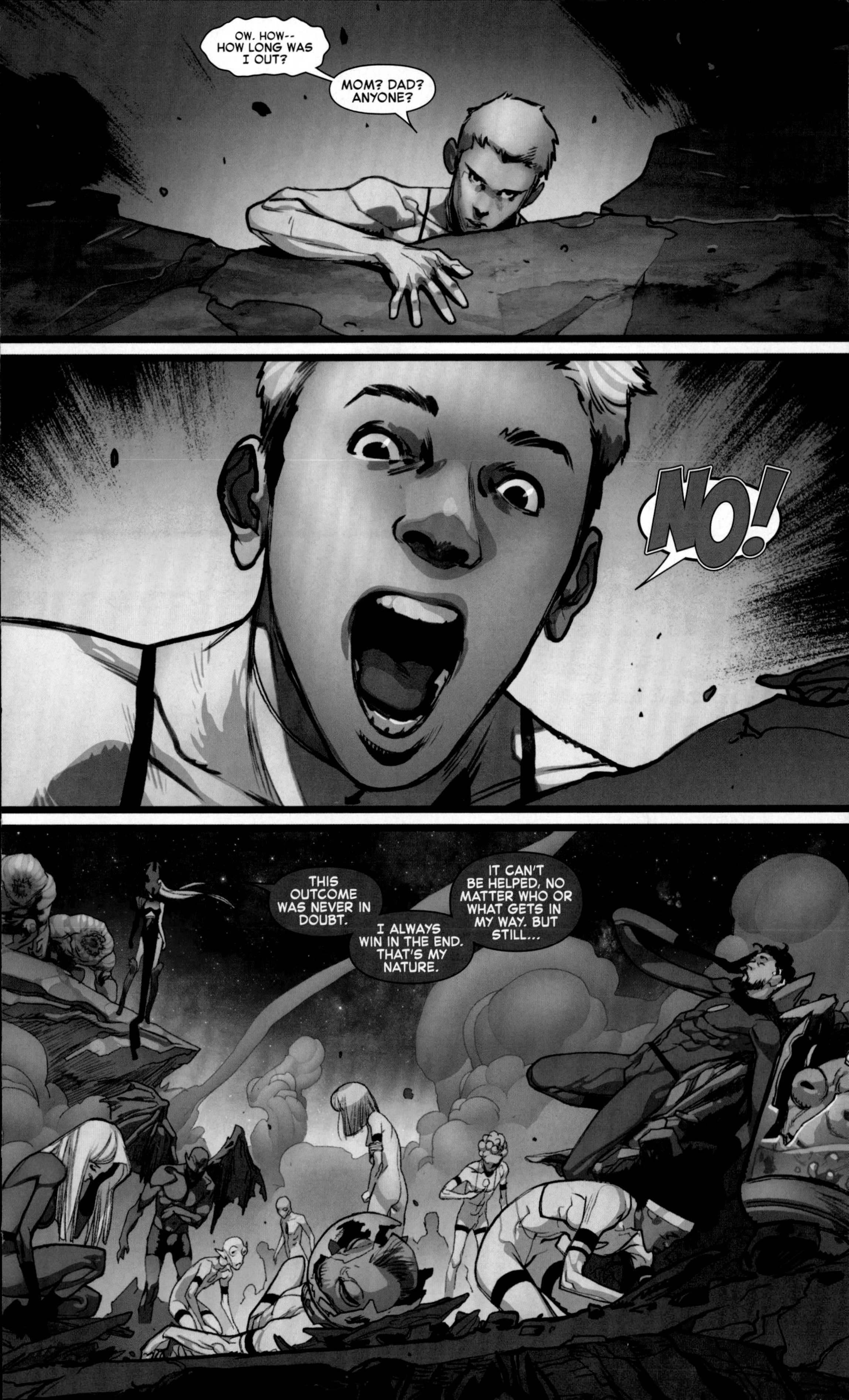
OW. HOW--
HOW LONG WAS I OUT?
MOM? DAD? ANYONE?
NO!
THIS OUTCOME WAS NEVER IN DOUBT.
I ALWAYS WIN IN THE END. THAT'S MY NATURE.
IT CAN'T BE HELPED, NO MATTER WHO OR WHAT GETS IN MY WAY. BUT STILL...

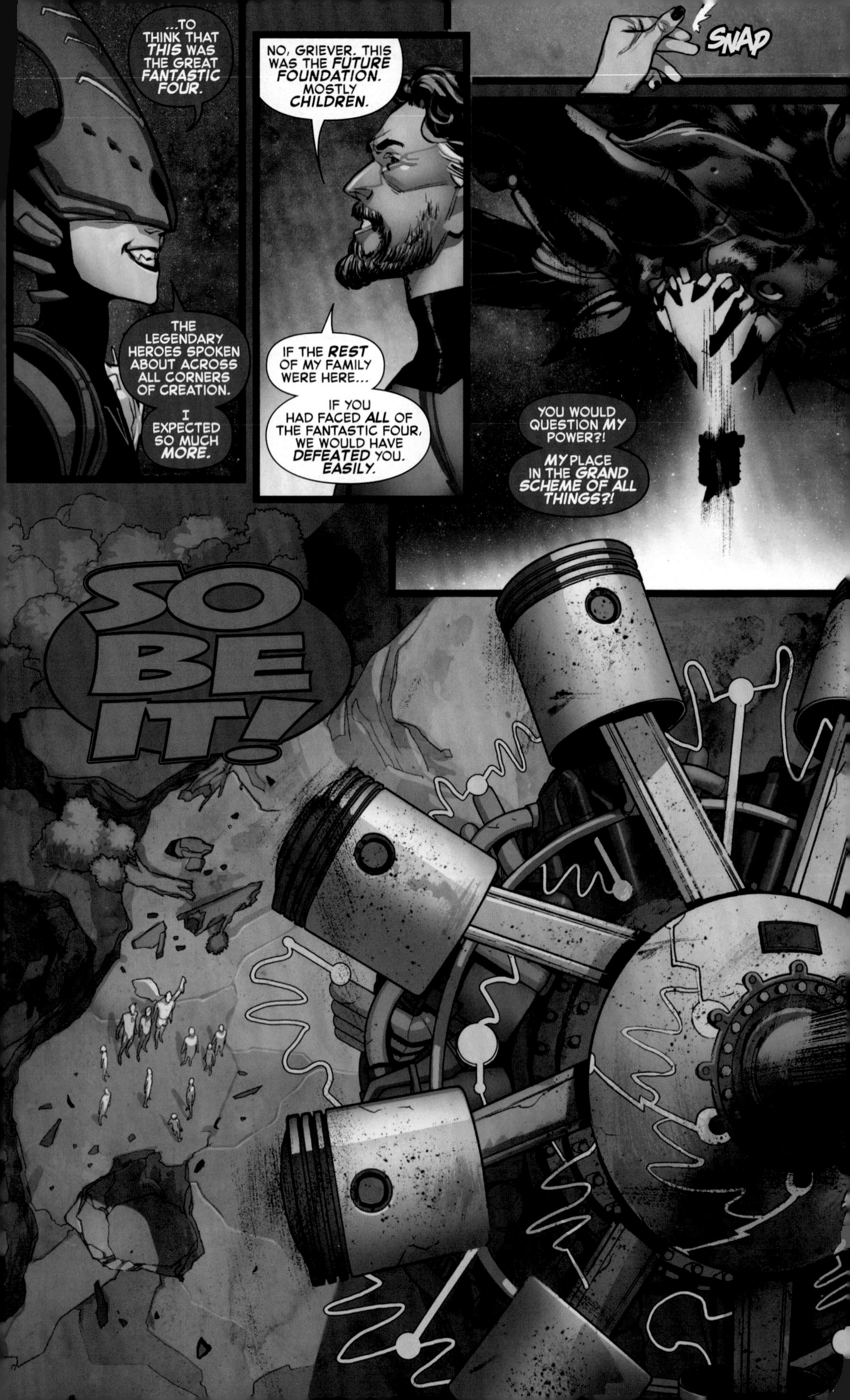
...TO THINK THAT THIS WAS THE GREAT FANTASTIC FOUR.
NO, GRIEVER. THIS WAS THE FUTURE FOUNDATION. MOSTLY CHILDREN.
SNAP
THE LEGENDARY HEROES SPOKEN ABOUT ACROSS ALL CORNERS OF CREATION.
I EXPECTED SO MUCH MORE.
IF THE REST OF MY FAMILY WERE HERE...
IF YOU HAD FACED ALL OF THE FANTASTIC FOUR, WE WOULD HAVE DEFEATED YOU. EASILY.
YOU WOULD QUESTION MY POWER?!
MY PLACE IN THE GRAND SCHEME OF ALL THINGS?!
SO BE IT!

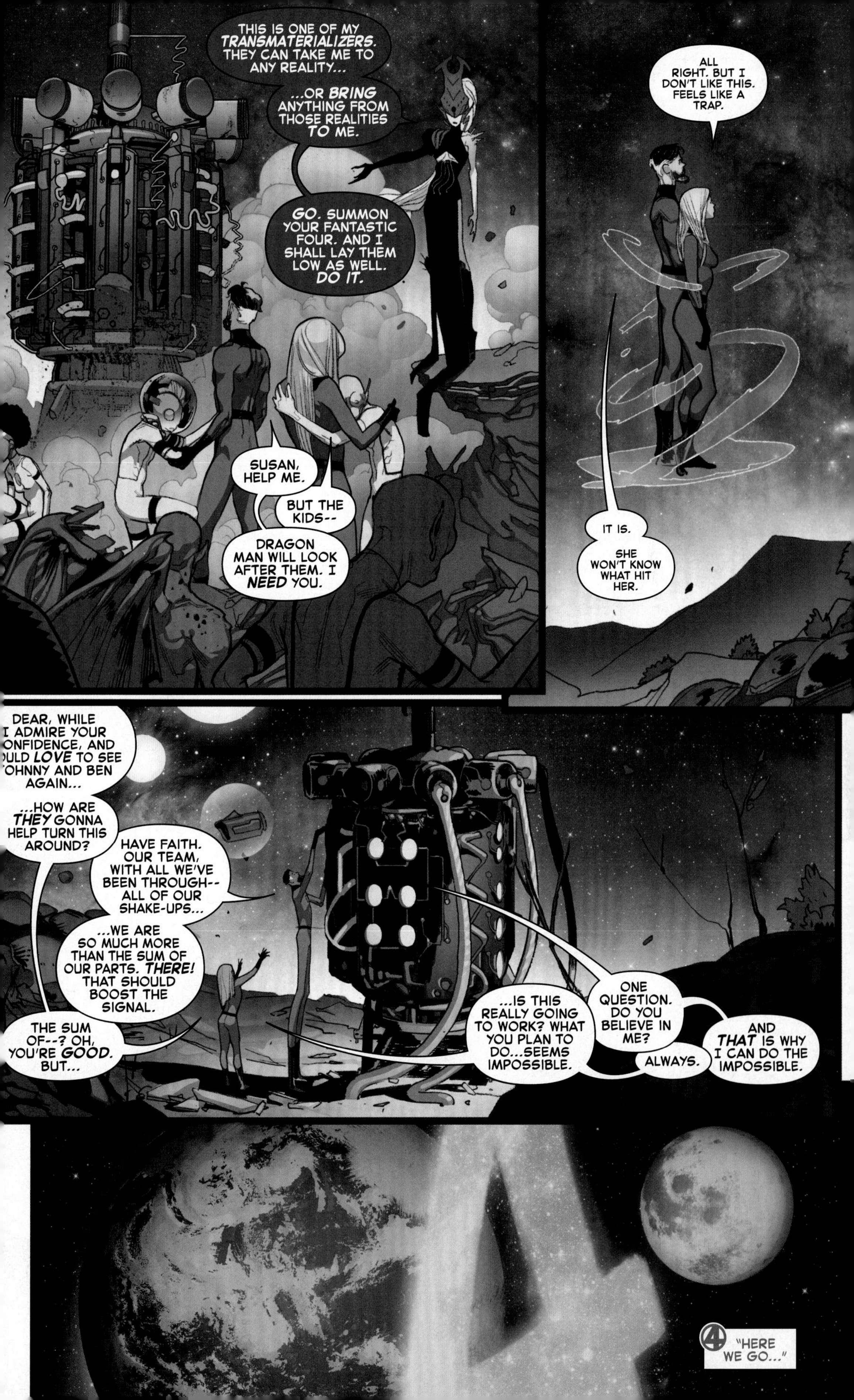
THIS IS ONE OF MY *TRANSMATERIALIZERS*. THEY CAN TAKE ME TO ANY REALITY...
...OR *BRING* ANYTHING FROM THOSE REALITIES *TO ME*.
GO. SUMMON YOUR FANTASTIC FOUR. AND I SHALL LAY THEM LOW AS WELL. *DO IT.*
SUSAN, HELP ME.
BUT THE KIDS--
DRAGON MAN WILL LOOK AFTER THEM. I *NEED* YOU.
ALL RIGHT. BUT I DON'T LIKE THIS. FEELS LIKE A TRAP.
IT IS.
SHE WON'T KNOW WHAT HIT HER.
DEAR, WHILE I ADMIRE YOUR ONFIDENCE, AND OULD *LOVE* TO SEE OHNNY AND BEN AGAIN...
...HOW ARE *THEY* GONNA HELP TURN THIS AROUND?
HAVE FAITH. OUR TEAM, WITH ALL WE'VE BEEN THROUGH-- ALL OF OUR SHAKE-UPS...
...WE ARE SO MUCH MORE THAN THE SUM OF OUR PARTS. *THERE!* THAT SHOULD BOOST THE SIGNAL.
THE SUM OF--? OH, YOU'RE *GOOD*. BUT...
...IS THIS REALLY GOING TO WORK? WHAT YOU PLAN TO DO...SEEMS IMPOSSIBLE.
ONE QUESTION. DO YOU BELIEVE IN ME?
ALWAYS.
AND *THAT* IS WHY I CAN DO THE IMPOSSIBLE.
"HERE WE GO..."

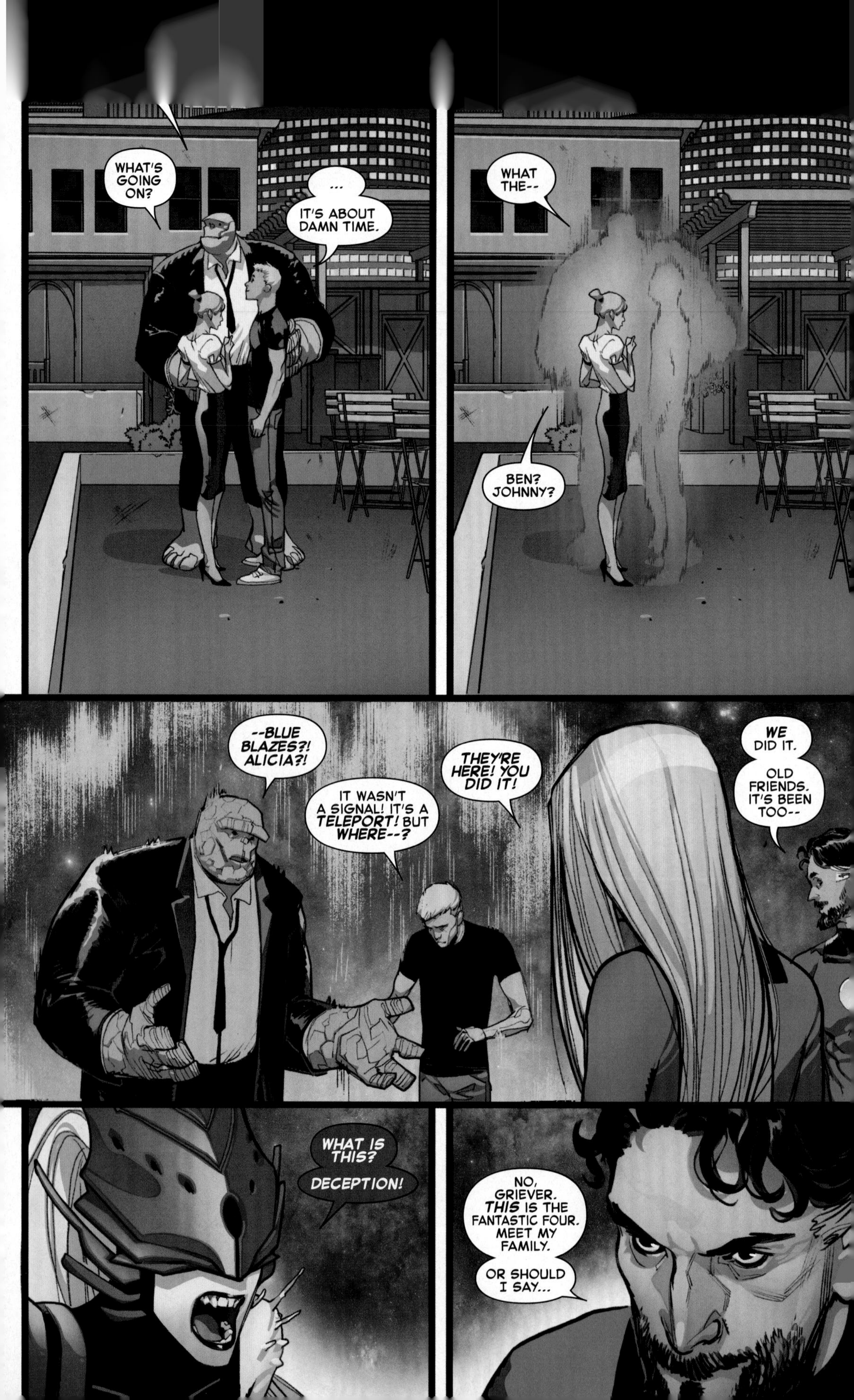
WHAT'S GOING ON?
...
IT'S ABOUT DAMN TIME.
WHAT THE--
BEN? JOHNNY?
--BLUE BLAZES?! ALICIA?!
IT WASN'T A SIGNAL! IT'S A TELEPORT! BUT WHERE--?
THEY'RE HERE! YOU DID IT!
WE DID IT.
OLD FRIENDS. IT'S BEEN TOO--
WHAT IS THIS?
DECEPTION!
NO, GRIEVER. THIS IS THE FANTASTIC FOUR. MEET MY FAMILY.
OR SHOULD I SAY...

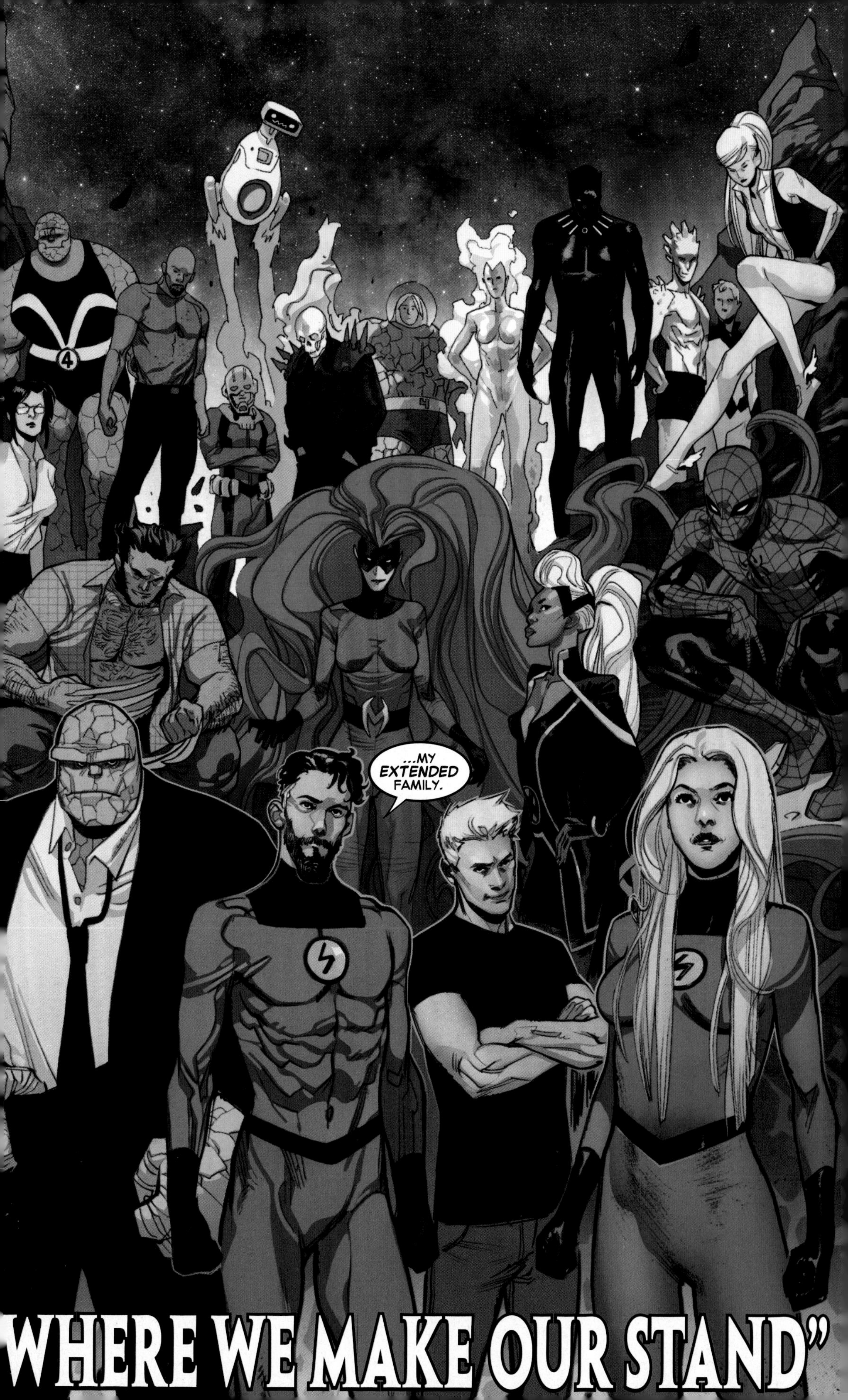
...MY EXTENDED FAMILY.
WHERE WE MAKE OUR STAND"

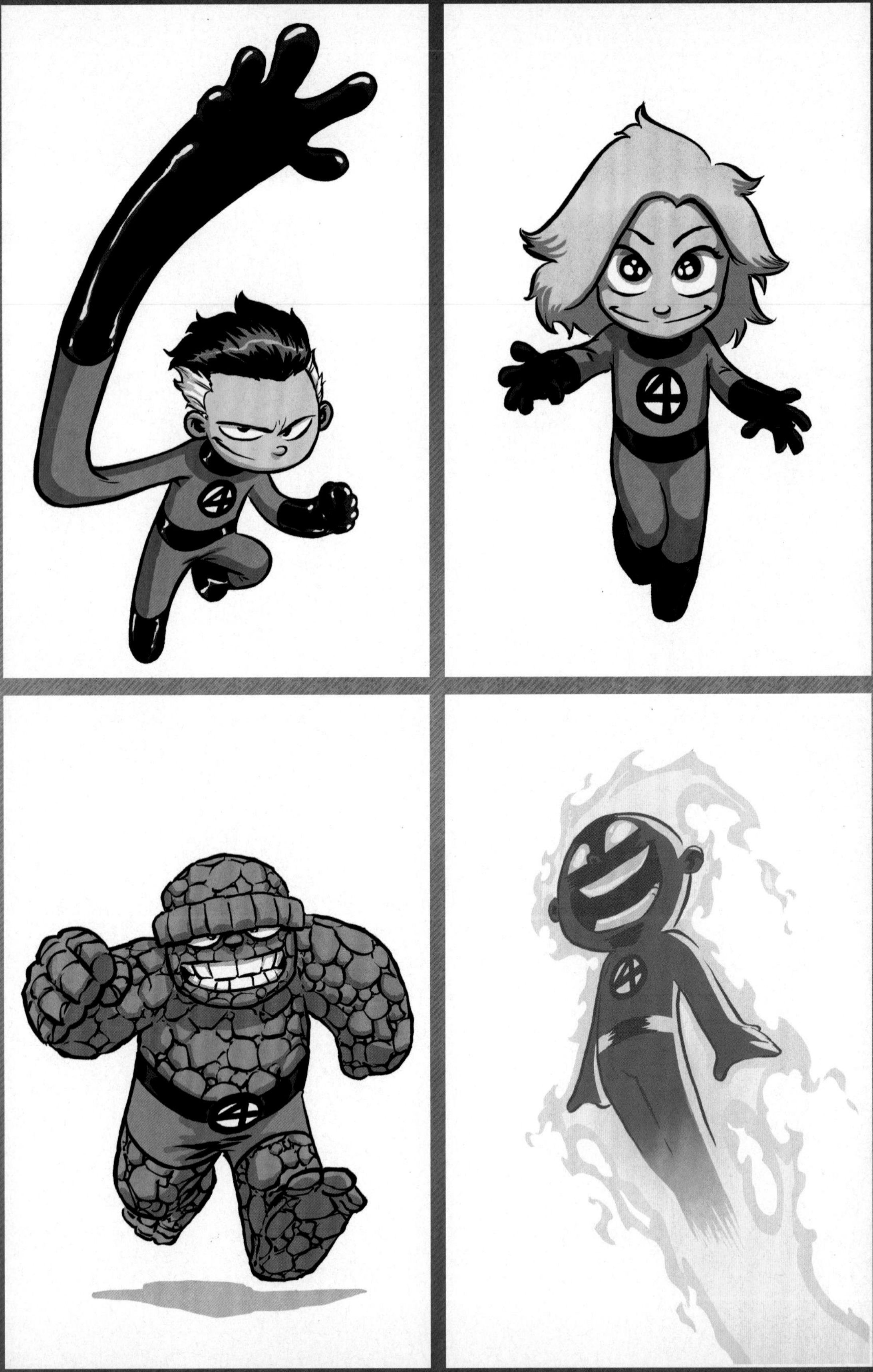

#1-4 variants by **Skottie Young**

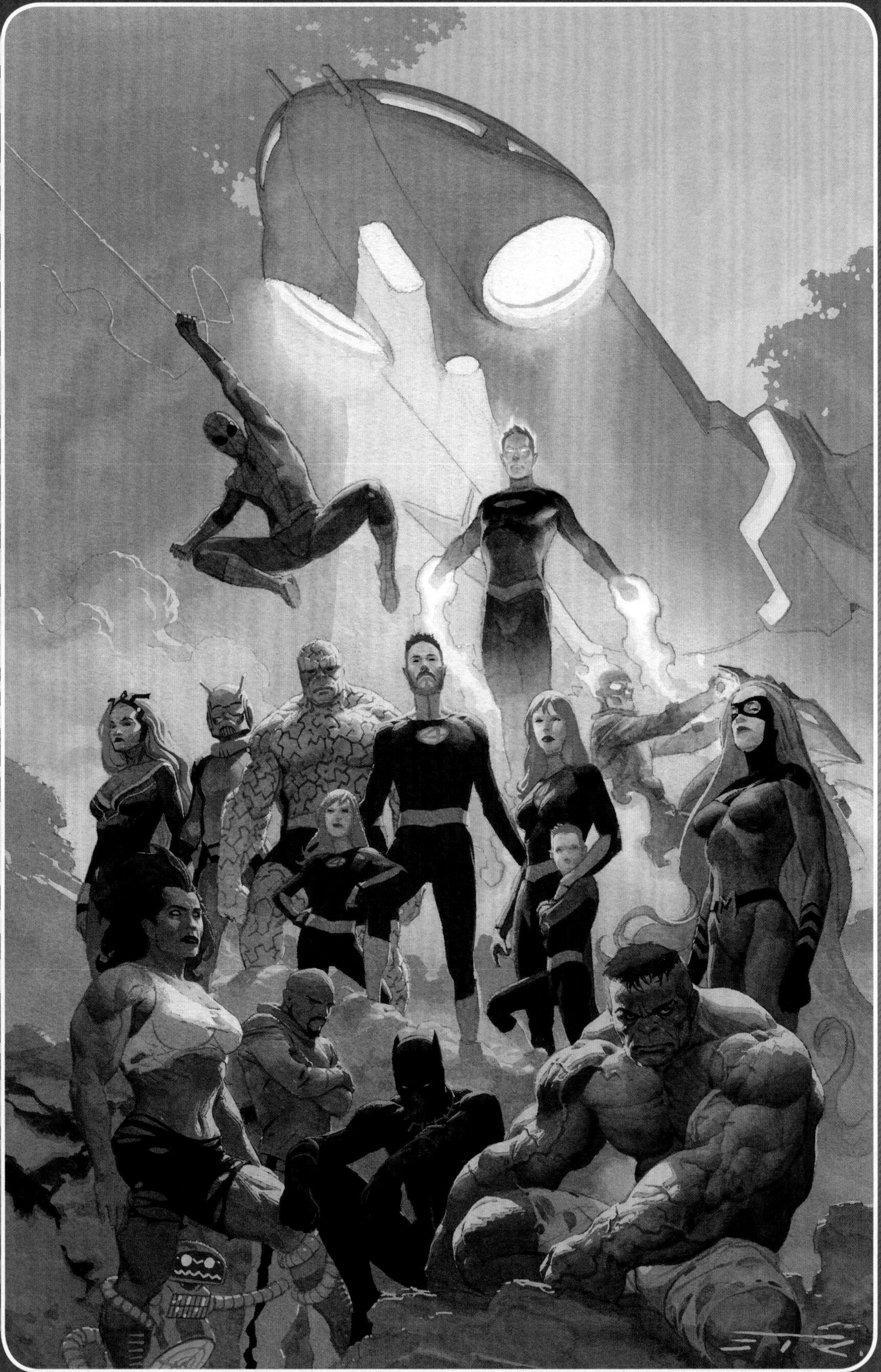

3

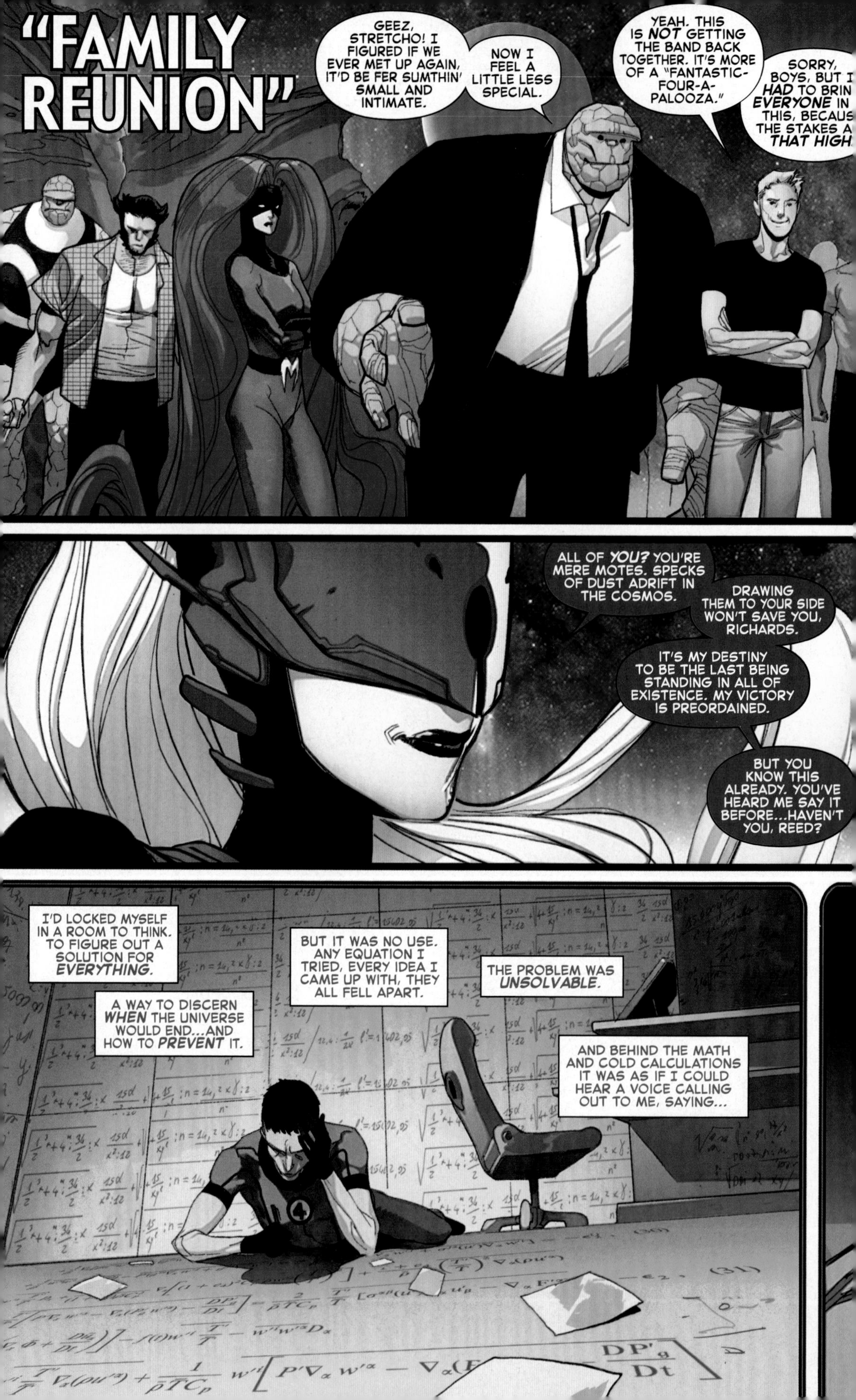
"FAMILY REUNION"
GEEZ, STRETCHO! I FIGURED IF WE EVER MET UP AGAIN, IT'D BE FER SUMTHIN' SMALL AND INTIMATE.
NOW I FEEL A LITTLE LESS SPECIAL.
YEAH. THIS IS NOT GETTING THE BAND BACK TOGETHER. IT'S MORE OF A "FANTASTIC-FOUR-A-PALOOZA."
SORRY, BOYS, BUT I HAD TO BRIN EVERYONE IN THIS, BECAUS THE STAKES A THAT HIGH.
ALL OF YOU? YOU'RE MERE MOTES. SPECKS OF DUST ADRIFT IN THE COSMOS.
DRAWING THEM TO YOUR SIDE WON'T SAVE YOU, RICHARDS.
IT'S MY DESTINY TO BE THE LAST BEING STANDING IN ALL OF EXISTENCE. MY VICTORY IS PREORDAINED.
BUT YOU KNOW THIS ALREADY. YOU'VE HEARD ME SAY IT BEFORE...HAVEN'T YOU, REED?
I'D LOCKED MYSELF IN A ROOM TO THINK. TO FIGURE OUT A SOLUTION FOR EVERYTHING.
A WAY TO DISCERN WHEN THE UNIVERSE WOULD END...AND HOW TO PREVENT IT.
BUT IT WAS NO USE. ANY EQUATION I TRIED, EVERY IDEA I CAME UP WITH, THEY ALL FELL APART.
THE PROBLEM WAS UNSOLVABLE.
AND BEHIND THE MATH AND COLD CALCULATIONS IT WAS AS IF I COULD HEAR A VOICE CALLING OUT TO ME, SAYING...

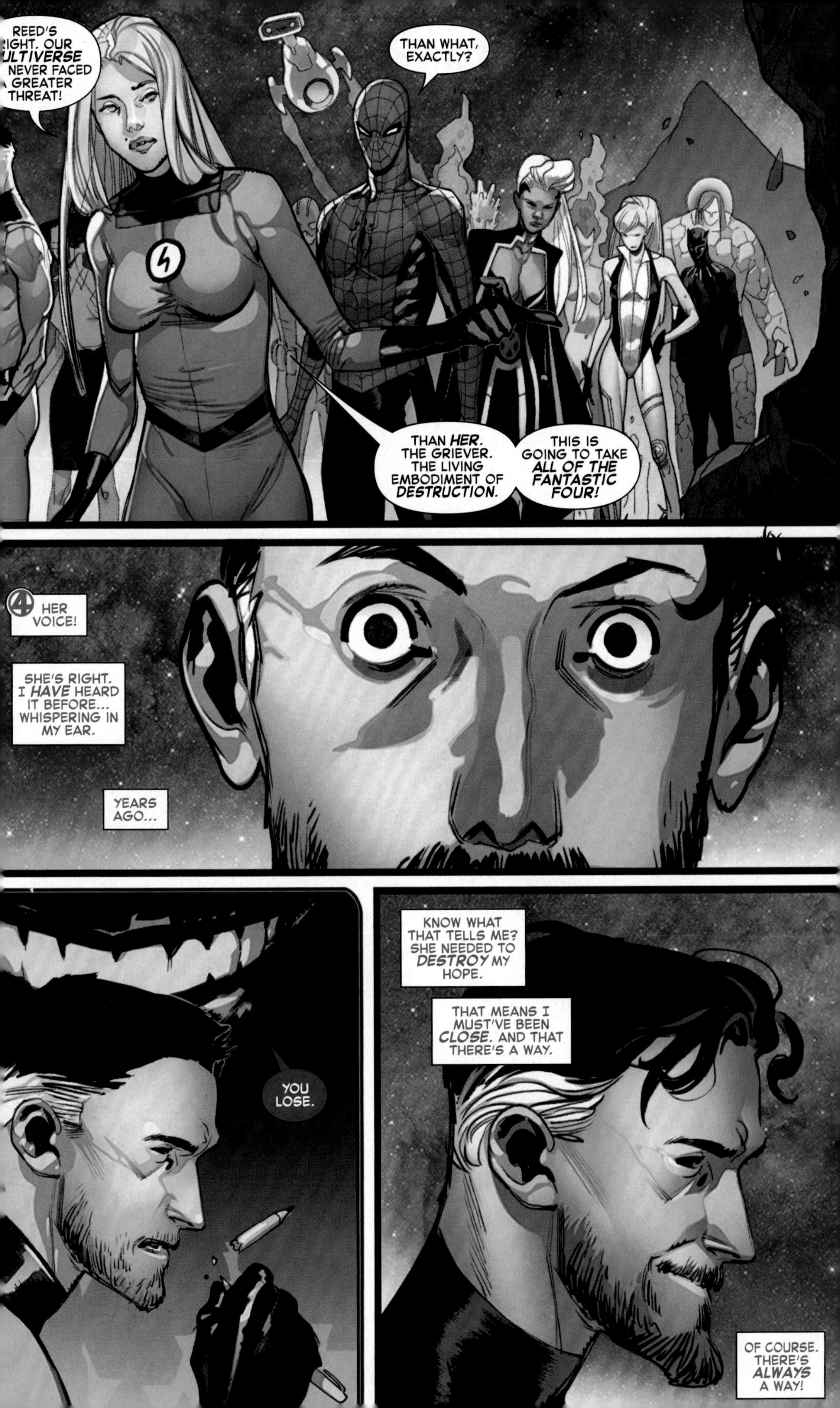
REED'S RIGHT. OUR MULTIVERSE NEVER FACED A GREATER THREAT!
THAN WHAT, EXACTLY?
THAN HER. THE GRIEVER. THE LIVING EMBODIMENT OF DESTRUCTION.
THIS IS GOING TO TAKE ALL OF THE FANTASTIC FOUR!
HER VOICE!
SHE'S RIGHT. I HAVE HEARD IT BEFORE... WHISPERING IN MY EAR.
YEARS AGO...
YOU LOSE.
KNOW WHAT THAT TELLS ME? SHE NEEDED TO DESTROY MY HOPE.
THAT MEANS I MUST'VE BEEN CLOSE. AND THAT THERE'S A WAY.
OF COURSE. THERE'S ALWAYS A WAY!

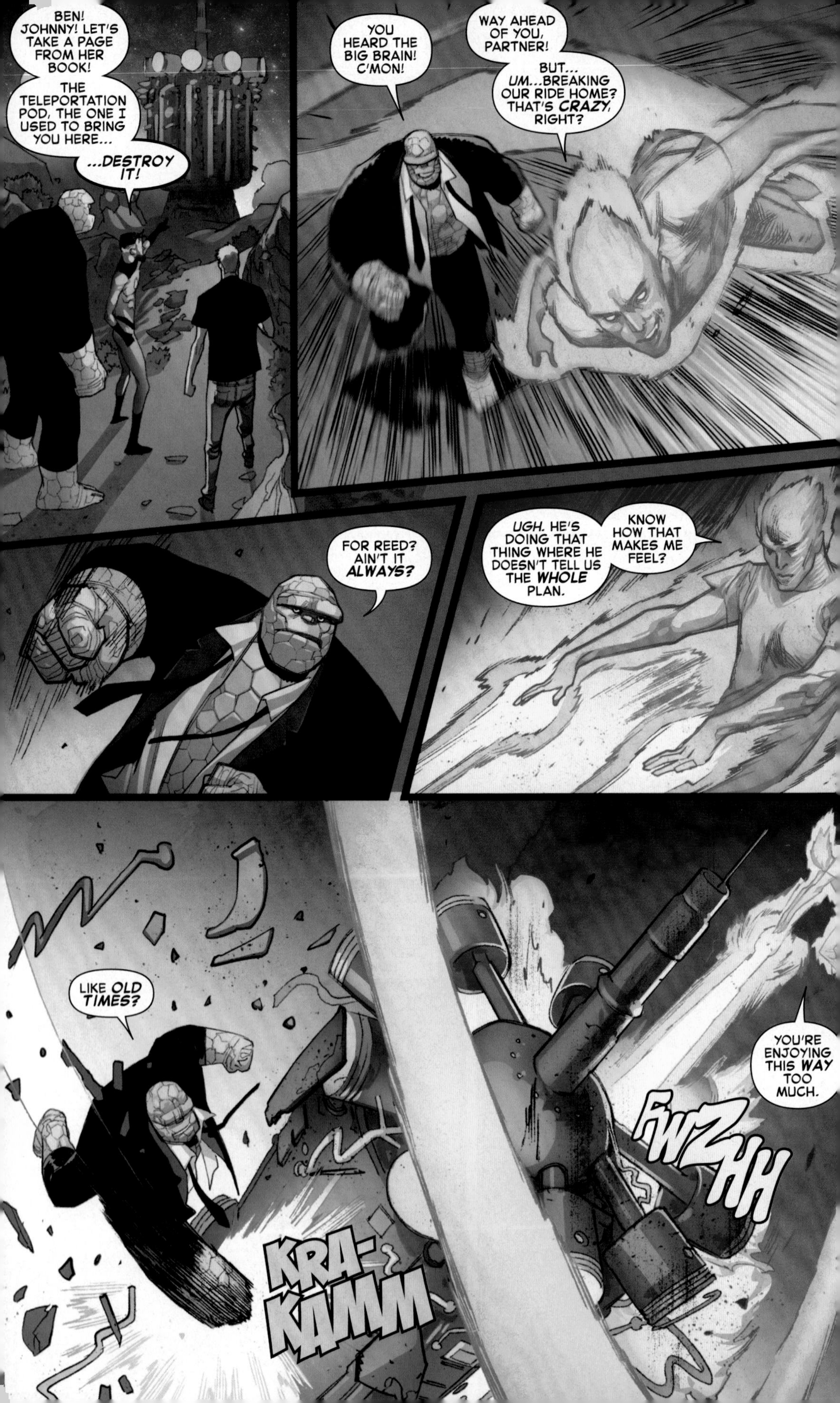
BEN! JOHNNY! LET'S TAKE A PAGE FROM HER BOOK!
THE TELEPORTATION POD, THE ONE I USED TO BRING YOU HERE...
...DESTROY IT!
YOU HEARD THE BIG BRAIN! C'MON!
WAY AHEAD OF YOU, PARTNER!
BUT... UM...BREAKING OUR RIDE HOME? THAT'S CRAZY, RIGHT?
FOR REED? AIN'T IT ALWAYS?
UGH. HE'S DOING THAT THING WHERE HE DOESN'T TELL US THE WHOLE PLAN.
KNOW HOW THAT MAKES ME FEEL?
LIKE OLD TIMES?
YOU'RE ENJOYING THIS WAY TOO MUCH.
FWZHH
KRA-KAMM

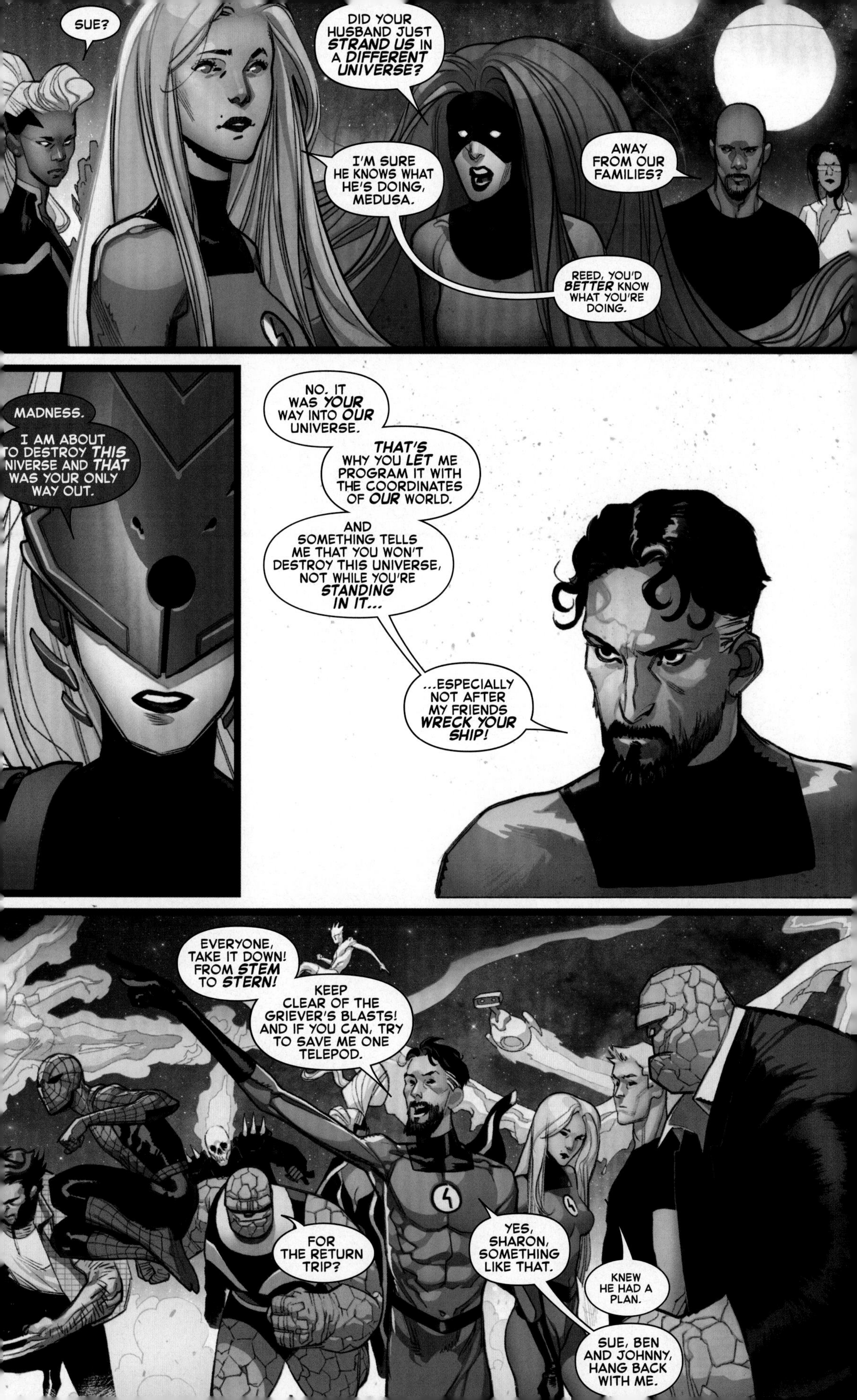
SUE?
DID YOUR HUSBAND JUST STRAND US IN A DIFFERENT UNIVERSE?
I'M SURE HE KNOWS WHAT HE'S DOING, MEDUSA.
AWAY FROM OUR FAMILIES?
REED, YOU'D BETTER KNOW WHAT YOU'RE DOING.
MADNESS.
I AM ABOUT TO DESTROY THIS NIVERSE AND THAT WAS YOUR ONLY WAY OUT.
NO. IT WAS YOUR WAY INTO OUR UNIVERSE.
THAT'S WHY YOU LET ME PROGRAM IT WITH THE COORDINATES OF OUR WORLD.
AND SOMETHING TELLS ME THAT YOU WON'T DESTROY THIS UNIVERSE, NOT WHILE YOU'RE STANDING IN IT...
...ESPECIALLY NOT AFTER MY FRIENDS WRECK YOUR SHIP!
EVERYONE, TAKE IT DOWN! FROM STEM TO STERN!
KEEP CLEAR OF THE GRIEVER'S BLASTS! AND IF YOU CAN, TRY TO SAVE ME ONE TELEPOD.
FOR THE RETURN TRIP?
YES, SHARON, SOMETHING LIKE THAT.
KNEW HE HAD A PLAN.
SUE, BEN AND JOHNNY, HANG BACK WITH ME.

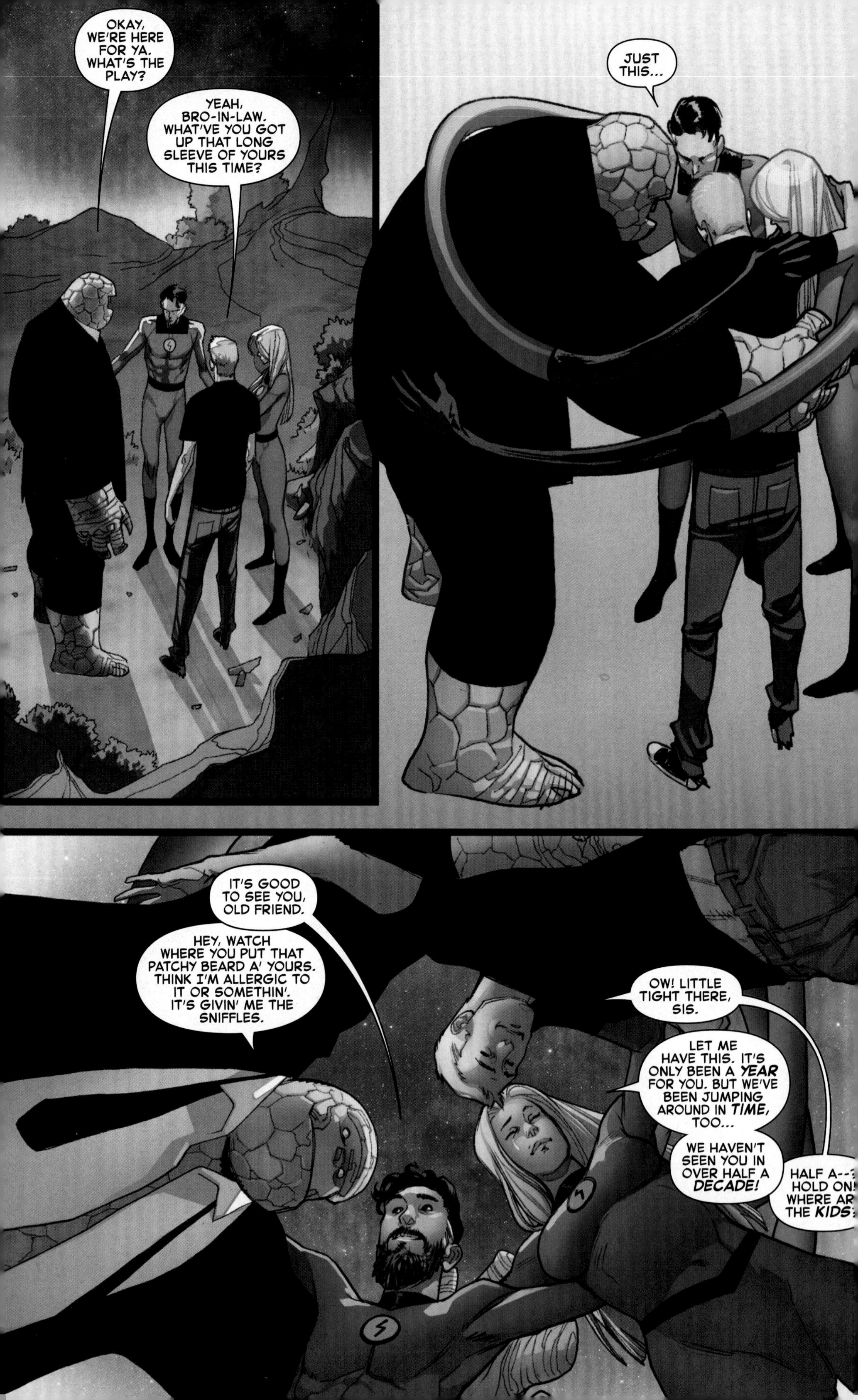
OKAY, WE'RE HERE FOR YA. WHAT'S THE PLAY?
YEAH, BRO-IN-LAW. WHAT'VE YOU GOT UP THAT LONG SLEEVE OF YOURS THIS TIME?
JUST THIS...
IT'S GOOD TO SEE YOU, OLD FRIEND.
HEY, WATCH WHERE YOU PUT THAT PATCHY BEARD A' YOURS. THINK I'M ALLERGIC TO IT OR SOMETHIN'. IT'S GIVIN' ME THE SNIFFLES.
OW! LITTLE TIGHT THERE, SIS.
LET ME HAVE THIS. IT'S ONLY BEEN A *YEAR* FOR YOU. BUT WE'VE BEEN JUMPING AROUND IN *TIME*, TOO...
WE HAVEN'T SEEN YOU IN OVER HALF A *DECADE!*
HALF A--? HOLD ON! WHERE AR THE *KIDS*?

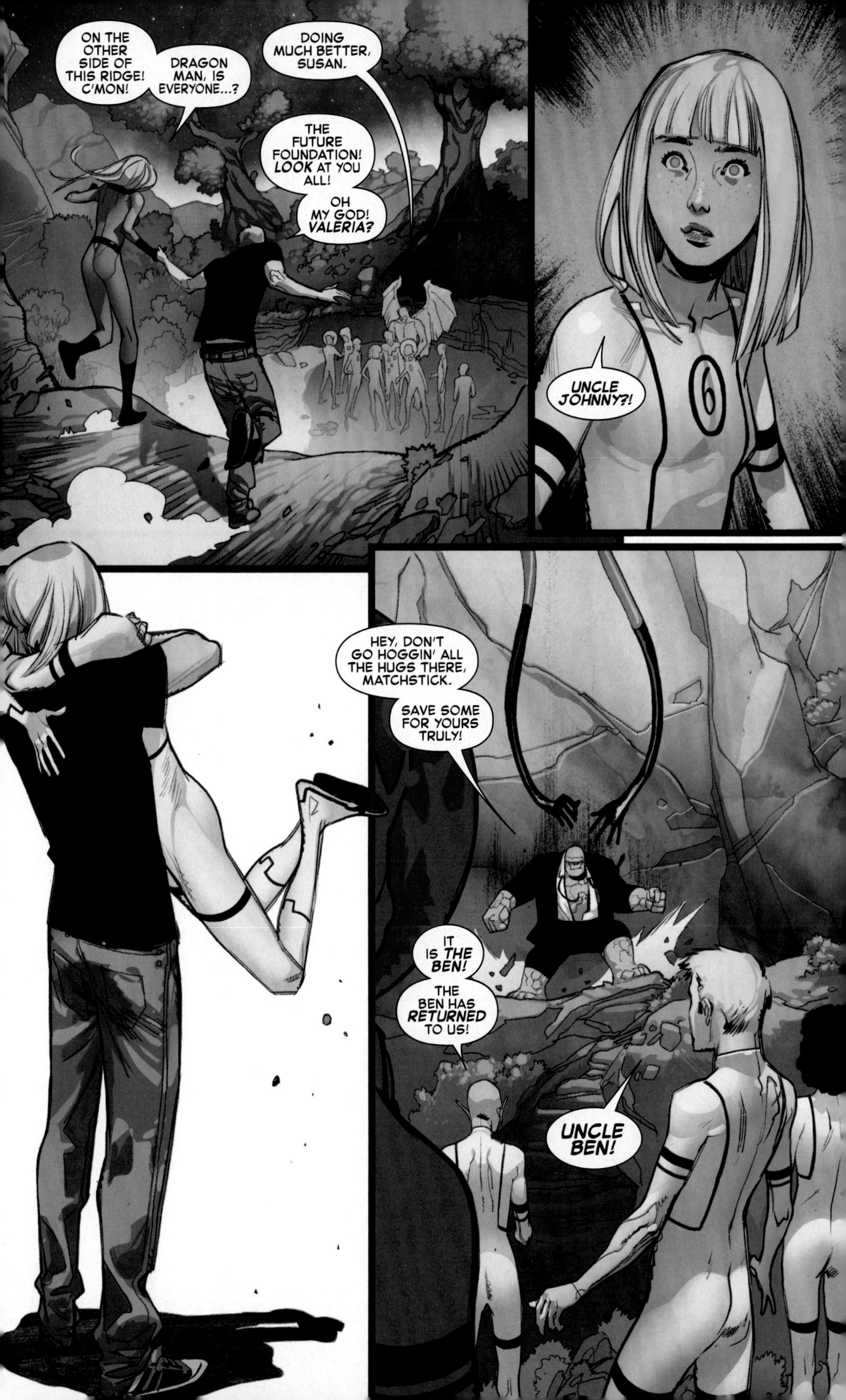
ON THE OTHER SIDE OF THIS RIDGE! C'MON!
DRAGON MAN, IS EVERYONE...?
DOING MUCH BETTER, SUSAN.
THE FUTURE FOUNDATION! LOOK AT YOU ALL!
OH MY GOD! VALERIA?
UNCLE JOHNNY?!
HEY, DON'T GO HOGGIN' ALL THE HUGS THERE, MATCHSTICK.
SAVE SOME FOR YOURS TRULY!
IT IS THE BEN!
THE BEN HAS RETURNED TO US!
UNCLE BEN!

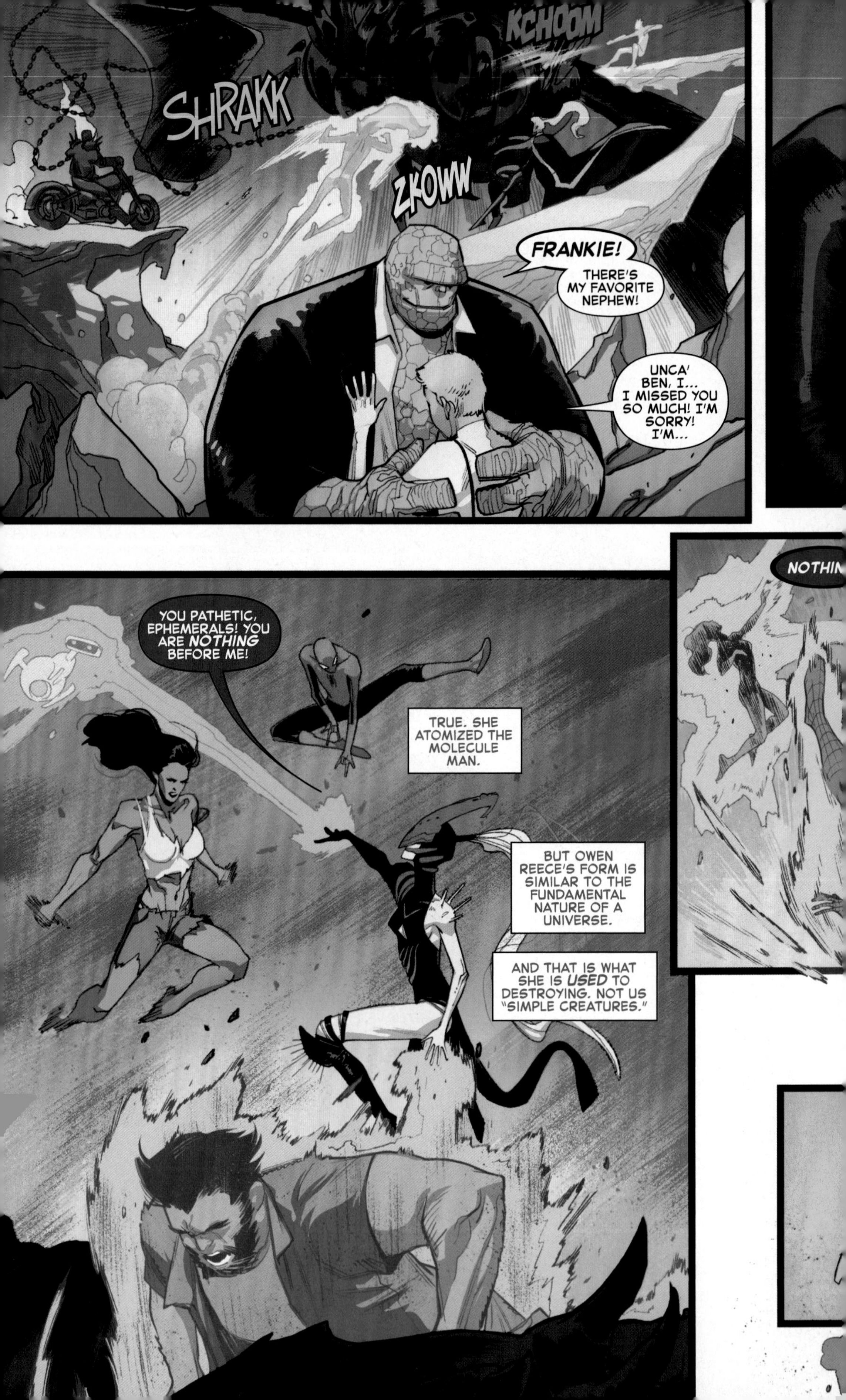
KCHOOM
SHRAKK
ZKOWW
FRANKIE! THERE'S MY FAVORITE NEPHEW!
UNCA' BEN, I... I MISSED YOU SO MUCH! I'M SORRY! I'M...
NOTHIN
YOU PATHETIC, EPHEMERALS! YOU ARE *NOTHING* BEFORE ME!
TRUE. SHE ATOMIZED THE MOLECULE MAN.
BUT OWEN REECE'S FORM IS SIMILAR TO THE FUNDAMENTAL NATURE OF A UNIVERSE.
AND THAT IS WHAT SHE IS *USED* TO DESTROYING. NOT US "SIMPLE CREATURES."

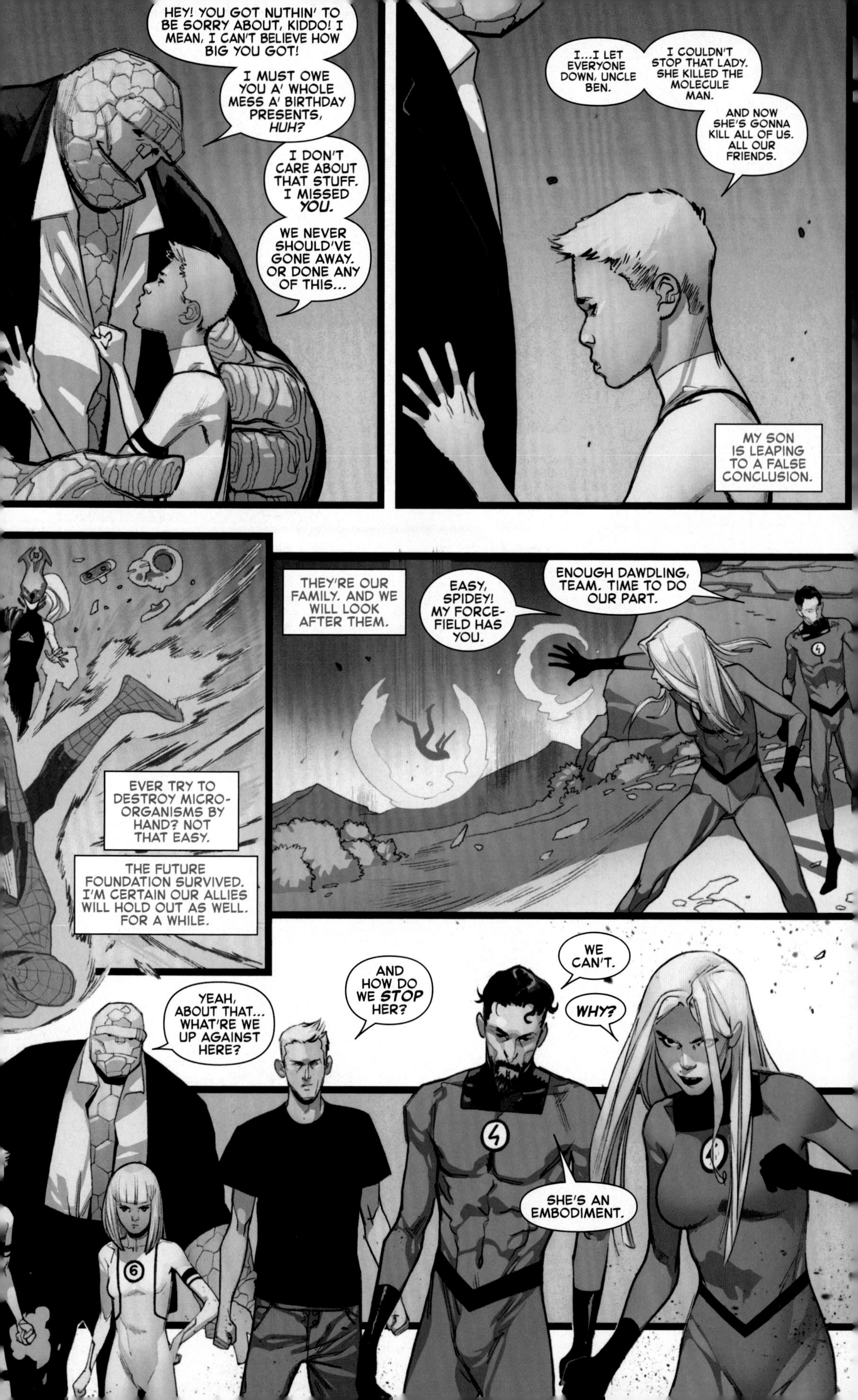
HEY! YOU GOT NUTHIN' TO BE SORRY ABOUT, KIDDO! I MEAN, I CAN'T BELIEVE HOW BIG YOU GOT!
I MUST OWE YOU A' WHOLE MESS A' BIRTHDAY PRESENTS, HUH?
I DON'T CARE ABOUT THAT STUFF. I MISSED YOU.
WE NEVER SHOULD'VE GONE AWAY. OR DONE ANY OF THIS...
I...I LET EVERYONE DOWN, UNCLE BEN.
I COULDN'T STOP THAT LADY. SHE KILLED THE MOLECULE MAN.
AND NOW SHE'S GONNA KILL ALL OF US. ALL OUR FRIENDS.
MY SON IS LEAPING TO A FALSE CONCLUSION.
EVER TRY TO DESTROY MICRO-ORGANISMS BY HAND? NOT THAT EASY.
THE FUTURE FOUNDATION SURVIVED. I'M CERTAIN OUR ALLIES WILL HOLD OUT AS WELL. FOR A WHILE.
THEY'RE OUR FAMILY. AND WE WILL LOOK AFTER THEM.
EASY, SPIDEY! MY FORCE-FIELD HAS YOU.
ENOUGH DAWDLING, TEAM. TIME TO DO OUR PART.
YEAH, ABOUT THAT... WHAT'RE WE UP AGAINST HERE?
AND HOW DO WE STOP HER?
WE CAN'T.
WHY?
SHE'S AN EMBODIMENT.

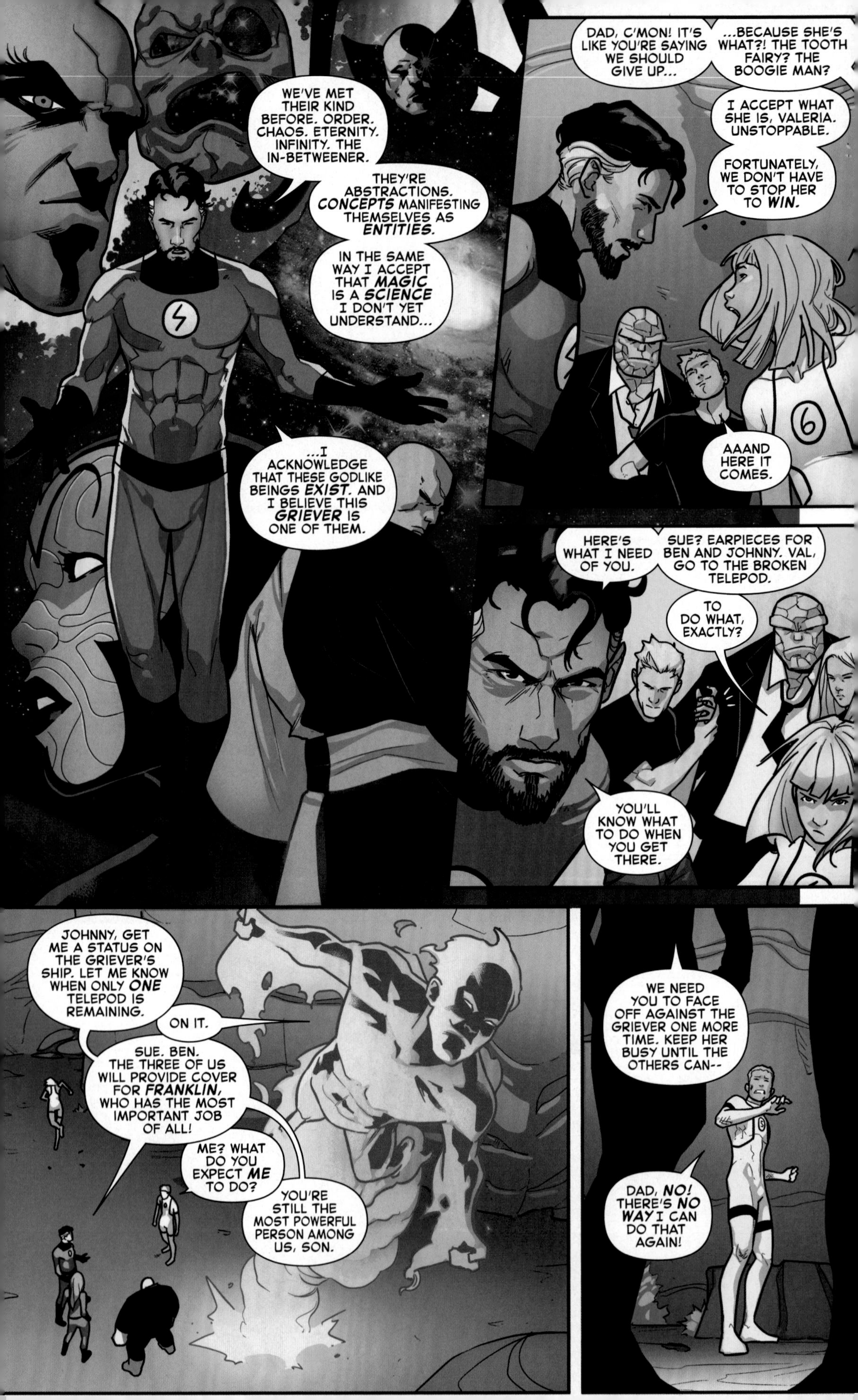
WE'VE MET THEIR KIND BEFORE. ORDER. CHAOS. ETERNITY. INFINITY. THE IN-BETWEENER.
THEY'RE ABSTRACTIONS. CONCEPTS MANIFESTING THEMSELVES AS ENTITIES.
IN THE SAME WAY I ACCEPT THAT MAGIC IS A SCIENCE I DON'T YET UNDERSTAND...
...I ACKNOWLEDGE THAT THESE GODLIKE BEINGS EXIST. AND I BELIEVE THIS GRIEVER IS ONE OF THEM.
DAD, C'MON! IT'S LIKE YOU'RE SAYING WE SHOULD GIVE UP...
...BECAUSE SHE'S WHAT?! THE TOOTH FAIRY? THE BOOGIE MAN?
I ACCEPT WHAT SHE IS, VALERIA. UNSTOPPABLE.
FORTUNATELY, WE DON'T HAVE TO STOP HER TO WIN.
AAAND HERE IT COMES.
HERE'S WHAT I NEED OF YOU.
SUE? EARPIECES FOR BEN AND JOHNNY. VAL, GO TO THE BROKEN TELEPOD.
TO DO WHAT, EXACTLY?
YOU'LL KNOW WHAT TO DO WHEN YOU GET THERE.
JOHNNY, GET ME A STATUS ON THE GRIEVER'S SHIP. LET ME KNOW WHEN ONLY ONE TELEPOD IS REMAINING.
ON IT.
SUE. BEN. THE THREE OF US WILL PROVIDE COVER FOR FRANKLIN, WHO HAS THE MOST IMPORTANT JOB OF ALL!
ME? WHAT DO YOU EXPECT ME TO DO?
YOU'RE STILL THE MOST POWERFUL PERSON AMONG US, SON.
WE NEED YOU TO FACE OFF AGAINST THE GRIEVER ONE MORE TIME. KEEP HER BUSY UNTIL THE OTHERS CAN--
DAD, NO! THERE'S NO WAY I CAN DO THAT AGAIN!

REED, BUDDY, THIS AIN'T RIGHT.

BEN, PLEASE. I BELIEVE IN YOU, SON. YOU CAN DO THIS!

BUT IF I SCREW UP AGAIN--

HONEY, NO, YOU *DIDN'T* SCREW UP. YOU WERE *SO BRAVE!*

YOU TRIED YOUR BEST. AND YOU DID IT TO KEEP ME, YOUR FATHER, YOUR SISTER AND ALL YOUR FRIENDS SAFE.

AND IF YOU REALLY DON'T WANT TO DO THIS, THERE'S NO SHAME IN--

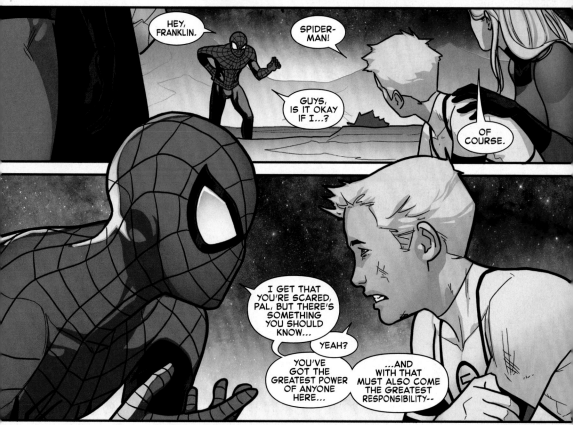

HEY, FRANKLIN.

SPIDER-MAN!

GUYS, IS IT OKAY IF I...?

OF COURSE.

I GET THAT YOU'RE SCARED, PAL, BUT THERE'S SOMETHING YOU SHOULD KNOW...

YEAH?

YOU'VE GOT THE GREATEST POWER OF ANYONE HERE...

...AND WITH THAT MUST ALSO COME THE GREATEST RESPONSIBILITY--

NOPE! NOT HAPPENING.

HEY!

SHUT UP! DON'T PUT ALL A' THAT ON THE KID'S BACK!

FRANKIE, DON'T PAY ATTENTION TO THIS YUTZ. LISTEN TO YOUR *UNCLE BEN.*

Y'KNOW HOW WE WIN IN TIMES LIKE THIS? SOMEBODY KNOCKS US DOWN, WE GET *BACK UP.*

AND WE *KEEP* GETTIN' BACK UP 'TIL WHAT NEEDS TO GET DONE *GETS DONE.*

BUT I CAN'T--

HEH. YOU DON'T HAVE TO. I SAID "*WE.*" YOU AIN'T DOIN' THIS *ALONE.*

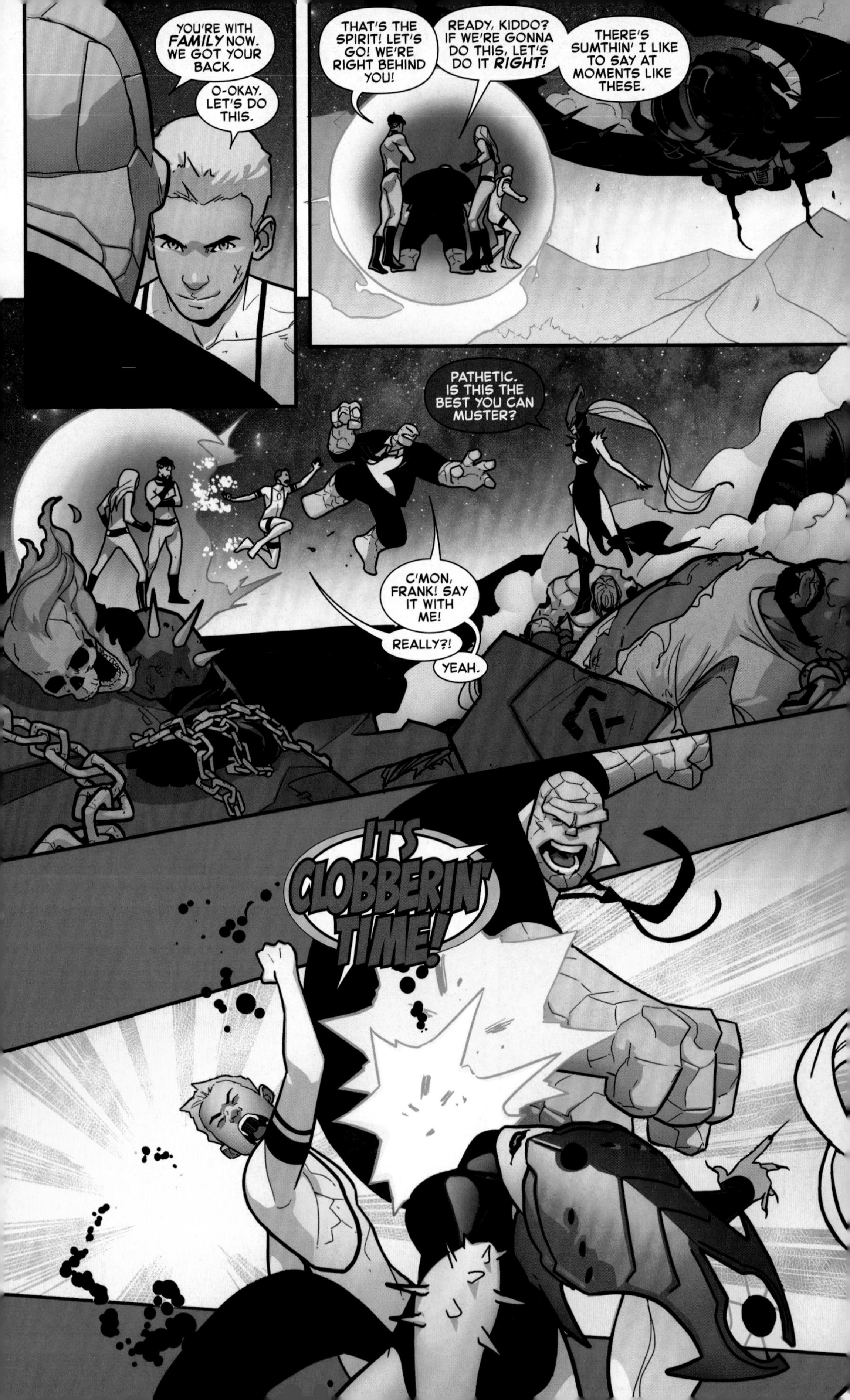
YOU'RE WITH FAMILY NOW. WE GOT YOUR BACK.
O-OKAY. LET'S DO THIS.
THAT'S THE SPIRIT! LET'S GO! WE'RE RIGHT BEHIND YOU!
READY, KIDDO? IF WE'RE GONNA DO THIS, LET'S DO IT RIGHT!
THERE'S SUMTHIN' I LIKE TO SAY AT MOMENTS LIKE THESE.
PATHETIC. IS THIS THE BEST YOU CAN MUSTER?
C'MON, FRANK! SAY IT WITH ME!
REALLY?!
YEAH.
IT'S CLOBBERIN' TIME!

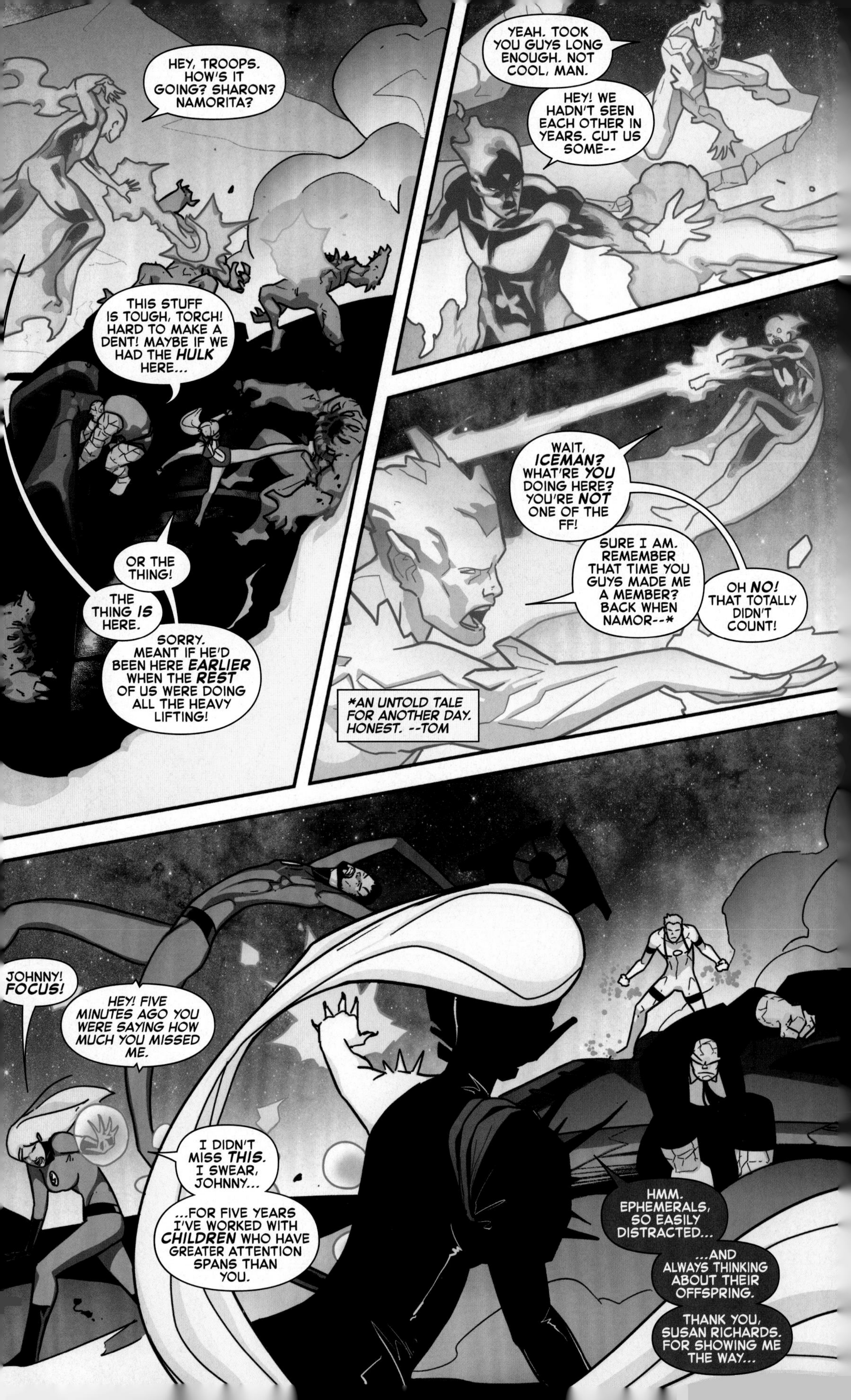
HEY, TROOPS. HOW'S IT GOING? SHARON? NAMORITA?
YEAH. TOOK YOU GUYS LONG ENOUGH. NOT COOL, MAN.
HEY! WE HADN'T SEEN EACH OTHER IN YEARS. CUT US SOME--
THIS STUFF IS TOUGH, TORCH! HARD TO MAKE A DENT! MAYBE IF WE HAD THE HULK HERE...
OR THE THING!
THE THING IS HERE.
SORRY. MEANT IF HE'D BEEN HERE EARLIER WHEN THE REST OF US WERE DOING ALL THE HEAVY LIFTING!
WAIT, ICEMAN? WHAT'RE YOU DOING HERE? YOU'RE NOT ONE OF THE FF!
SURE I AM. REMEMBER THAT TIME YOU GUYS MADE ME A MEMBER? BACK WHEN NAMOR--*
OH NO! THAT TOTALLY DIDN'T COUNT!
*AN UNTOLD TALE FOR ANOTHER DAY. HONEST. --TOM
JOHNNY! FOCUS!
HEY! FIVE MINUTES AGO YOU WERE SAYING HOW MUCH YOU MISSED ME.
I DIDN'T MISS THIS. I SWEAR, JOHNNY...
...FOR FIVE YEARS I'VE WORKED WITH CHILDREN WHO HAVE GREATER ATTENTION SPANS THAN YOU.
HMM. EPHEMERALS, SO EASILY DISTRACTED...
...AND ALWAYS THINKING ABOUT THEIR OFFSPRING.
THANK YOU, SUSAN RICHARDS. FOR SHOWING ME THE WAY...

LISTEN TO ME, MY ENDLINGS.

THE ADULTS? LEAVE THEM BE.

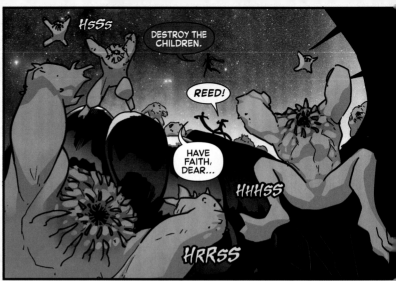

HSSS

DESTROY THE CHILDREN.

REED!

HAVE FAITH, DEAR...

HHHSS

HRRSS

"...WE'VE TRAINED THE FUTURE FOUNDATION WELL.

"AND REMEMBER, IT'S LIKE BEN SAID...

EVERYONE, GET READY! ONOME?

I AM PREPARED, ALEX. DRAGON MAN?

I WILL KEEP WATCH OVER THE YOUNGER ONES.

"...NONE OF US ARE ALONE. WE'RE WITH FAMILY."

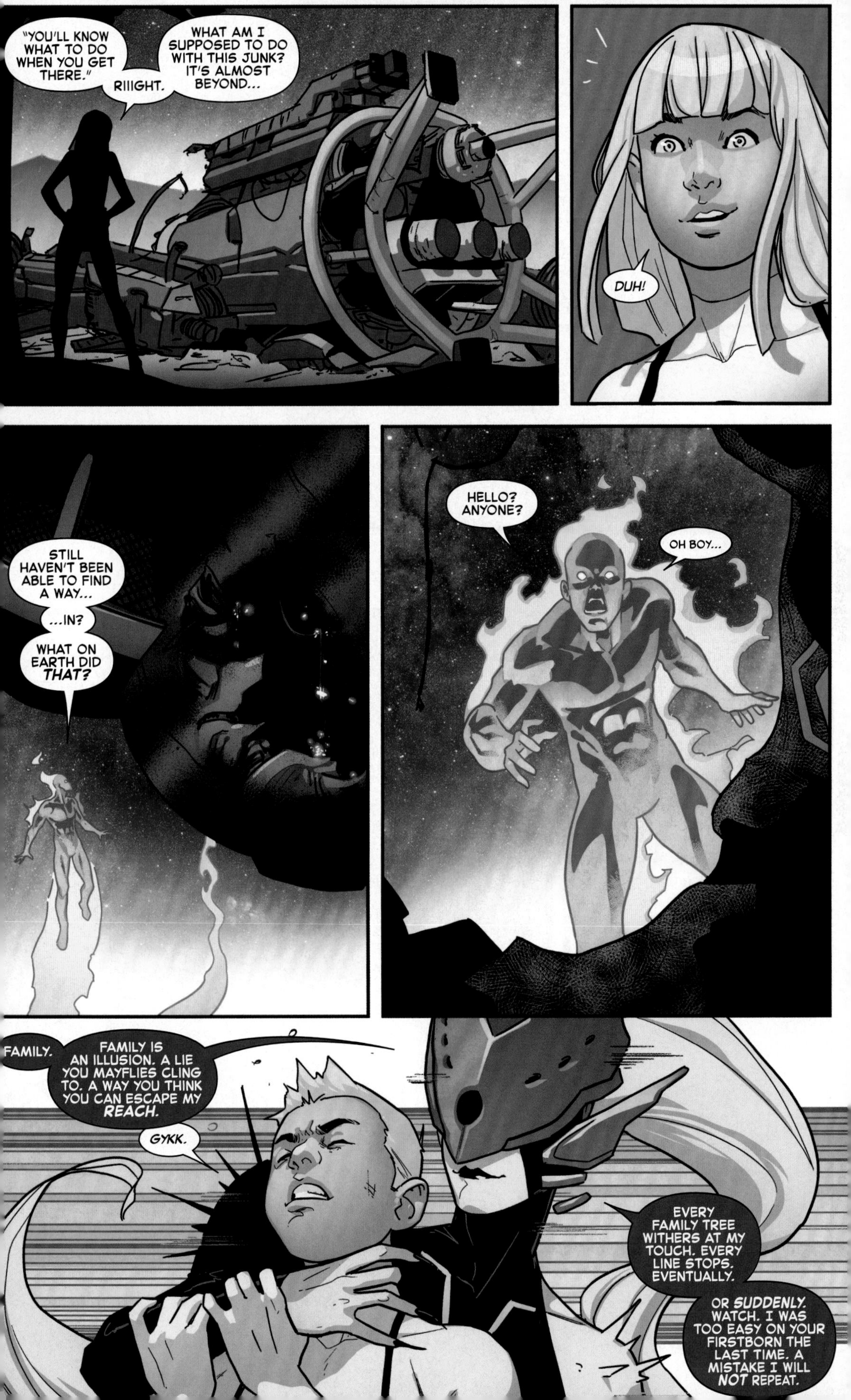
"YOU'LL KNOW WHAT TO DO WHEN YOU GET THERE."
RIIIGHT.
WHAT AM I SUPPOSED TO DO WITH THIS JUNK? IT'S ALMOST BEYOND...
DUH!
STILL HAVEN'T BEEN ABLE TO FIND A WAY...
...IN?
WHAT ON EARTH DID *THAT?*
HELLO? ANYONE?
OH BOY...
FAMILY.
FAMILY IS AN ILLUSION. A LIE YOU MAYFLIES CLING TO. A WAY YOU THINK YOU CAN ESCAPE MY *REACH.*
GYKK.
EVERY FAMILY TREE WITHERS AT MY TOUCH. EVERY LINE STOPS. EVENTUALLY.
OR *SUDDENLY.* WATCH. I WAS TOO EASY ON YOUR FIRSTBORN THE LAST TIME. A MISTAKE I WILL *NOT* REPEAT.

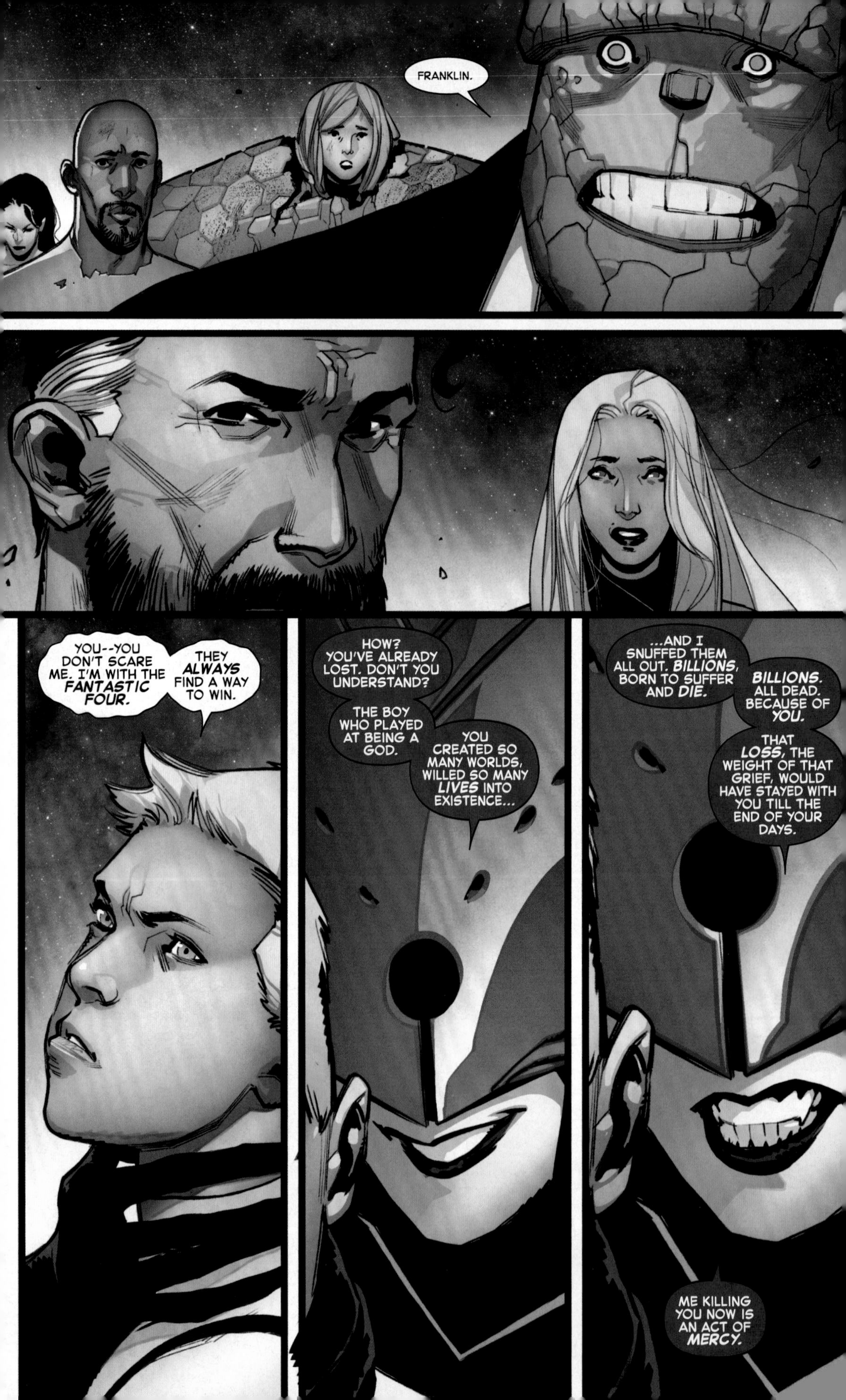
FRANKLIN.
YOU--YOU DON'T SCARE ME. I'M WITH THE FANTASTIC FOUR.
THEY ALWAYS FIND A WAY TO WIN.
HOW? YOU'VE ALREADY LOST. DON'T YOU UNDERSTAND?
THE BOY WHO PLAYED AT BEING A GOD.
YOU CREATED SO MANY WORLDS, WILLED SO MANY LIVES INTO EXISTENCE...
...AND I SNUFFED THEM ALL OUT. BILLIONS, BORN TO SUFFER AND DIE.
BILLIONS. ALL DEAD. BECAUSE OF YOU.
THAT LOSS, THE WEIGHT OF THAT GRIEF, WOULD HAVE STAYED WITH YOU TILL THE END OF YOUR DAYS.
ME KILLING YOU NOW IS AN ACT OF MERCY.

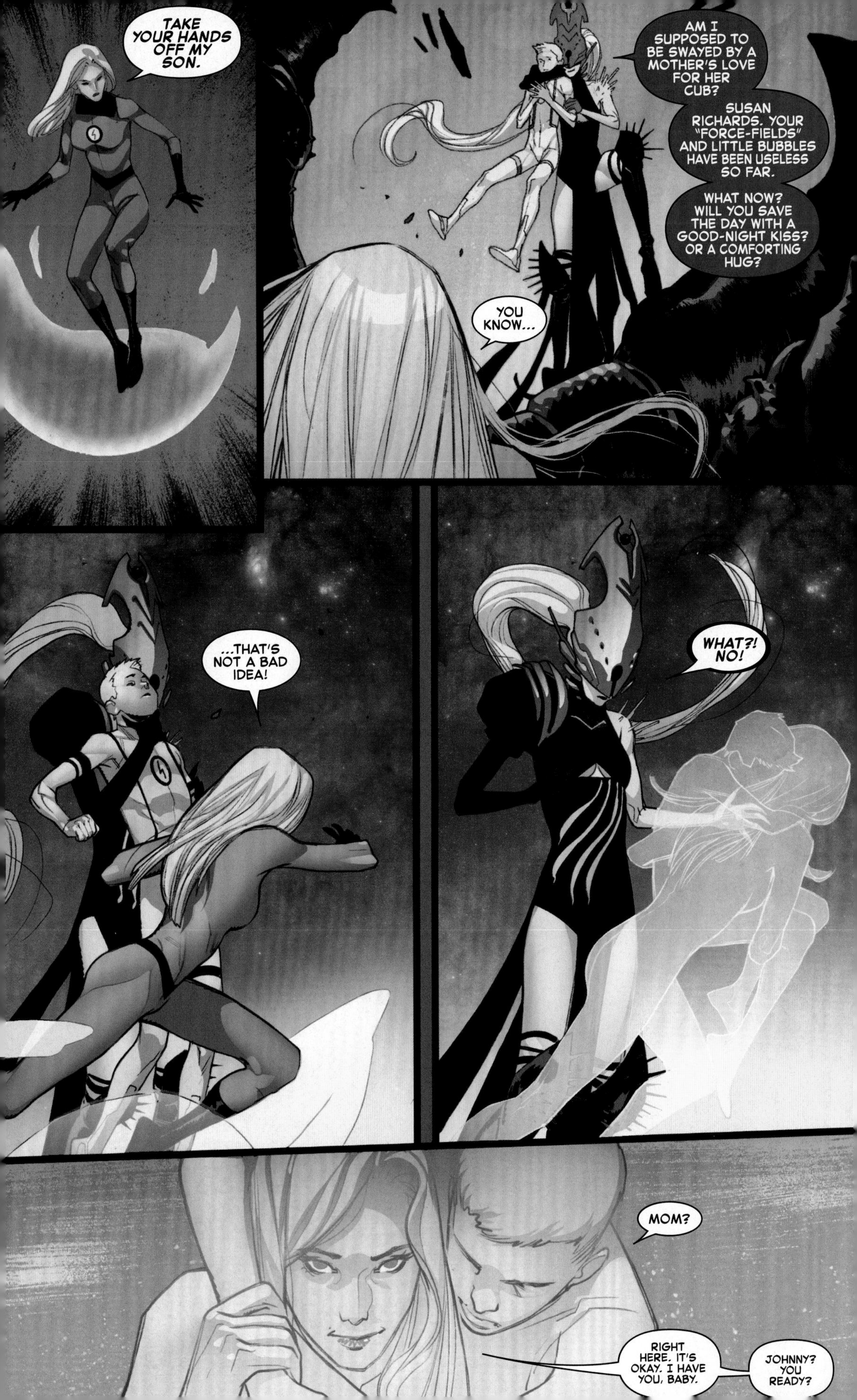
TAKE YOUR HANDS OFF MY SON.
AM I SUPPOSED TO BE SWAYED BY A MOTHER'S LOVE FOR HER CUB?
SUSAN RICHARDS. YOUR "FORCE-FIELDS" AND LITTLE BUBBLES HAVE BEEN USELESS SO FAR.
WHAT NOW? WILL YOU SAVE THE DAY WITH A GOOD-NIGHT KISS? OR A COMFORTING HUG?
YOU KNOW...
...THAT'S NOT A BAD IDEA!
WHAT?! NO!
MOM?
RIGHT HERE. IT'S OKAY. I HAVE YOU, BABY.
JOHNNY? YOU READY?

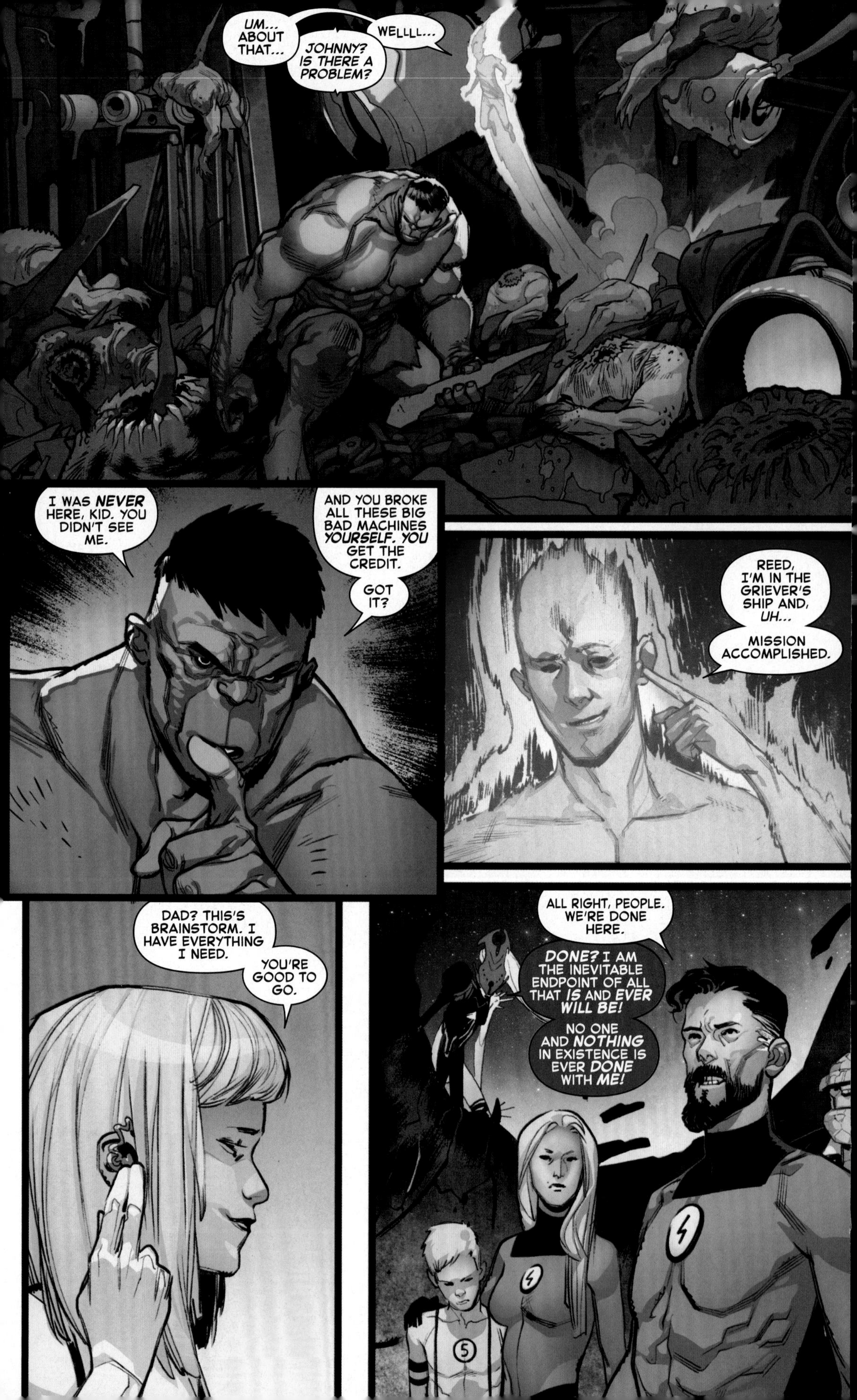
JOHNNY? IS THERE A PROBLEM?
UM... ABOUT THAT...
WELLLL...
I WAS NEVER HERE, KID. YOU DIDN'T SEE ME.
AND YOU BROKE ALL THESE BIG BAD MACHINES YOURSELF. YOU GET THE CREDIT.
GOT IT?
REED, I'M IN THE GRIEVER'S SHIP AND, UH...
MISSION ACCOMPLISHED.
DAD? THIS'S BRAINSTORM. I HAVE EVERYTHING I NEED.
YOU'RE GOOD TO GO.
ALL RIGHT, PEOPLE. WE'RE DONE HERE.
DONE? I AM THE INEVITABLE ENDPOINT OF ALL THAT IS AND EVER WILL BE!
NO ONE AND NOTHING IN EXISTENCE IS EVER DONE WITH ME!

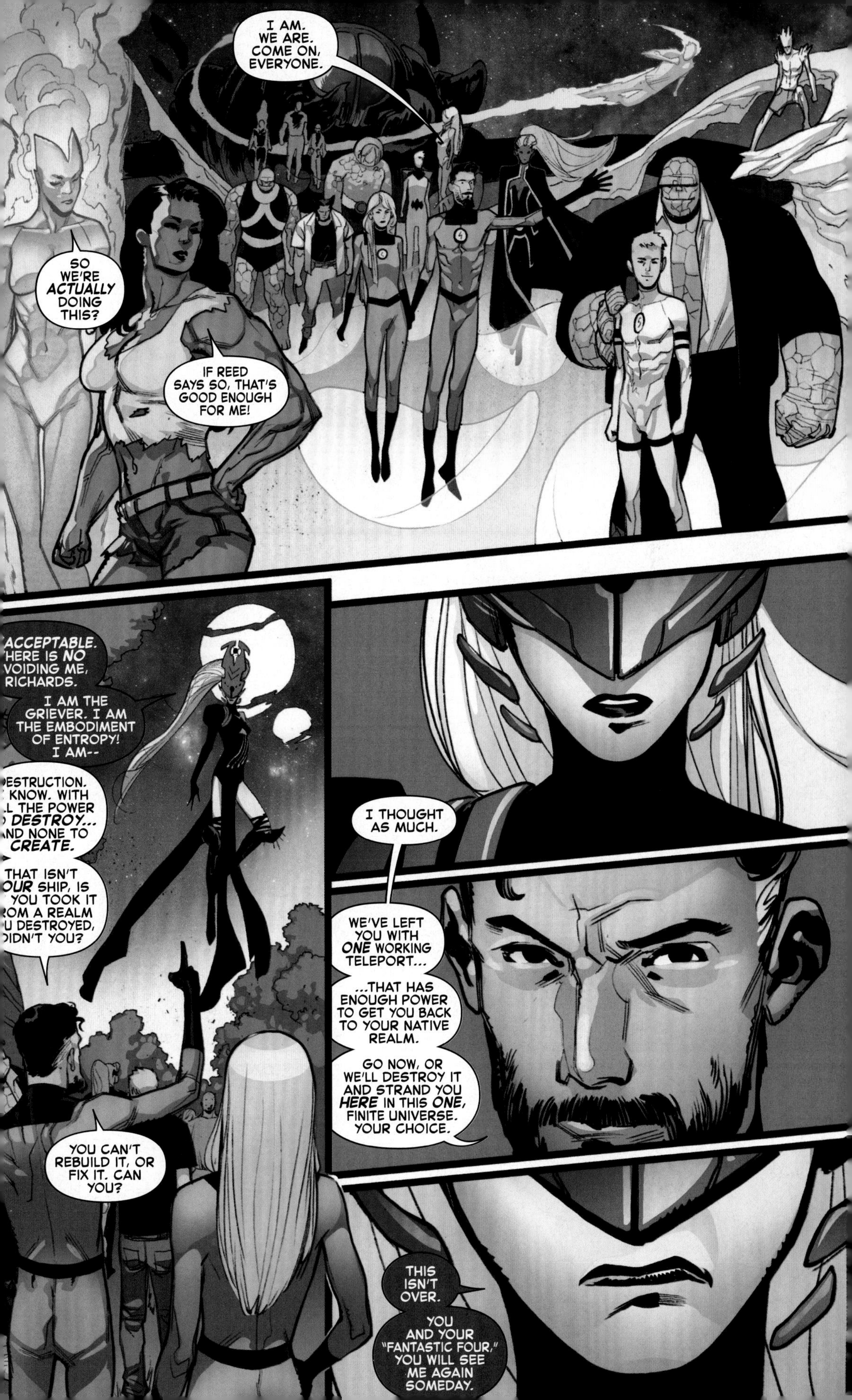

I AM. WE ARE. COME ON, EVERYONE.
SO WE'RE ACTUALLY DOING THIS?
IF REED SAYS SO, THAT'S GOOD ENOUGH FOR ME!
ACCEPTABLE. HERE IS NO VOIDING ME, RICHARDS.
I AM THE GRIEVER. I AM THE EMBODIMENT OF ENTROPY! I AM--
DESTRUCTION. KNOW. WITH L THE POWER DESTROY... AND NONE TO CREATE.
THAT ISN'T OUR SHIP, IS YOU TOOK IT ROM A REALM U DESTROYED, DIDN'T YOU?
YOU CAN'T REBUILD IT, OR FIX IT. CAN YOU?
I THOUGHT AS MUCH.
WE'VE LEFT YOU WITH ONE WORKING TELEPORT...
...THAT HAS ENOUGH POWER TO GET YOU BACK TO YOUR NATIVE REALM.
GO NOW, OR WE'LL DESTROY IT AND STRAND YOU HERE IN THIS ONE, FINITE UNIVERSE. YOUR CHOICE.
THIS ISN'T OVER.
YOU AND YOUR "FANTASTIC FOUR," YOU WILL SEE ME AGAIN SOMEDAY.

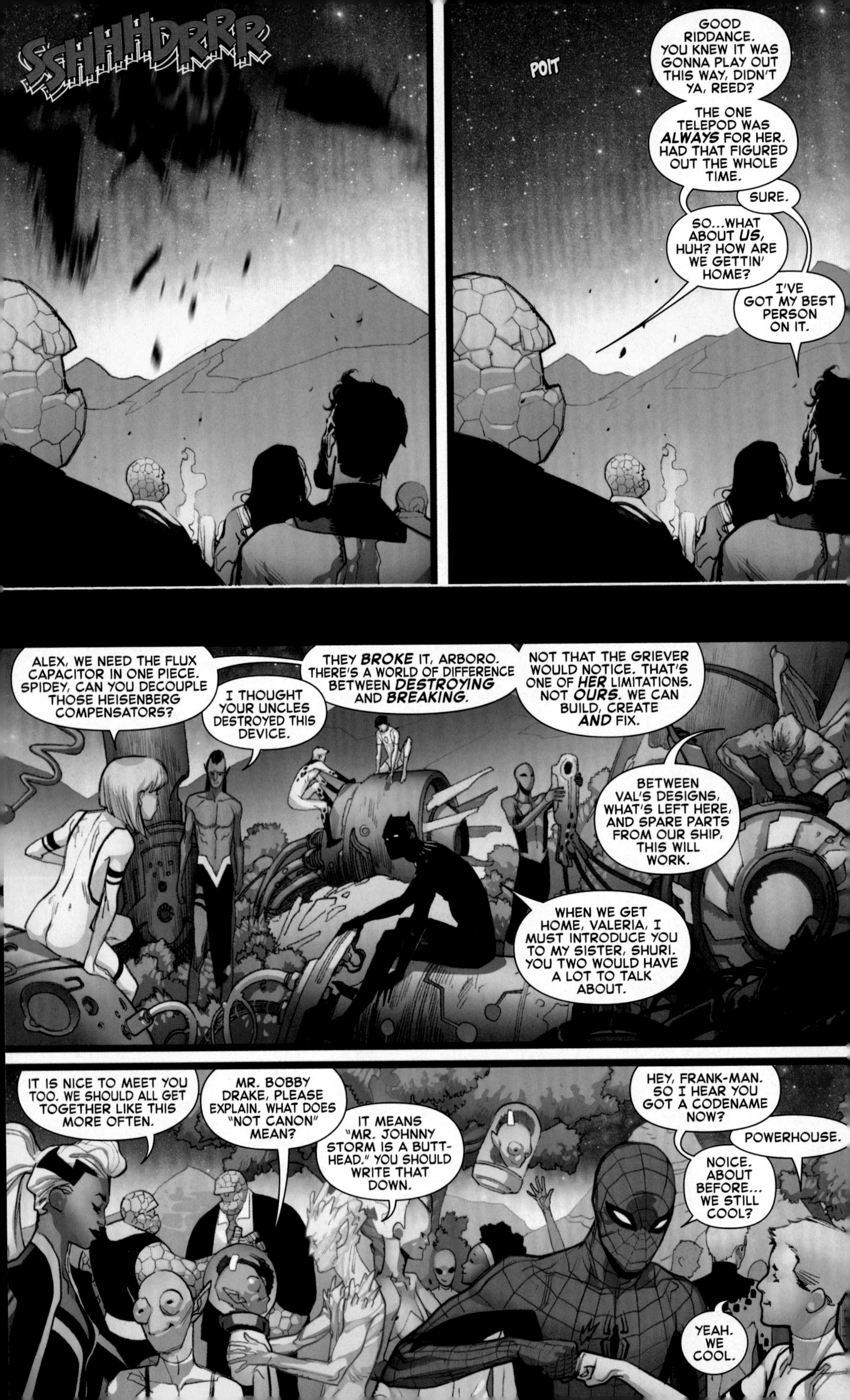
SSHHHDRRR
POIT
GOOD RIDDANCE. YOU KNEW IT WAS GONNA PLAY OUT THIS WAY, DIDN'T YA, REED?
THE ONE TELEPOD WAS ALWAYS FOR HER. HAD THAT FIGURED OUT THE WHOLE TIME.
SURE.
SO...WHAT ABOUT US, HUH? HOW ARE WE GETTIN' HOME?
I'VE GOT MY BEST PERSON ON IT.
ALEX, WE NEED THE FLUX CAPACITOR IN ONE PIECE. SPIDEY, CAN YOU DECOUPLE THOSE HEISENBERG COMPENSATORS?
I THOUGHT YOUR UNCLES DESTROYED THIS DEVICE.
THEY BROKE IT, ARBORO. THERE'S A WORLD OF DIFFERENCE BETWEEN DESTROYING AND BREAKING.
NOT THAT THE GRIEVER WOULD NOTICE. THAT'S ONE OF HER LIMITATIONS. NOT OURS. WE CAN BUILD, CREATE AND FIX.
BETWEEN VAL'S DESIGNS, WHAT'S LEFT HERE, AND SPARE PARTS FROM OUR SHIP, THIS WILL WORK.
WHEN WE GET HOME, VALERIA, I MUST INTRODUCE YOU TO MY SISTER, SHURI. YOU TWO WOULD HAVE A LOT TO TALK ABOUT.
IT IS NICE TO MEET YOU TOO. WE SHOULD ALL GET TOGETHER LIKE THIS MORE OFTEN.
MR. BOBBY DRAKE, PLEASE EXPLAIN. WHAT DOES "NOT CANON" MEAN?
IT MEANS "MR. JOHNNY STORM IS A BUTT-HEAD." YOU SHOULD WRITE THAT DOWN.
HEY, FRANK-MAN. SO I HEAR YOU GOT A CODENAME NOW?
POWERHOUSE.
NOICE. ABOUT BEFORE... WE STILL COOL?
YEAH. WE COOL.

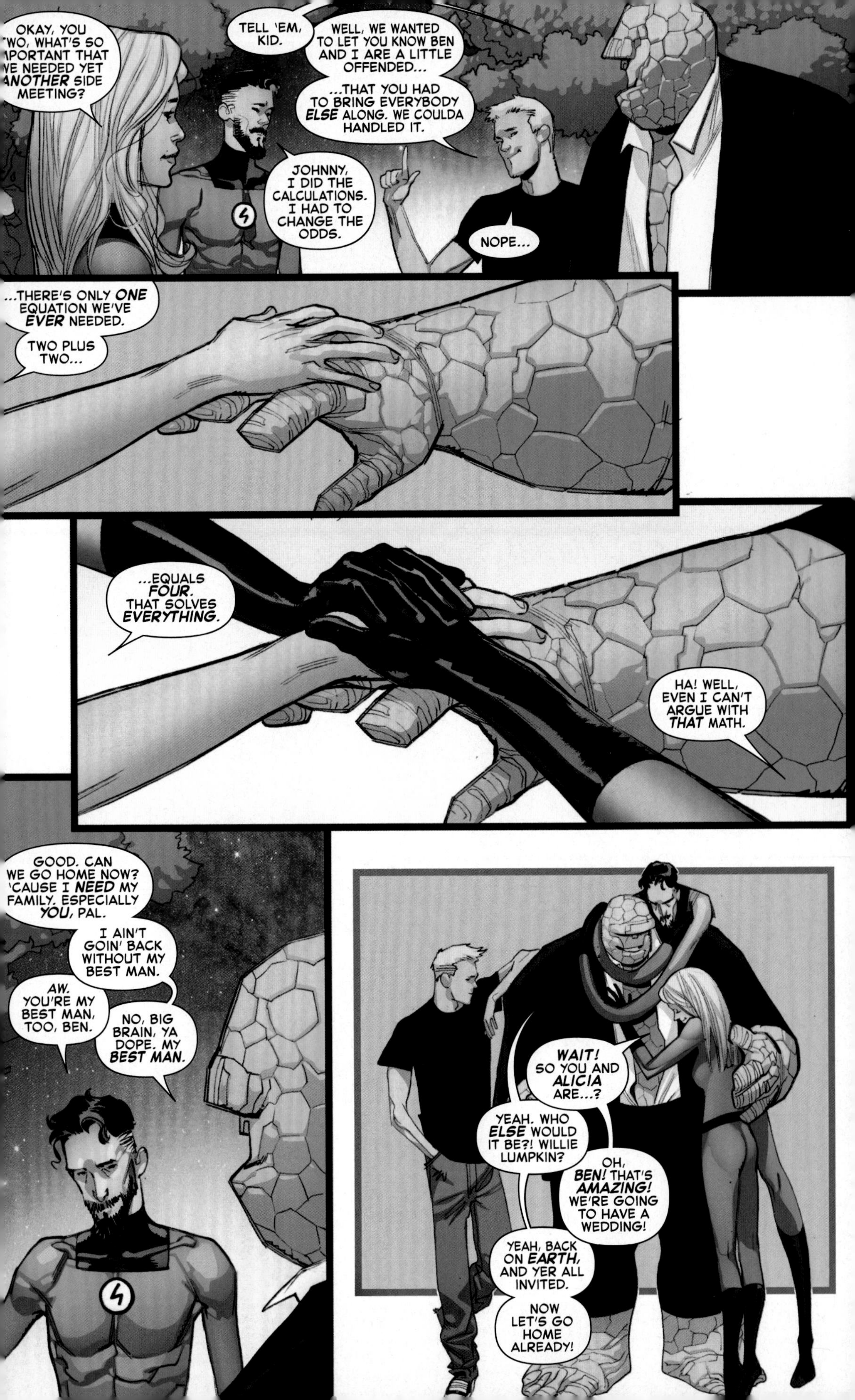
OKAY, YOU TWO, WHAT'S SO IMPORTANT THAT WE NEEDED YET ANOTHER SIDE MEETING?
TELL 'EM, KID.
WELL, WE WANTED TO LET YOU KNOW BEN AND I ARE A LITTLE OFFENDED...
...THAT YOU HAD TO BRING EVERYBODY ELSE ALONG. WE COULDA HANDLED IT.
JOHNNY, I DID THE CALCULATIONS. I HAD TO CHANGE THE ODDS.
NOPE...
...THERE'S ONLY ONE EQUATION WE'VE EVER NEEDED.
TWO PLUS TWO...
...EQUALS FOUR. THAT SOLVES EVERYTHING.
HA! WELL, EVEN I CAN'T ARGUE WITH THAT MATH.
GOOD. CAN WE GO HOME NOW? 'CAUSE I NEED MY FAMILY. ESPECIALLY YOU, PAL.
I AIN'T GOIN' BACK WITHOUT MY BEST MAN.
AW. YOU'RE MY BEST MAN, TOO, BEN.
NO, BIG BRAIN, YA DOPE. MY BEST MAN.
WAIT! SO YOU AND ALICIA ARE...?
YEAH. WHO ELSE WOULD IT BE?! WILLIE LUMPKIN?
OH, BEN! THAT'S AMAZING! WE'RE GOING TO HAVE A WEDDING!
YEAH, BACK ON EARTH, AND YER ALL INVITED.
NOW LET'S GO HOME ALREADY!

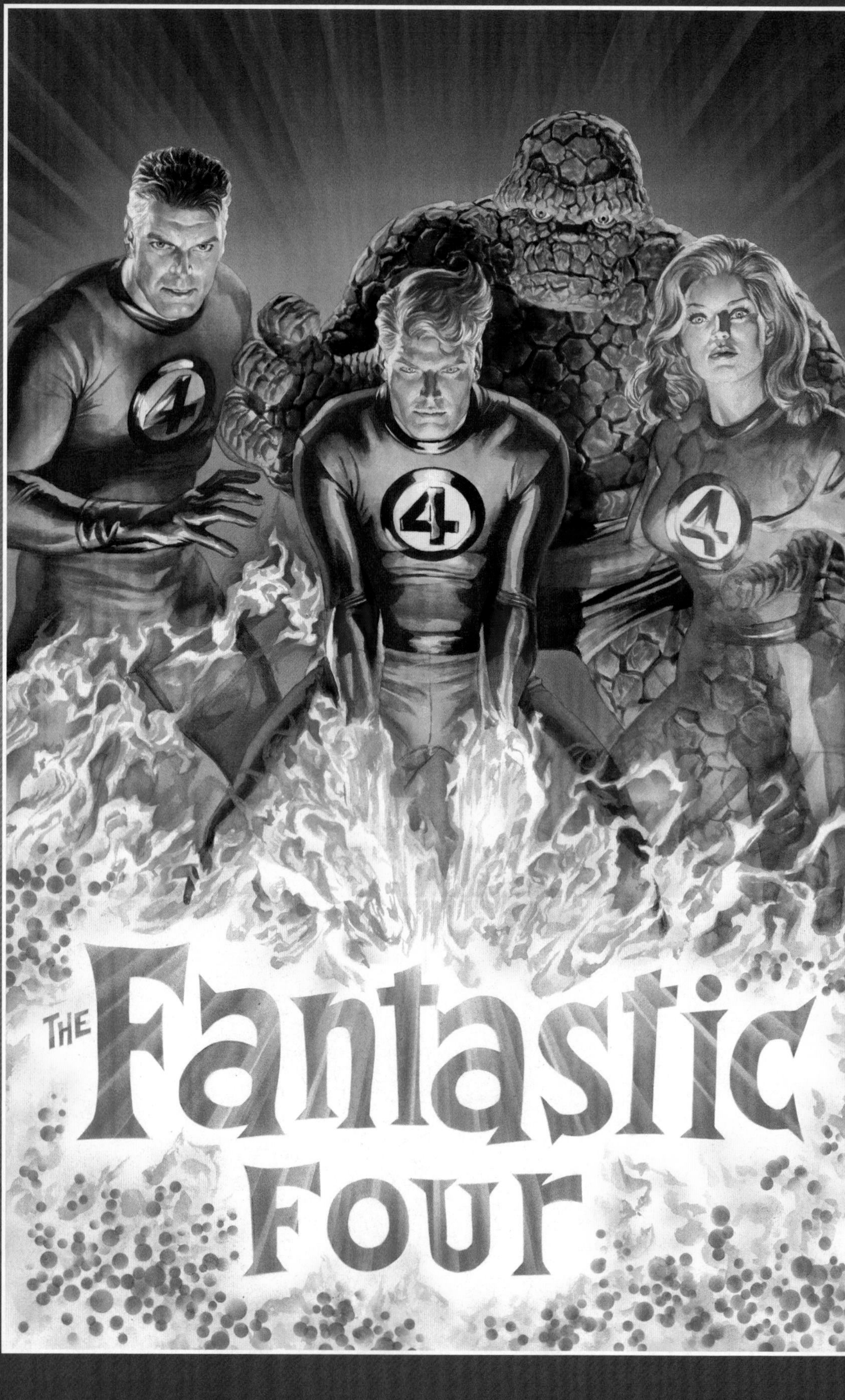
THE
Fantastic
Four

#1 variant by **Alex Ross**

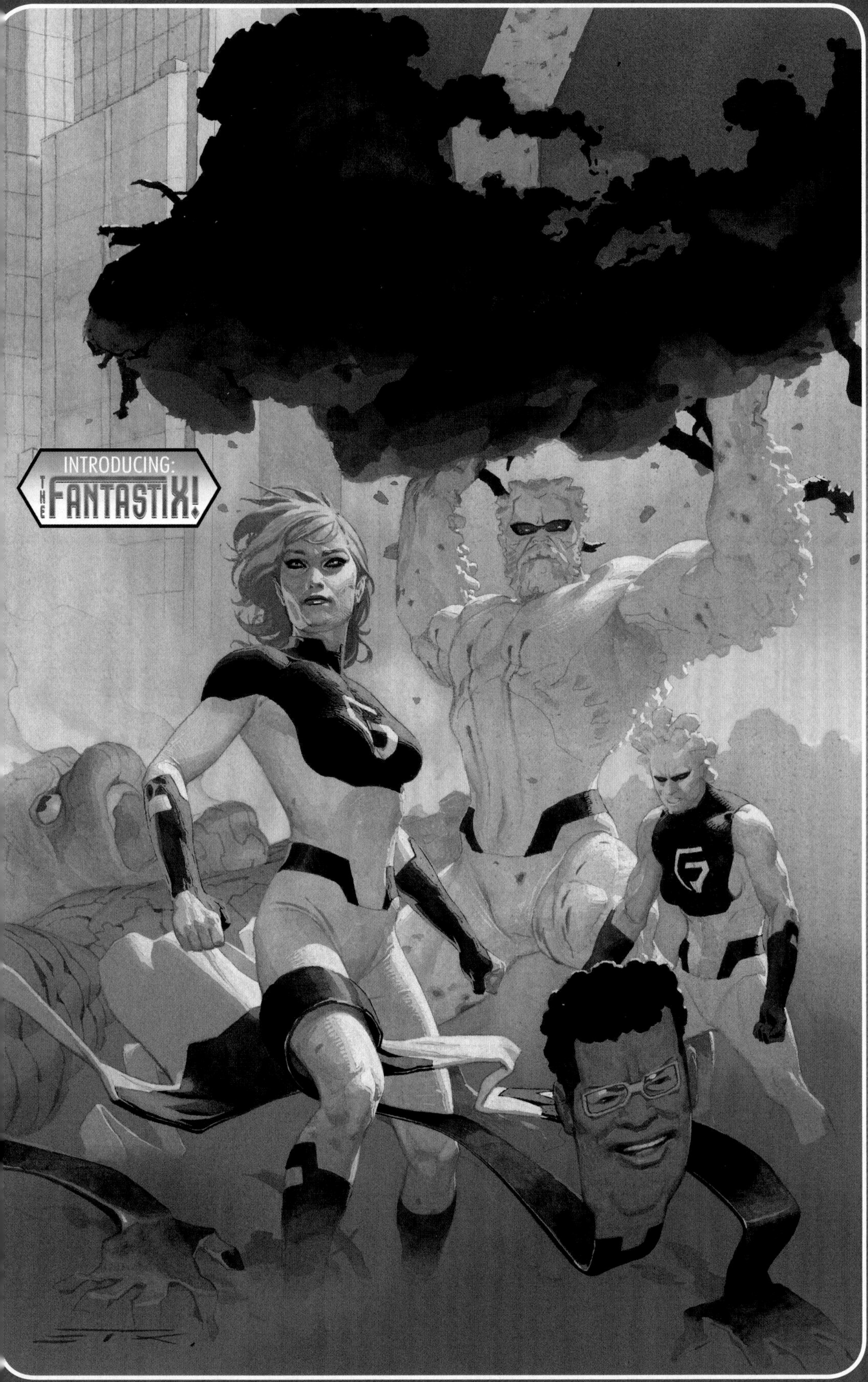
INTRODUCING:
THE FANTASTIX!

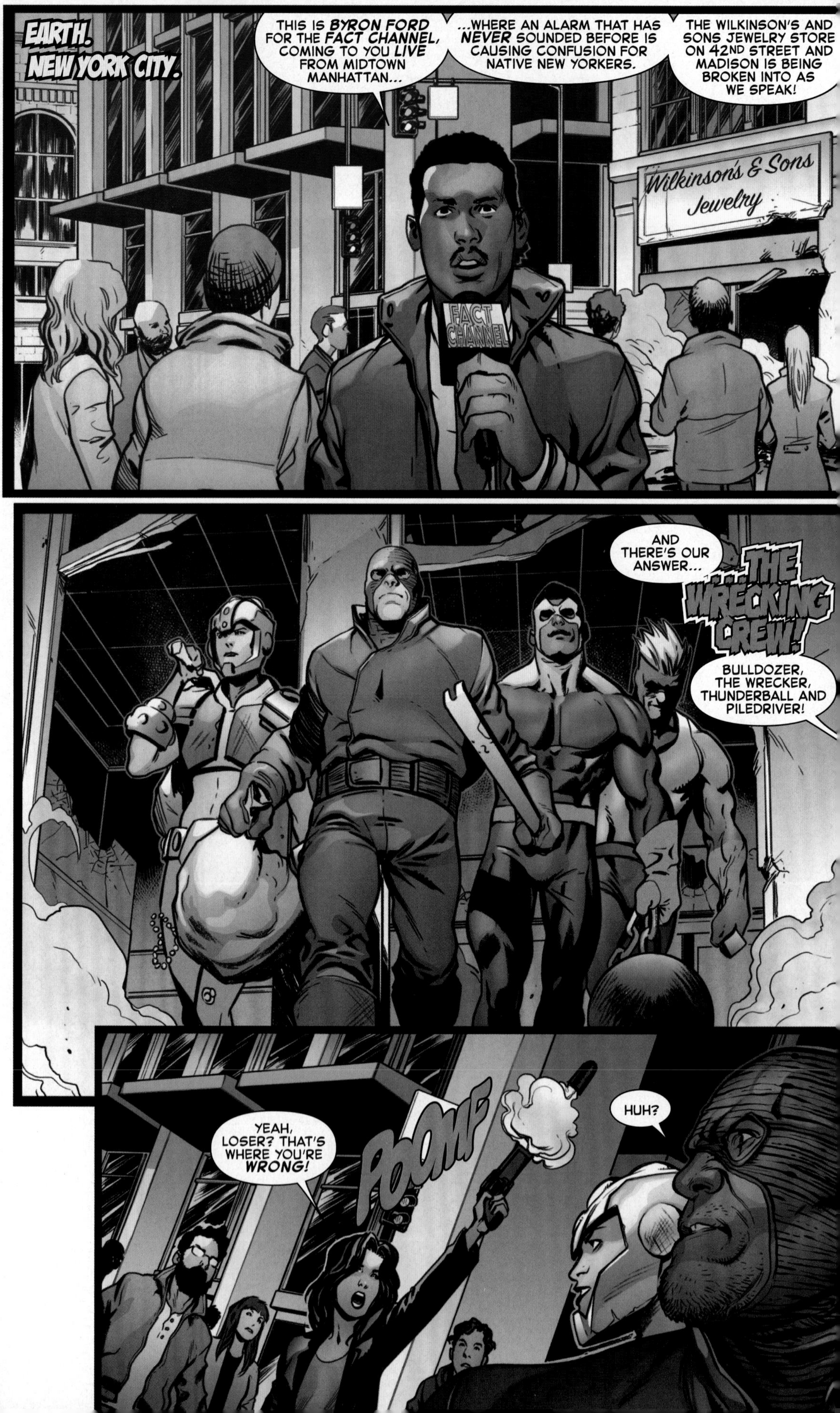

EARTH. NEW YORK CITY.
THIS IS BYRON FORD FOR THE FACT CHANNEL, COMING TO YOU LIVE FROM MIDTOWN MANHATTAN...
...WHERE AN ALARM THAT HAS NEVER SOUNDED BEFORE IS CAUSING CONFUSION FOR NATIVE NEW YORKERS.
THE WILKINSON'S AND SONS JEWELRY STORE ON 42ND STREET AND MADISON IS BEING BROKEN INTO AS WE SPEAK!
Wilkinson's & Sons Jewelry
FACT CHANNEL
AND THERE'S OUR ANSWER...
...THE WRECKING CREW!
BULLDOZER, THE WRECKER, THUNDERBALL AND PILEDRIVER!
YEAH, LOSER? THAT'S WHERE YOU'RE WRONG!
POOMF
HUH?

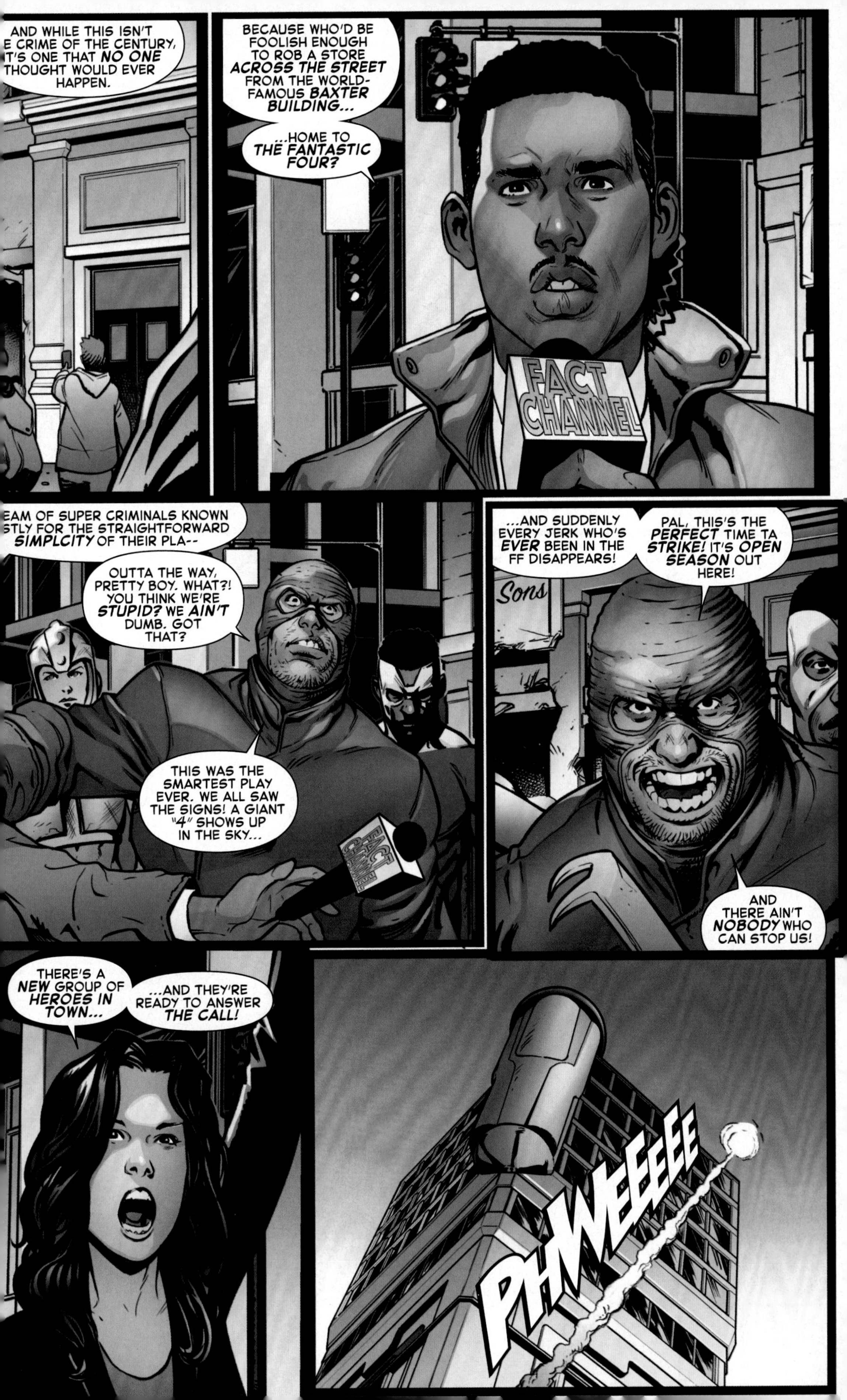
AND WHILE THIS ISN'T
E CRIME OF THE CENTURY,
'T'S ONE THAT NO ONE
THOUGHT WOULD EVER
HAPPEN.
BECAUSE WHO'D BE FOOLISH ENOUGH TO ROB A STORE ACROSS THE STREET FROM THE WORLD-FAMOUS BAXTER BUILDING...
...HOME TO THE FANTASTIC FOUR?
FACT CHANNEL
EAM OF SUPER CRIMINALS KNOWN
STLY FOR THE STRAIGHTFORWARD
SIMPLCITY OF THEIR PLA--
OUTTA THE WAY, PRETTY BOY. WHAT?! YOU THINK WE'RE STUPID? WE AIN'T DUMB. GOT THAT?
THIS WAS THE SMARTEST PLAY EVER. WE ALL SAW THE SIGNS! A GIANT "4" SHOWS UP IN THE SKY...
FACT CHANNEL
...AND SUDDENLY EVERY JERK WHO'S EVER BEEN IN THE FF DISAPPEARS!
PAL, THIS'S THE PERFECT TIME TA STRIKE! IT'S OPEN SEASON OUT HERE!
Sons
AND THERE AIN'T NOBODY WHO CAN STOP US!
THERE'S A NEW GROUP OF HEROES IN TOWN...
...AND THEY'RE READY TO ANSWER THE CALL!
PHWEEEEE

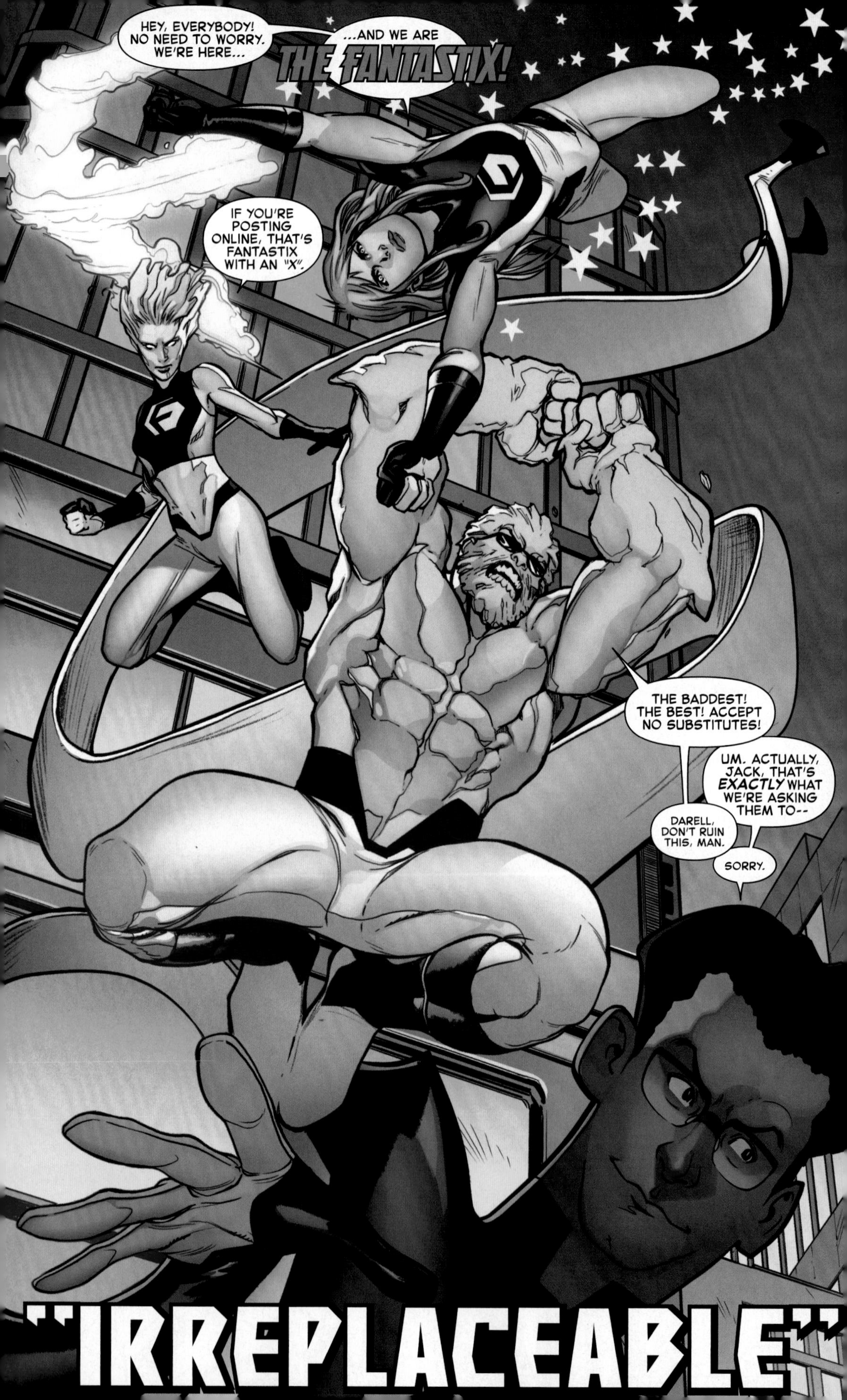
HEY, EVERYBODY! NO NEED TO WORRY. WE'RE HERE...
...AND WE ARE
THE FANTASTIX!
IF YOU'RE POSTING ONLINE, THAT'S FANTASTIX WITH AN "X".
THE BADDEST! THE BEST! ACCEPT NO SUBSTITUTES!
UM. ACTUALLY, JACK, THAT'S EXACTLY WHAT WE'RE ASKING THEM TO--
DARELL, DON'T RUIN THIS, MAN.
SORRY.
"IRREPLACEABLE"

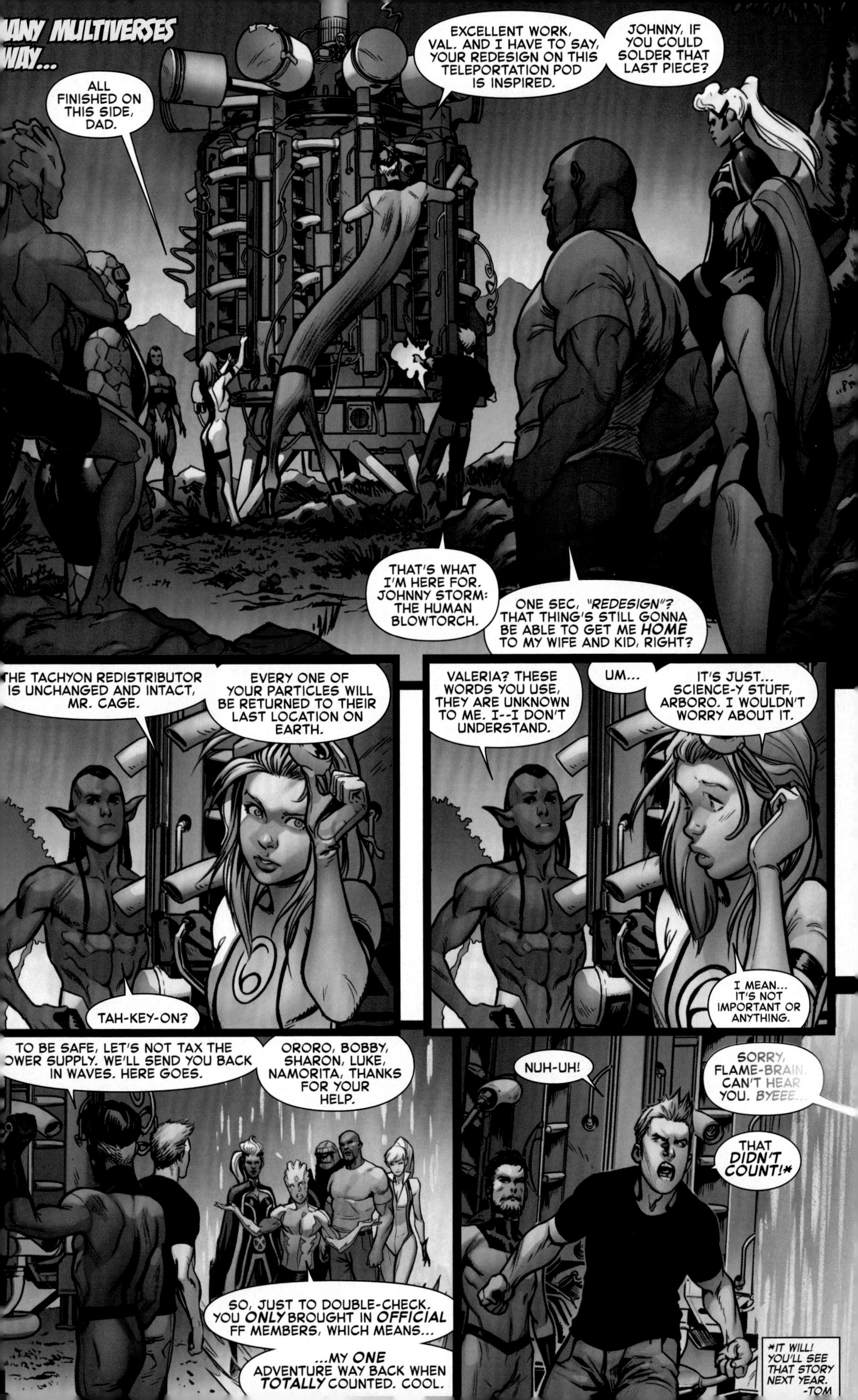

ANY MULTIVERSES WAY...
ALL FINISHED ON THIS SIDE, DAD.
EXCELLENT WORK, VAL. AND I HAVE TO SAY, YOUR REDESIGN ON THIS TELEPORTATION POD IS INSPIRED.
JOHNNY, IF YOU COULD SOLDER THAT LAST PIECE?
THAT'S WHAT I'M HERE FOR. JOHNNY STORM: THE HUMAN BLOWTORCH.
ONE SEC, "REDESIGN"? THAT THING'S STILL GONNA BE ABLE TO GET ME HOME TO MY WIFE AND KID, RIGHT?
THE TACHYON REDISTRIBUTOR IS UNCHANGED AND INTACT, MR. CAGE.
EVERY ONE OF YOUR PARTICLES WILL BE RETURNED TO THEIR LAST LOCATION ON EARTH.
TAH-KEY-ON?
VALERIA? THESE WORDS YOU USE, THEY ARE UNKNOWN TO ME. I--I DON'T UNDERSTAND.
UM...
IT'S JUST... SCIENCE-Y STUFF, ARBORO. I WOULDN'T WORRY ABOUT IT.
I MEAN... IT'S NOT IMPORTANT OR ANYTHING.
TO BE SAFE, LET'S NOT TAX THE OWER SUPPLY. WE'LL SEND YOU BACK IN WAVES. HERE GOES.
ORORO, BOBBY, SHARON, LUKE, NAMORITA, THANKS FOR YOUR HELP.
SO, JUST TO DOUBLE-CHECK. YOU ONLY BROUGHT IN OFFICIAL FF MEMBERS, WHICH MEANS...
...MY ONE ADVENTURE WAY BACK WHEN TOTALLY COUNTED. COOL.
NUH-UH!
SORRY, FLAME-BRAIN. CAN'T HEAR YOU. BYEEE...
THAT DIDN'T COUNT!*
*IT WILL! YOU'LL SEE THAT STORY NEXT YEAR. -TOM

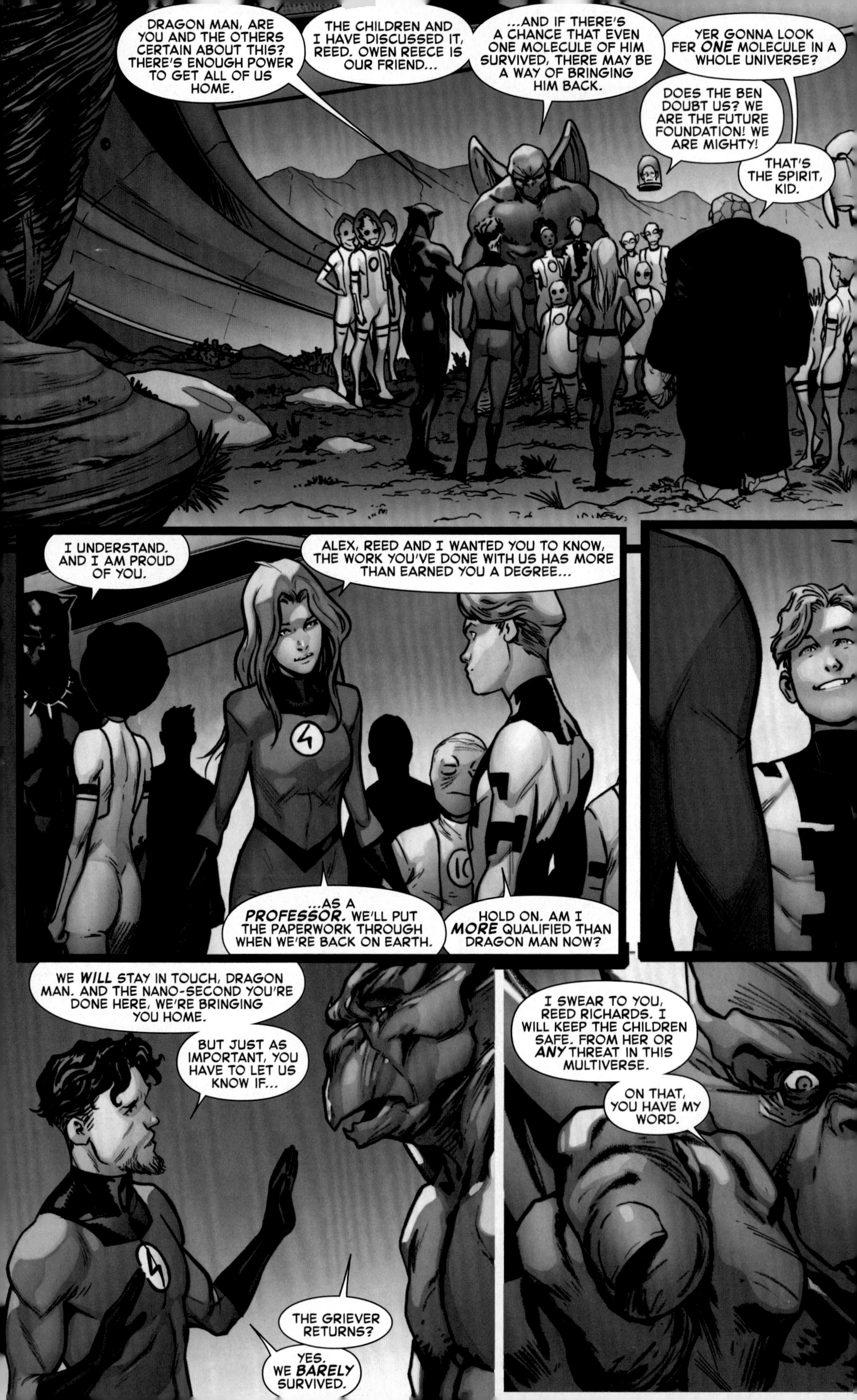
DRAGON MAN, ARE YOU AND THE OTHERS CERTAIN ABOUT THIS? THERE'S ENOUGH POWER TO GET ALL OF US HOME.
THE CHILDREN AND I HAVE DISCUSSED IT, REED. OWEN REECE IS OUR FRIEND...
...AND IF THERE'S A CHANCE THAT EVEN ONE MOLECULE OF HIM SURVIVED, THERE MAY BE A WAY OF BRINGING HIM BACK.
YER GONNA LOOK FER *ONE* MOLECULE IN A WHOLE UNIVERSE?
DOES THE BEN DOUBT US? WE ARE THE FUTURE FOUNDATION! WE ARE MIGHTY!
THAT'S THE SPIRIT, KID.
I UNDERSTAND. AND I AM PROUD OF YOU.
ALEX, REED AND I WANTED YOU TO KNOW, THE WORK YOU'VE DONE WITH US HAS MORE THAN EARNED YOU A DEGREE...
...AS A *PROFESSOR.* WE'LL PUT THE PAPERWORK THROUGH WHEN WE'RE BACK ON EARTH.
HOLD ON. AM I *MORE* QUALIFIED THAN DRAGON MAN NOW?
WE *WILL* STAY IN TOUCH, DRAGON MAN. AND THE NANO-SECOND YOU'RE DONE HERE, WE'RE BRINGING YOU HOME.
BUT JUST AS IMPORTANT, YOU HAVE TO LET US KNOW IF...
THE GRIEVER RETURNS?
YES. WE *BARELY* SURVIVED.
I SWEAR TO YOU, REED RICHARDS. I WILL KEEP THE CHILDREN SAFE. FROM HER OR *ANY* THREAT IN THIS MULTIVERSE.
ON THAT, YOU HAVE MY WORD.

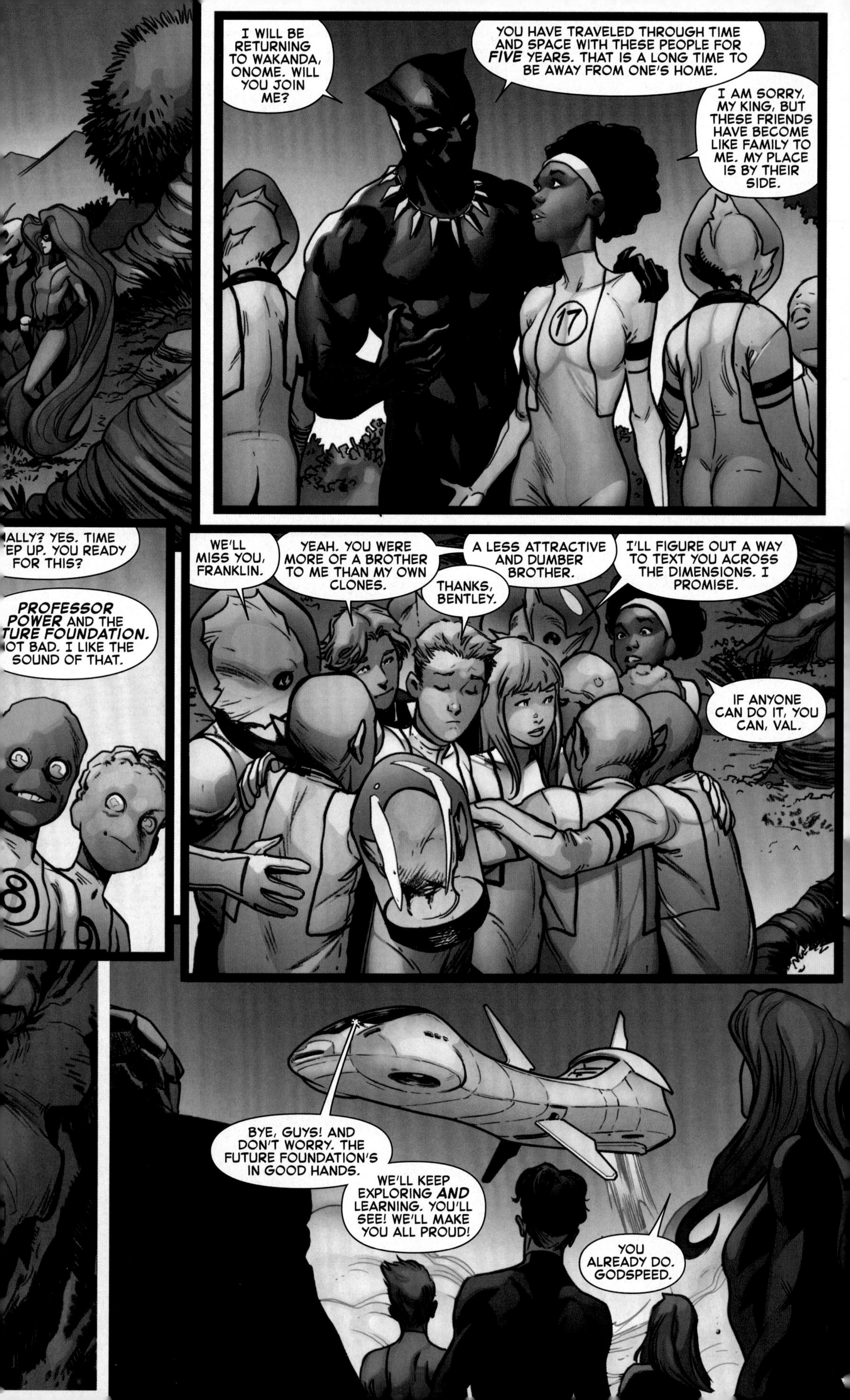
I WILL BE RETURNING TO WAKANDA, ONOME. WILL YOU JOIN ME?
YOU HAVE TRAVELED THROUGH TIME AND SPACE WITH THESE PEOPLE FOR *FIVE* YEARS. THAT IS A LONG TIME TO BE AWAY FROM ONE'S HOME.
I AM SORRY, MY KING, BUT THESE FRIENDS HAVE BECOME LIKE FAMILY TO ME. MY PLACE IS BY THEIR SIDE.
17
ALLY? YES. TIME EP UP. YOU READY FOR THIS?
PROFESSOR POWER AND THE *TURE FOUNDATION.* OT BAD. I LIKE THE SOUND OF THAT.
WE'LL MISS YOU, FRANKLIN.
YEAH. YOU WERE MORE OF A BROTHER TO ME THAN MY OWN CLONES.
THANKS, BENTLEY.
A LESS ATTRACTIVE AND DUMBER BROTHER.
I'LL FIGURE OUT A WAY TO TEXT YOU ACROSS THE DIMENSIONS. I PROMISE.
IF ANYONE CAN DO IT, YOU CAN, VAL.
BYE, GUYS! AND DON'T WORRY. THE FUTURE FOUNDATION'S IN GOOD HANDS.
WE'LL KEEP EXPLORING *AND* LEARNING. YOU'LL SEE! WE'LL MAKE YOU ALL PROUD!
YOU ALREADY DO. GODSPEED.

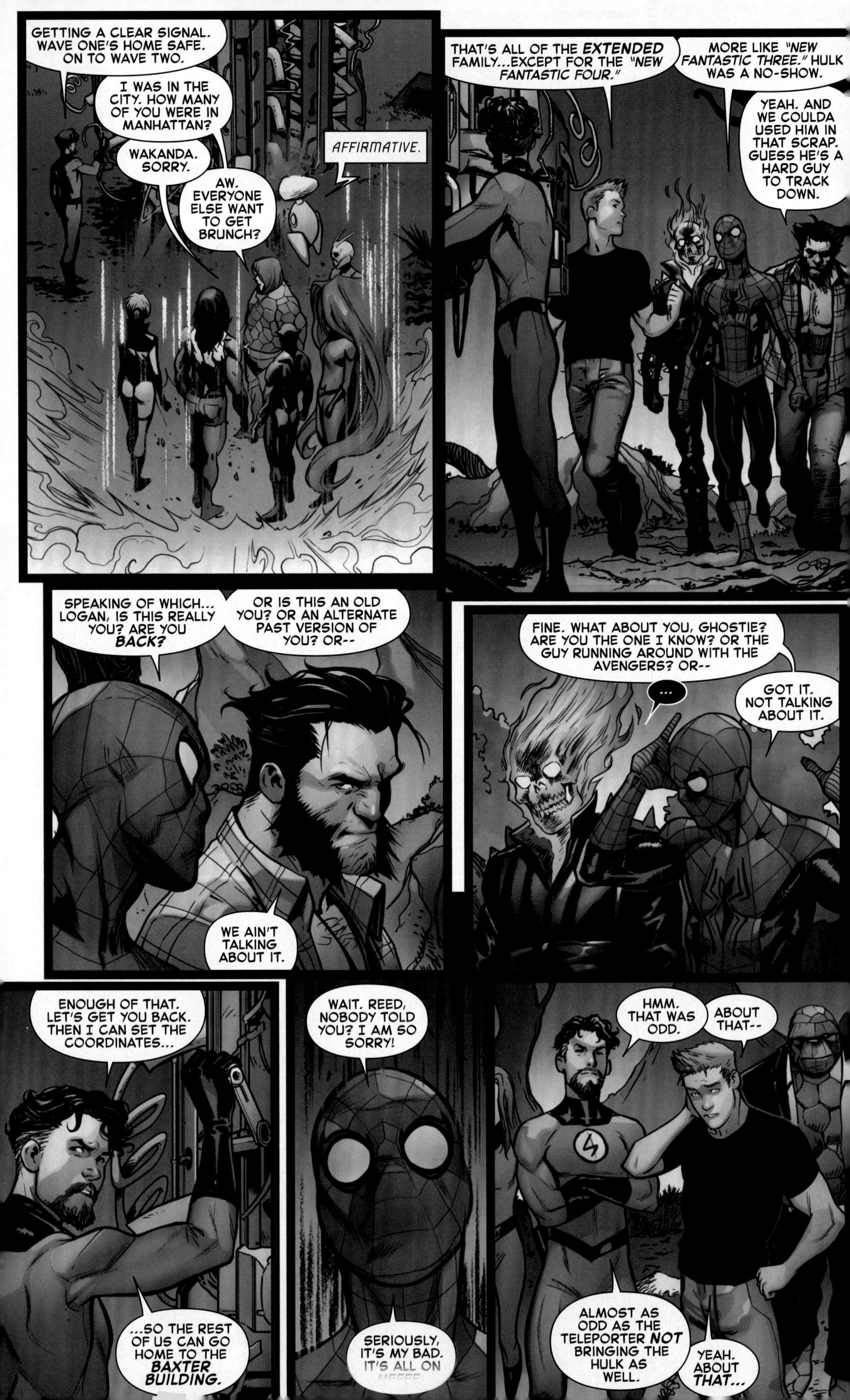
GETTING A CLEAR SIGNAL. WAVE ONE'S HOME SAFE. ON TO WAVE TWO.
I WAS IN THE CITY. HOW MANY OF YOU WERE IN MANHATTAN?
WAKANDA. SORRY.
AW. EVERYONE ELSE WANT TO GET BRUNCH?
AFFIRMATIVE.
THAT'S ALL OF THE EXTENDED FAMILY...EXCEPT FOR THE "NEW FANTASTIC FOUR."
MORE LIKE "NEW FANTASTIC THREE." HULK WAS A NO-SHOW.
YEAH. AND WE COULDA USED HIM IN THAT SCRAP. GUESS HE'S A HARD GUY TO TRACK DOWN.
SPEAKING OF WHICH... LOGAN, IS THIS REALLY YOU? ARE YOU BACK?
OR IS THIS AN OLD YOU? OR AN ALTERNATE PAST VERSION OF YOU? OR--
WE AIN'T TALKING ABOUT IT.
FINE. WHAT ABOUT YOU, GHOSTIE? ARE YOU THE ONE I KNOW? OR THE GUY RUNNING AROUND WITH THE AVENGERS? OR--
...
GOT IT. NOT TALKING ABOUT IT.
ENOUGH OF THAT. LET'S GET YOU BACK. THEN I CAN SET THE COORDINATES...
...SO THE REST OF US CAN GO HOME TO THE BAXTER BUILDING.
WAIT. REED, NOBODY TOLD YOU? I AM SO SORRY!
SERIOUSLY, IT'S MY BAD. IT'S ALL ON
HMM. THAT WAS ODD.
ABOUT THAT--
ALMOST AS ODD AS THE TELEPORTER NOT BRINGING THE HULK AS WELL.
YEAH. ABOUT THAT...

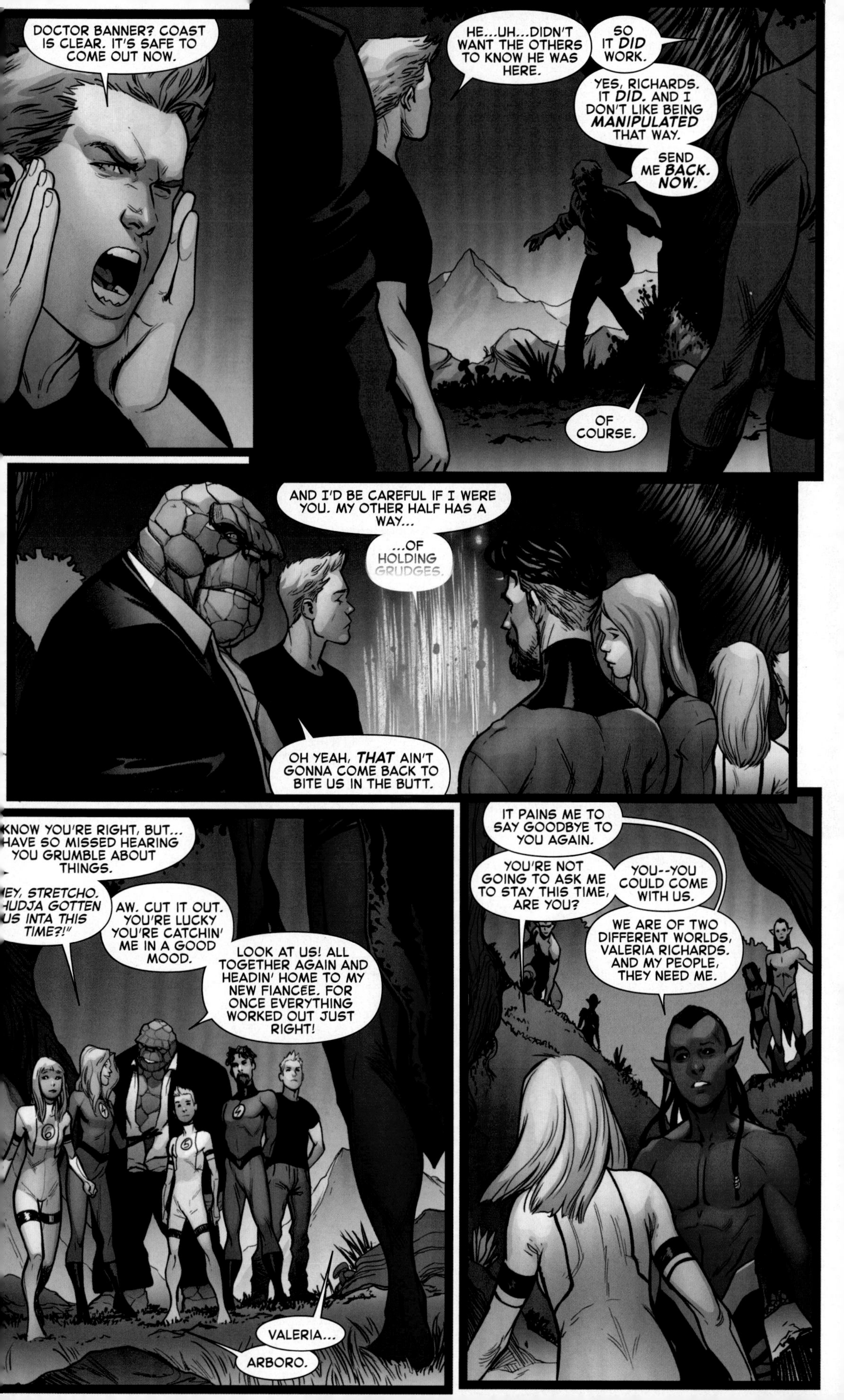
DOCTOR BANNER? COAST IS CLEAR. IT'S SAFE TO COME OUT NOW.
HE...UH...DIDN'T WANT THE OTHERS TO KNOW HE WAS HERE.
SO IT *DID* WORK.
YES, RICHARDS. IT *DID.* AND I DON'T LIKE BEING *MANIPULATED* THAT WAY.
SEND ME *BACK.* *NOW.*
OF COURSE.
AND I'D BE CAREFUL IF I WERE YOU. MY OTHER HALF HAS A WAY...
...OF HOLDING GRUDGES.
OH YEAH, *THAT* AIN'T GONNA COME BACK TO BITE US IN THE BUTT.
KNOW YOU'RE RIGHT, BUT... HAVE SO MISSED HEARING YOU GRUMBLE ABOUT THINGS.
EY, STRETCHO. HUDJA GOTTEN US INTA THIS TIME?!"
AW. CUT IT OUT. YOU'RE LUCKY YOU'RE CATCHIN' ME IN A GOOD MOOD.
LOOK AT US! ALL TOGETHER AGAIN AND HEADIN' HOME TO MY NEW FIANCÉE. FOR ONCE EVERYTHING WORKED OUT JUST RIGHT!
VALERIA...
ARBORO.
IT PAINS ME TO SAY GOODBYE TO YOU AGAIN.
YOU'RE NOT GOING TO ASK ME TO STAY THIS TIME, ARE YOU?
YOU--YOU COULD COME WITH US.
WE ARE OF TWO DIFFERENT WORLDS, VALERIA RICHARDS. AND MY PEOPLE, THEY NEED ME.

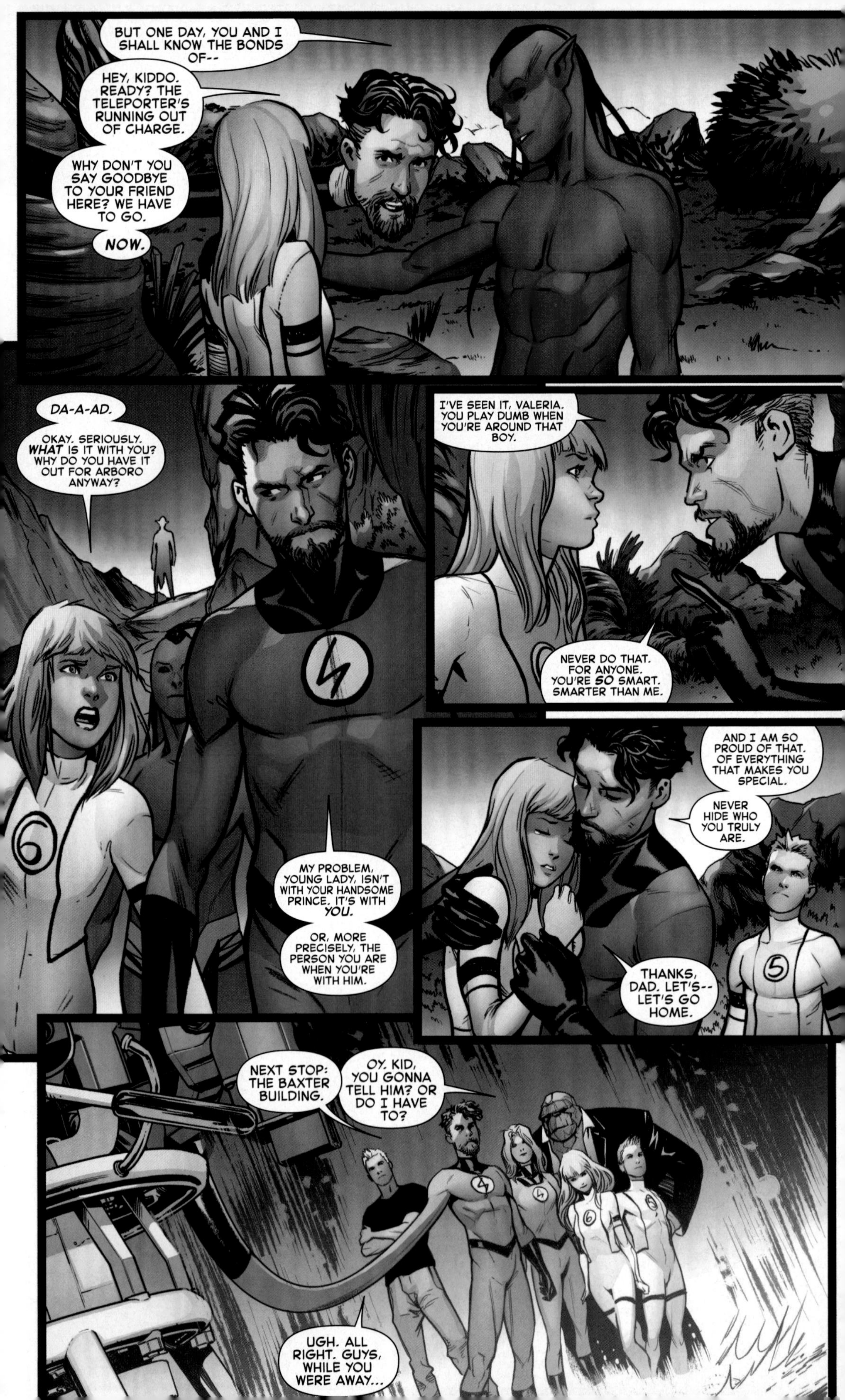

BUT ONE DAY, YOU AND I SHALL KNOW THE BONDS OF--
HEY, KIDDO. READY? THE TELEPORTER'S RUNNING OUT OF CHARGE.
WHY DON'T YOU SAY GOODBYE TO YOUR FRIEND HERE? WE HAVE TO GO.
NOW.
DA-A-AD.
OKAY. SERIOUSLY. WHAT IS IT WITH YOU? WHY DO YOU HAVE IT OUT FOR ARBORO ANYWAY?
MY PROBLEM, YOUNG LADY, ISN'T WITH YOUR HANDSOME PRINCE. IT'S WITH YOU.
OR, MORE PRECISELY, THE PERSON YOU ARE WHEN YOU'RE WITH HIM.
I'VE SEEN IT, VALERIA. YOU PLAY DUMB WHEN YOU'RE AROUND THAT BOY.
NEVER DO THAT. FOR ANYONE. YOU'RE SO SMART. SMARTER THAN ME.
AND I AM SO PROUD OF THAT. OF EVERYTHING THAT MAKES YOU SPECIAL.
NEVER HIDE WHO YOU TRULY ARE.
THANKS, DAD. LET'S-- LET'S GO HOME.
NEXT STOP: THE BAXTER BUILDING.
OY. KID, YOU GONNA TELL HIM? OR DO I HAVE TO?
UGH. ALL RIGHT. GUYS, WHILE YOU WERE AWAY...

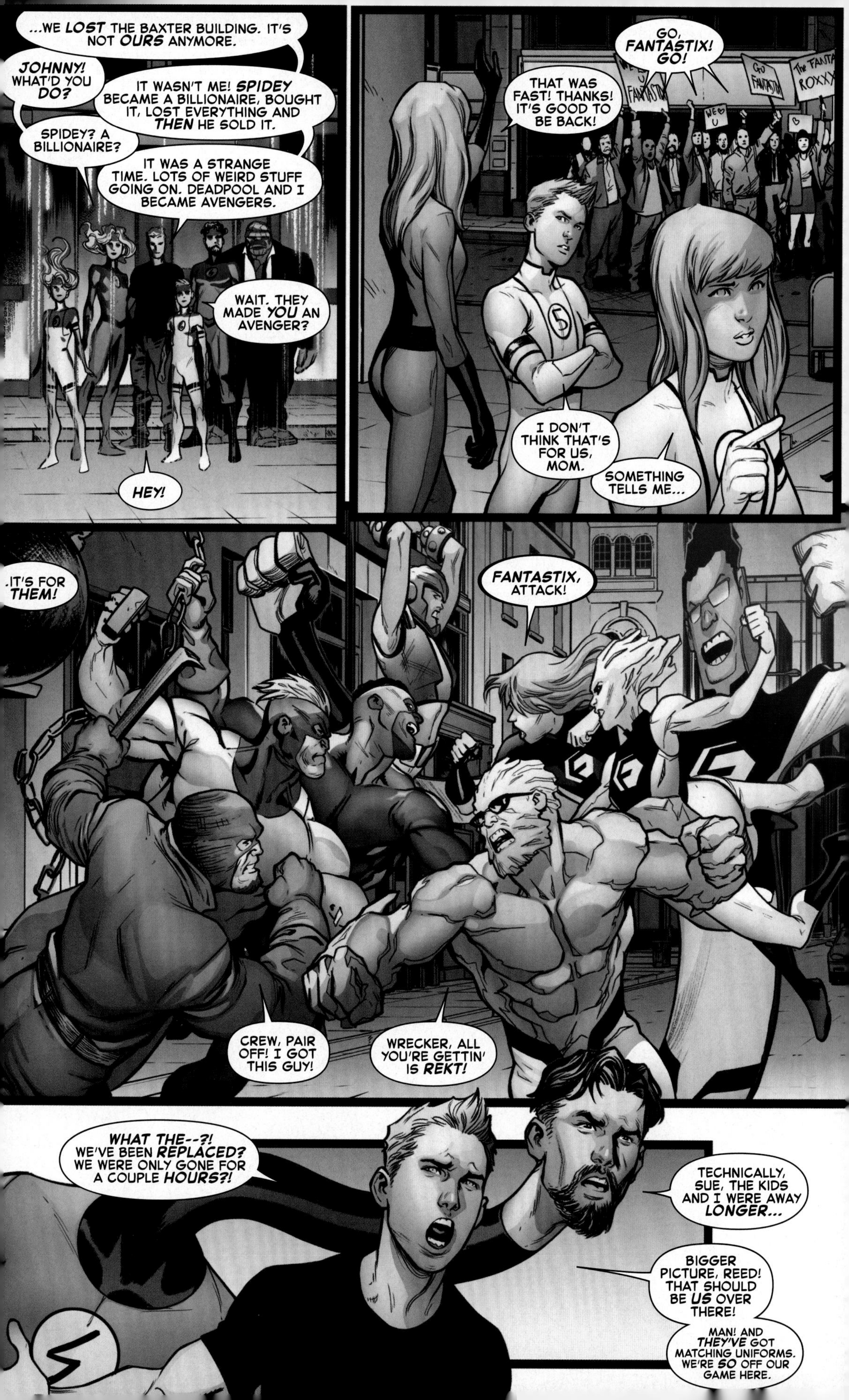

...WE LOST THE BAXTER BUILDING. IT'S NOT OURS ANYMORE.
JOHNNY! WHAT'D YOU DO?
IT WASN'T ME! SPIDEY BECAME A BILLIONAIRE, BOUGHT IT, LOST EVERYTHING AND THEN HE SOLD IT.
SPIDEY? A BILLIONAIRE?
IT WAS A STRANGE TIME. LOTS OF WEIRD STUFF GOING ON. DEADPOOL AND I BECAME AVENGERS.
WAIT. THEY MADE YOU AN AVENGER?
HEY!
GO, FANTASTIX! GO!
THAT WAS FAST! THANKS! IT'S GOOD TO BE BACK!
GO FANTASTIX
WE ♡ U
The FANTA ROXXX
I DON'T THINK THAT'S FOR US, MOM.
SOMETHING TELLS ME...
...IT'S FOR THEM!
FANTASTIX, ATTACK!
CREW, PAIR OFF! I GOT THIS GUY!
WRECKER, ALL YOU'RE GETTIN' IS REKT!
WHAT THE--?! WE'VE BEEN REPLACED? WE WERE ONLY GONE FOR A COUPLE HOURS?!
TECHNICALLY, SUE, THE KIDS AND I WERE AWAY LONGER...
BIGGER PICTURE, REED! THAT SHOULD BE US OVER THERE!
MAN! AND THEY'VE GOT MATCHING UNIFORMS. WE'RE SO OFF OUR GAME HERE.

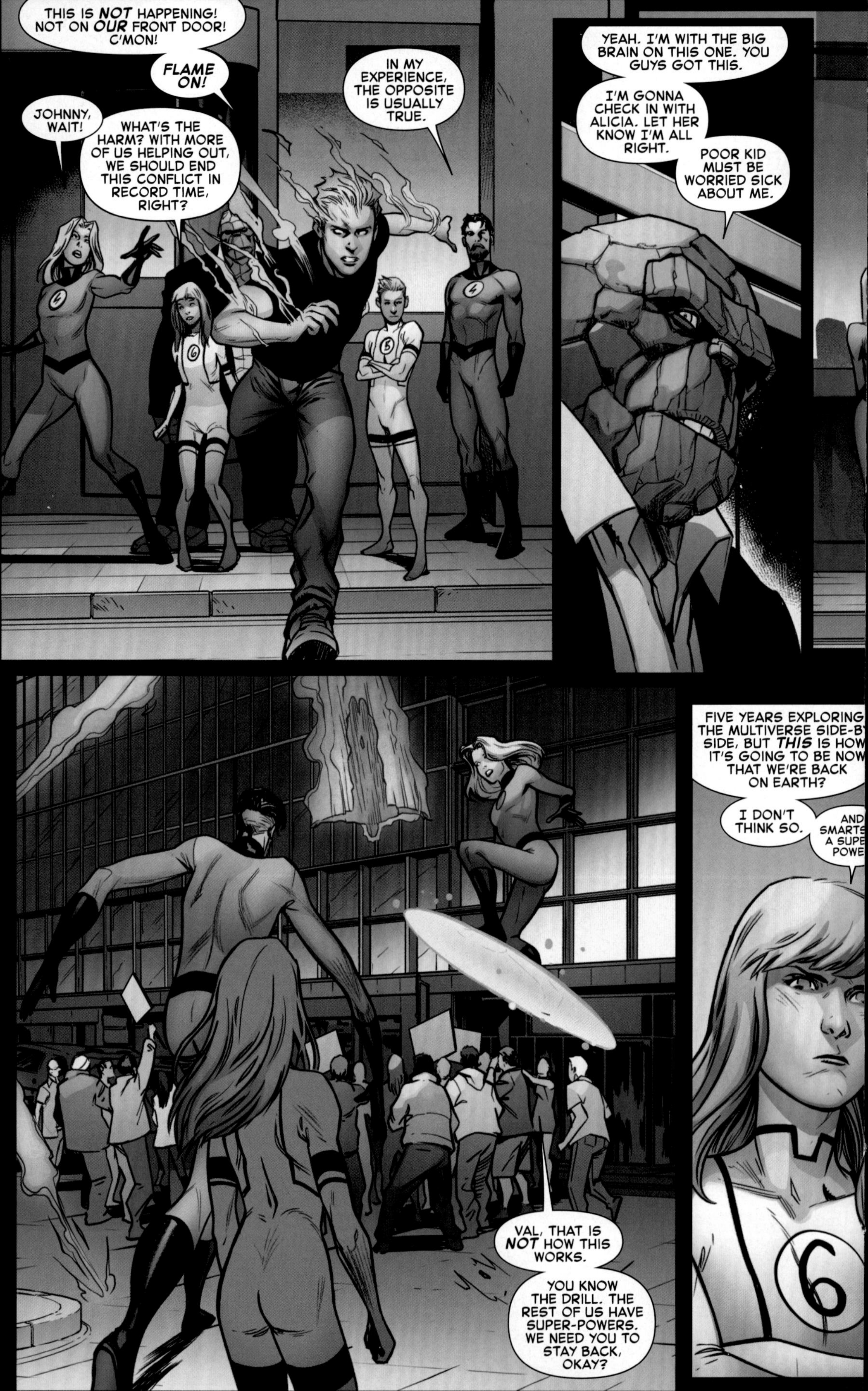

THIS IS NOT HAPPENING! NOT ON OUR FRONT DOOR! C'MON!
FLAME ON!
JOHNNY, WAIT!
WHAT'S THE HARM? WITH MORE OF US HELPING OUT, WE SHOULD END THIS CONFLICT IN RECORD TIME, RIGHT?
IN MY EXPERIENCE, THE OPPOSITE IS USUALLY TRUE.
YEAH. I'M WITH THE BIG BRAIN ON THIS ONE. YOU GUYS GOT THIS.
I'M GONNA CHECK IN WITH ALICIA. LET HER KNOW I'M ALL RIGHT.
POOR KID MUST BE WORRIED SICK ABOUT ME.
VAL, THAT IS NOT HOW THIS WORKS.
YOU KNOW THE DRILL. THE REST OF US HAVE SUPER-POWERS. WE NEED YOU TO STAY BACK, OKAY?
FIVE YEARS EXPLORING THE MULTIVERSE SIDE-BY SIDE, BUT THIS IS HOW IT'S GOING TO BE NOW THAT WE'RE BACK ON EARTH?
I DON'T THINK SO.

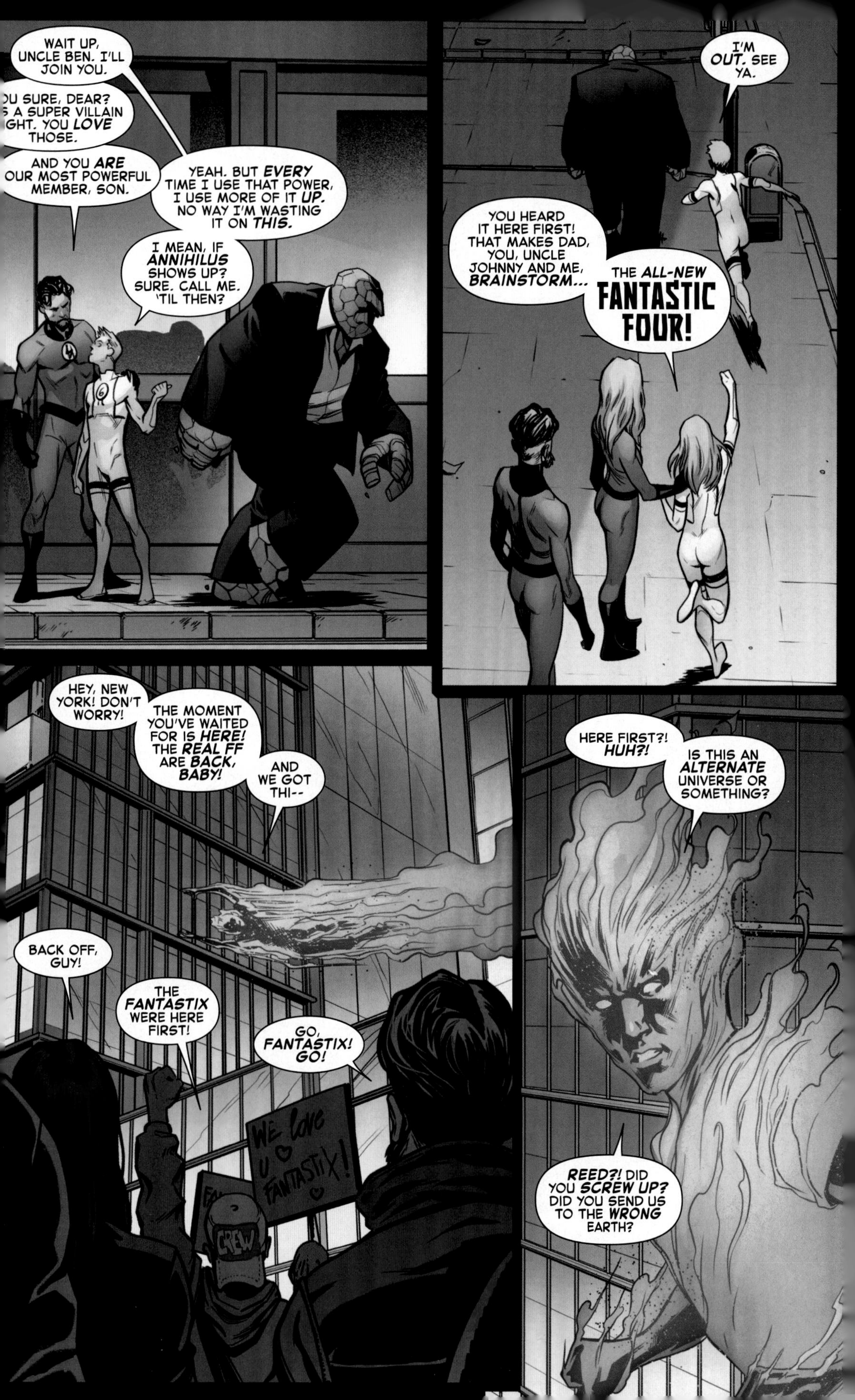
WAIT UP, UNCLE BEN. I'LL JOIN YOU.
OU SURE, DEAR? S A SUPER VILLAIN IGHT. YOU LOVE THOSE.
AND YOU ARE OUR MOST POWERFUL MEMBER, SON.
YEAH. BUT EVERY TIME I USE THAT POWER, I USE MORE OF IT UP. NO WAY I'M WASTING IT ON THIS.
I MEAN, IF ANNIHILUS SHOWS UP? SURE. CALL ME. 'TIL THEN?
I'M OUT. SEE YA.
YOU HEARD IT HERE FIRST! THAT MAKES DAD, YOU, UNCLE JOHNNY AND ME, BRAINSTORM...
THE ALL-NEW FANTASTIC FOUR!
HEY, NEW YORK! DON'T WORRY!
THE MOMENT YOU'VE WAITED FOR IS HERE! THE REAL FF ARE BACK, BABY!
AND WE GOT THI--
BACK OFF, GUY!
THE FANTASTIX WERE HERE FIRST!
GO, FANTASTIX! GO!
WE LOVE U FANTASTIX!
CREW
HERE FIRST?! HUH?!
IS THIS AN ALTERNATE UNIVERSE OR SOMETHING?
REED?! DID YOU SCREW UP? DID YOU SEND US TO THE WRONG EARTH?

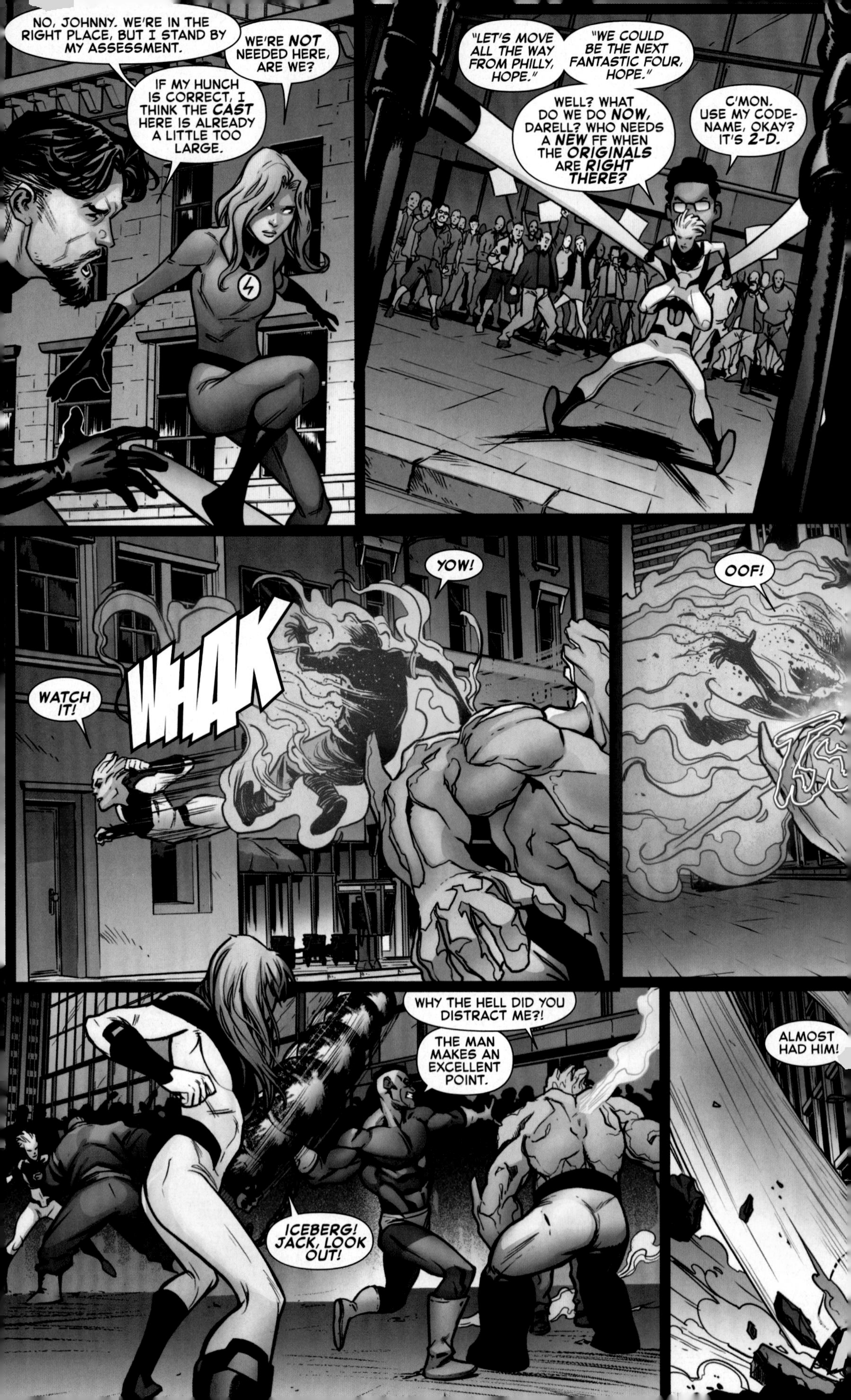
NO, JOHNNY. WE'RE IN THE RIGHT PLACE, BUT I STAND BY MY ASSESSMENT.
WE'RE NOT NEEDED HERE, ARE WE?
IF MY HUNCH IS CORRECT, I THINK THE CAST HERE IS ALREADY A LITTLE TOO LARGE.
"LET'S MOVE ALL THE WAY FROM PHILLY, HOPE."
"WE COULD BE THE NEXT FANTASTIC FOUR, HOPE."
WELL? WHAT DO WE DO NOW, DARELL? WHO NEEDS A NEW FF WHEN THE ORIGINALS ARE RIGHT THERE?
C'MON. USE MY CODE-NAME, OKAY? IT'S 2-D.
YOW!
WHAK
WATCH IT!
OOF!
WHY THE HELL DID YOU DISTRACT ME?!
THE MAN MAKES AN EXCELLENT POINT.
ICEBERG! JACK, LOOK OUT!
ALMOST HAD HIM!

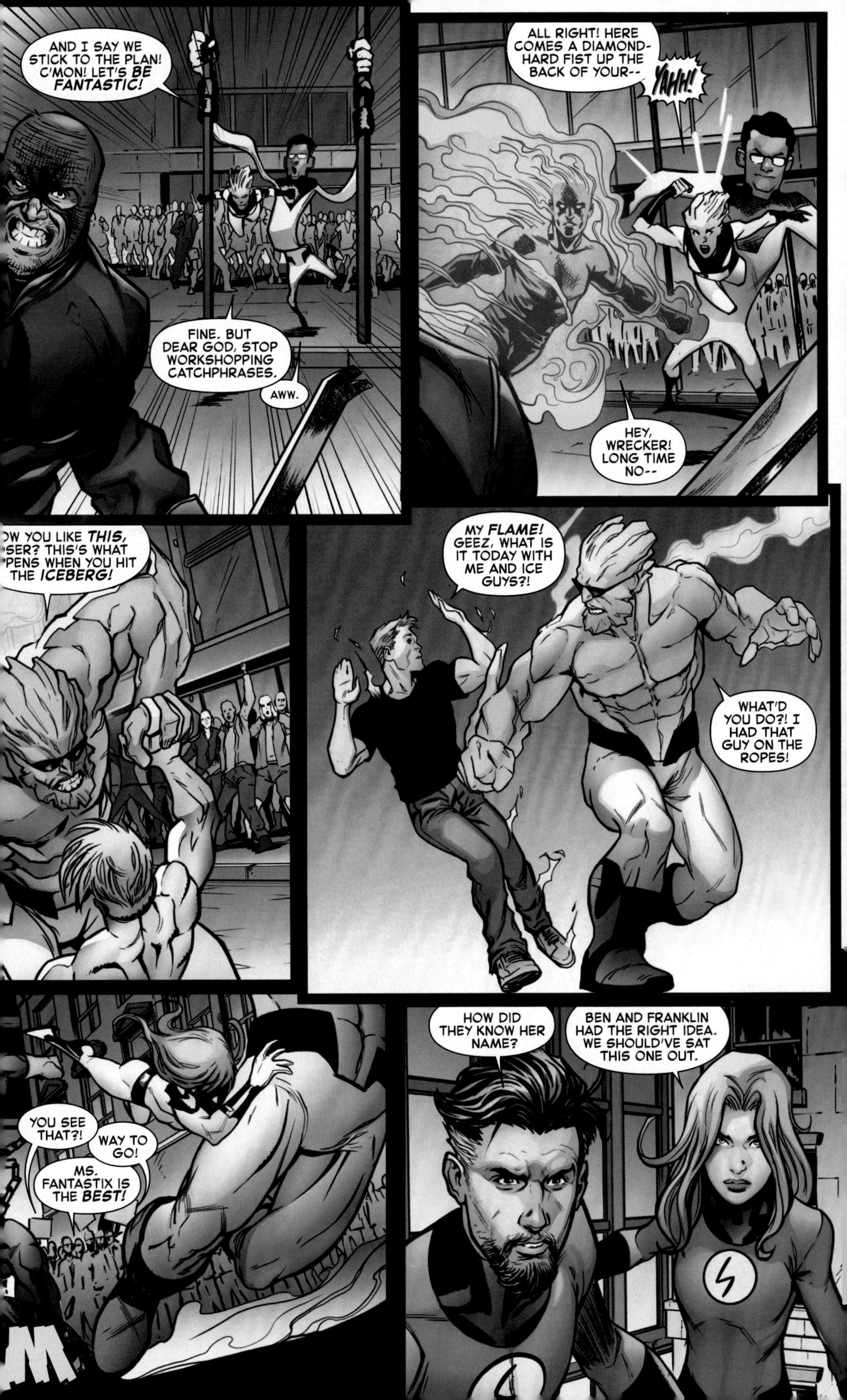

AND I SAY WE STICK TO THE PLAN! C'MON! LET'S *BE FANTASTIC!*
FINE. BUT DEAR GOD, STOP WORKSHOPPING CATCHPHRASES.
AWW.
ALL RIGHT! HERE COMES A DIAMOND-HARD FIST UP THE BACK OF YOUR--
YAHH!
HEY, WRECKER! LONG TIME NO--
OW YOU LIKE *THIS,* SER? THIS'S WHAT PENS WHEN YOU HIT THE *ICEBERG!*
MY *FLAME!* GEEZ, WHAT IS IT TODAY WITH ME AND ICE GUYS?!
WHAT'D YOU DO?! I HAD THAT GUY ON THE ROPES!
YOU SEE THAT?!
WAY TO GO!
MS. FANTASTIX IS THE *BEST!*
HOW DID THEY KNOW HER NAME?
BEN AND FRANKLIN HAD THE RIGHT IDEA. WE SHOULD'VE SAT THIS ONE OUT.

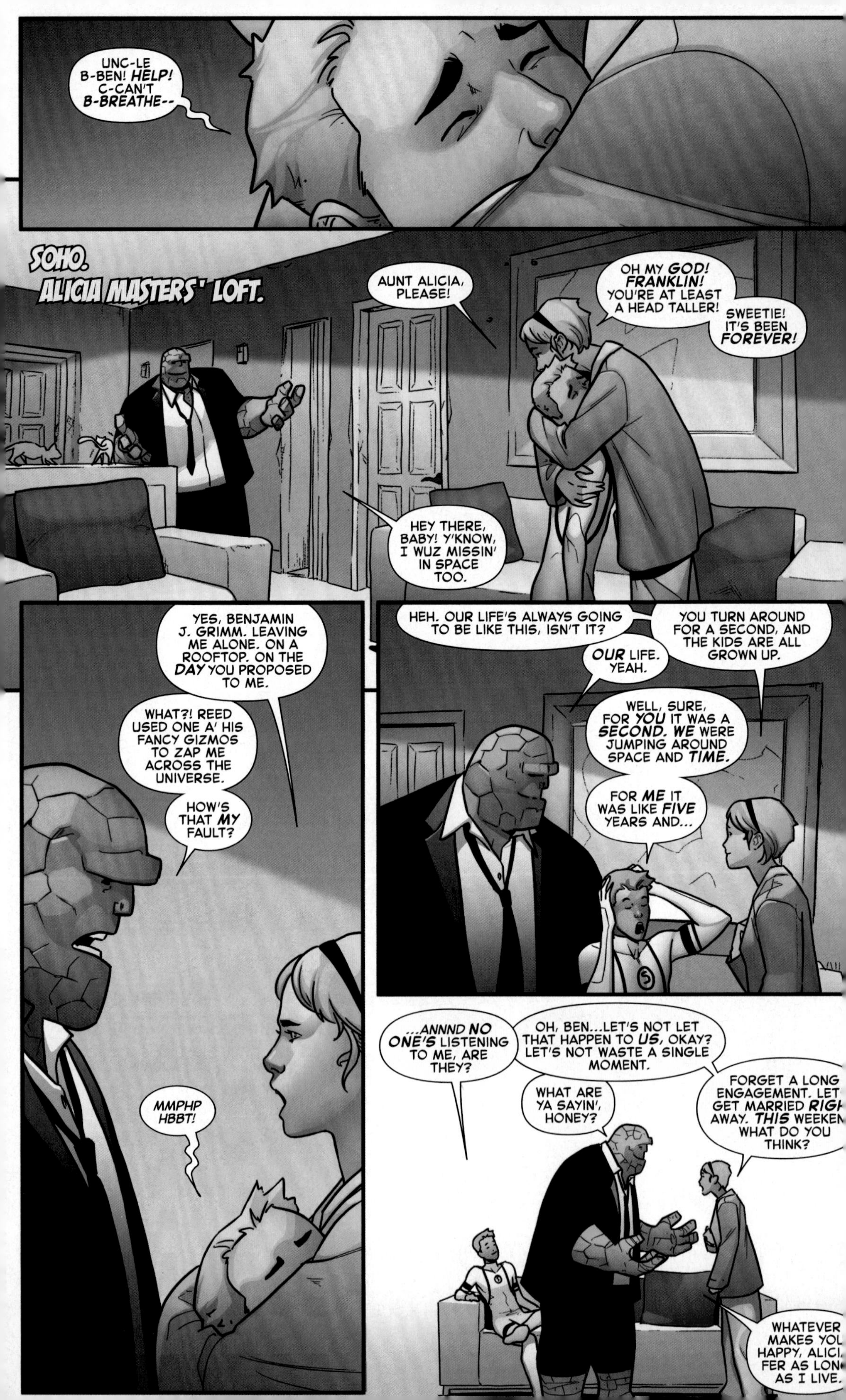
UNC-LE B-BEN! HELP! C-CAN'T B-BREATHE--
SOHO. ALICIA MASTERS' LOFT.
AUNT ALICIA, PLEASE!
OH MY GOD! FRANKLIN! YOU'RE AT LEAST A HEAD TALLER!
SWEETIE! IT'S BEEN FOREVER!
HEY THERE, BABY! Y'KNOW, I WUZ MISSIN' IN SPACE TOO.
YES, BENJAMIN J. GRIMM. LEAVING ME ALONE. ON A ROOFTOP. ON THE DAY YOU PROPOSED TO ME.
WHAT?! REED USED ONE A' HIS FANCY GIZMOS TO ZAP ME ACROSS THE UNIVERSE.
HOW'S THAT MY FAULT?
MMPHP HBBT!
HEH. OUR LIFE'S ALWAYS GOING TO BE LIKE THIS, ISN'T IT?
YOU TURN AROUND FOR A SECOND, AND THE KIDS ARE ALL GROWN UP.
OUR LIFE. YEAH.
WELL, SURE, FOR YOU IT WAS A SECOND. WE WERE JUMPING AROUND SPACE AND TIME.
FOR ME IT WAS LIKE FIVE YEARS AND...
...ANNND NO ONE'S LISTENING TO ME, ARE THEY?
OH, BEN...LET'S NOT LET THAT HAPPEN TO US, OKAY? LET'S NOT WASTE A SINGLE MOMENT.
FORGET A LONG ENGAGEMENT. LET GET MARRIED RIGH AWAY. THIS WEEKEN WHAT DO YOU THINK?
WHAT ARE YA SAYIN', HONEY?
WHATEVER MAKES YOU HAPPY, ALICI FER AS LON AS I LIVE.

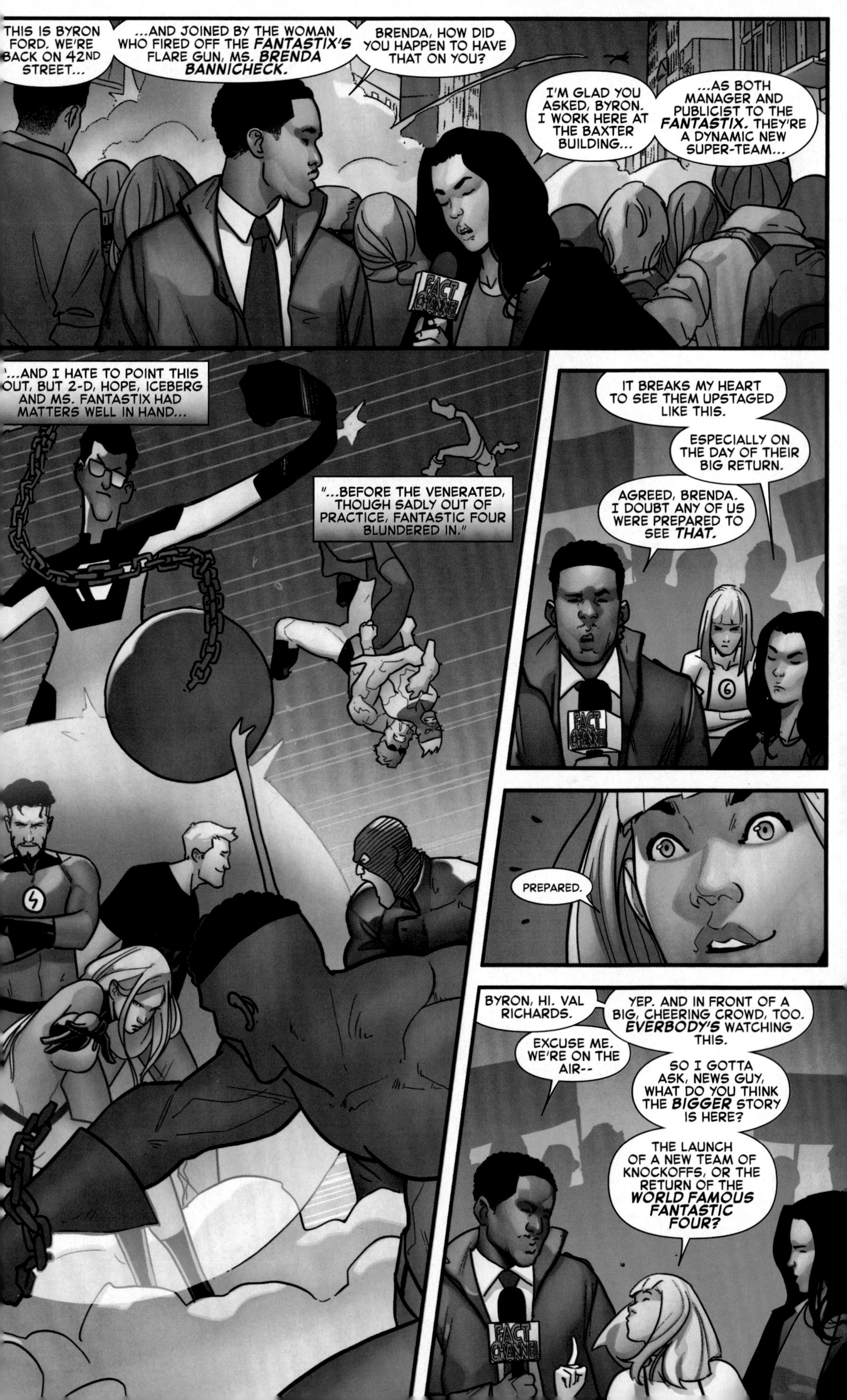
THIS IS BYRON FORD. WE'RE BACK ON 42ND STREET...
...AND JOINED BY THE WOMAN WHO FIRED OFF THE FANTASTIX'S FLARE GUN, MS. BRENDA BANNICHECK.
BRENDA, HOW DID YOU HAPPEN TO HAVE THAT ON YOU?
I'M GLAD YOU ASKED, BYRON. I WORK HERE AT THE BAXTER BUILDING...
...AS BOTH MANAGER AND PUBLICIST TO THE FANTASTIX. THEY'RE A DYNAMIC NEW SUPER-TEAM...
FACT CHANNEL
"...AND I HATE TO POINT THIS OUT, BUT 2-D, HOPE, ICEBERG AND MS. FANTASTIX HAD MATTERS WELL IN HAND...
"...BEFORE THE VENERATED, THOUGH SADLY OUT OF PRACTICE, FANTASTIC FOUR BLUNDERED IN."
IT BREAKS MY HEART TO SEE THEM UPSTAGED LIKE THIS.
ESPECIALLY ON THE DAY OF THEIR BIG RETURN.
AGREED, BRENDA. I DOUBT ANY OF US WERE PREPARED TO SEE THAT.
FACT CHANNEL
PREPARED.
BYRON, HI. VAL RICHARDS.
EXCUSE ME. WE'RE ON THE AIR--
YEP. AND IN FRONT OF A BIG, CHEERING CROWD, TOO. EVERBODY'S WATCHING THIS.
SO I GOTTA ASK, NEWS GUY, WHAT DO YOU THINK THE BIGGER STORY IS HERE?
THE LAUNCH OF A NEW TEAM OF KNOCKOFFS, OR THE RETURN OF THE WORLD FAMOUS FANTASTIC FOUR?
FACT CHANNEL

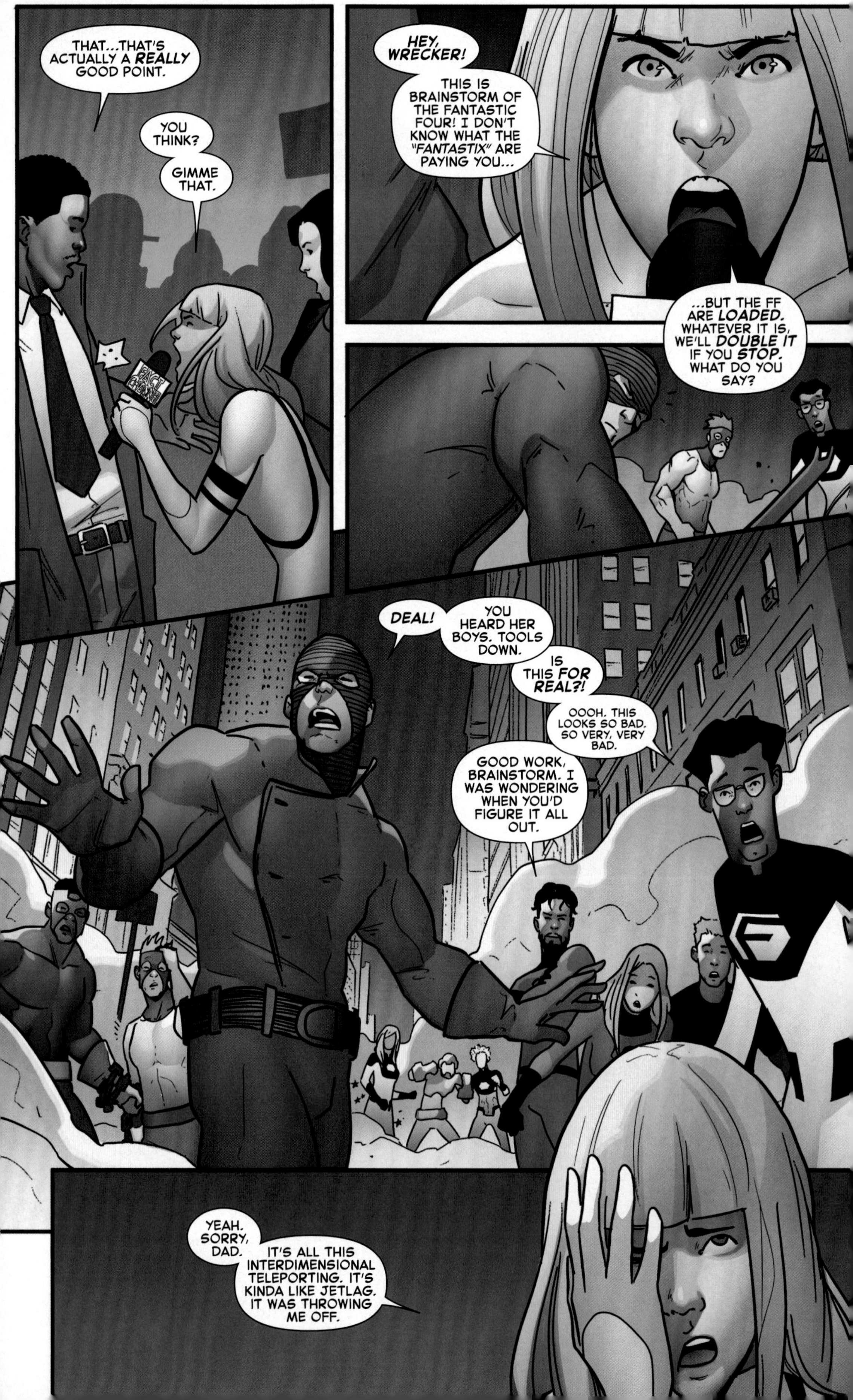
THAT...THAT'S ACTUALLY A REALLY GOOD POINT.
YOU THINK?
GIMME THAT.
FACT CHANNEL
HEY, WRECKER!
THIS IS BRAINSTORM OF THE FANTASTIC FOUR! I DON'T KNOW WHAT THE "FANTASTIX" ARE PAYING YOU...
...BUT THE FF ARE LOADED. WHATEVER IT IS, WE'LL DOUBLE IT IF YOU STOP. WHAT DO YOU SAY?
DEAL!
YOU HEARD HER BOYS. TOOLS DOWN.
IS THIS FOR REAL?!
OOOH. THIS LOOKS SO BAD. SO VERY, VERY BAD.
GOOD WORK, BRAINSTORM. I WAS WONDERING WHEN YOU'D FIGURE IT ALL OUT.
YEAH. SORRY, DAD.
IT'S ALL THIS INTERDIMENSIONAL TELEPORTING. IT'S KINDA LIKE JETLAG. IT WAS THROWING ME OFF.

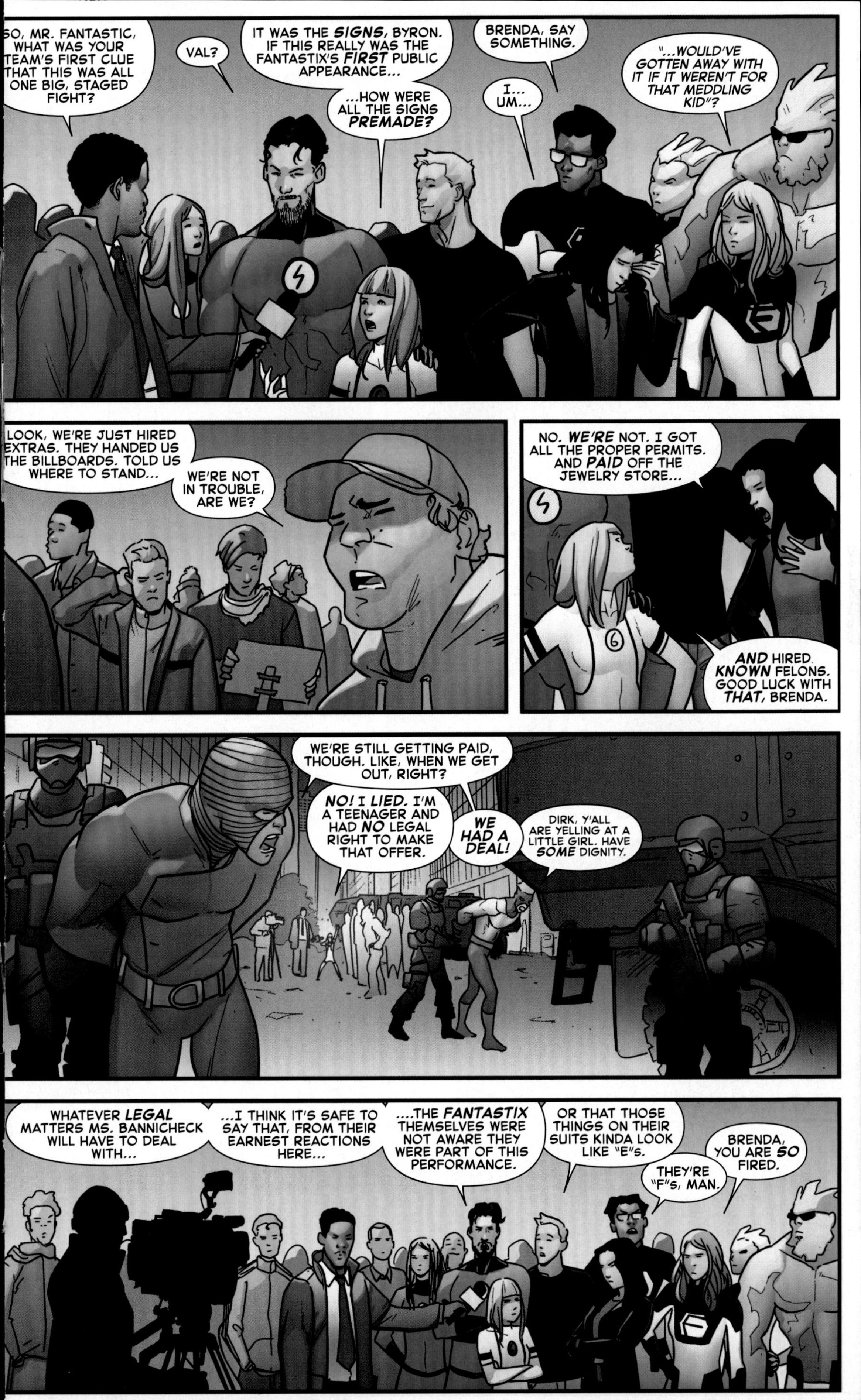
SO, MR. FANTASTIC, WHAT WAS YOUR TEAM'S FIRST CLUE THAT THIS WAS ALL ONE BIG, STAGED FIGHT?
VAL?
IT WAS THE SIGNS, BYRON. IF THIS REALLY WAS THE FANTASTIX'S FIRST PUBLIC APPEARANCE...
...HOW WERE ALL THE SIGNS PREMADE?
BRENDA, SAY SOMETHING.
I... UM...
"...WOULD'VE GOTTEN AWAY WITH IT IF IT WEREN'T FOR THAT MEDDLING KID"?
LOOK, WE'RE JUST HIRED EXTRAS. THEY HANDED US THE BILLBOARDS. TOLD US WHERE TO STAND...
WE'RE NOT IN TROUBLE, ARE WE?
NO. WE'RE NOT. I GOT ALL THE PROPER PERMITS. AND PAID OFF THE JEWELRY STORE...
AND HIRED KNOWN FELONS. GOOD LUCK WITH THAT, BRENDA.
WE'RE STILL GETTING PAID, THOUGH. LIKE, WHEN WE GET OUT, RIGHT?
NO! I LIED. I'M A TEENAGER AND HAD NO LEGAL RIGHT TO MAKE THAT OFFER.
WE HAD A DEAL!
DIRK, Y'ALL ARE YELLING AT A LITTLE GIRL. HAVE SOME DIGNITY.
WHATEVER LEGAL MATTERS MS. BANNICHECK WILL HAVE TO DEAL WITH...
...I THINK IT'S SAFE TO SAY THAT, FROM THEIR EARNEST REACTIONS HERE...
....THE FANTASTIX THEMSELVES WERE NOT AWARE THEY WERE PART OF THIS PERFORMANCE.
OR THAT THOSE THINGS ON THEIR SUITS KINDA LOOK LIKE "E"s.
THEY'RE "F"s, MAN.
BRENDA, YOU ARE SO FIRED.

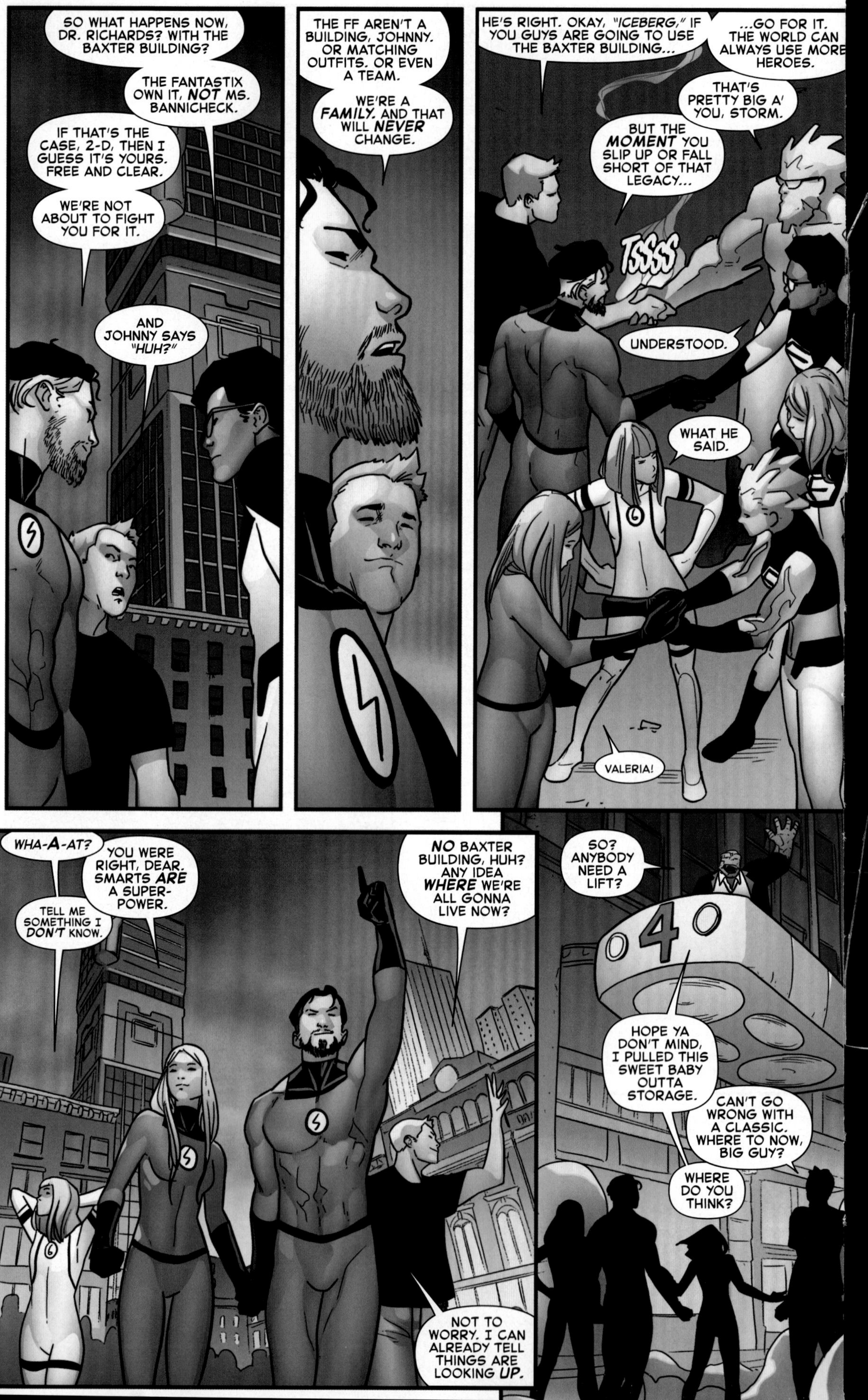
SO WHAT HAPPENS NOW, DR. RICHARDS? WITH THE BAXTER BUILDING?
THE FANTASTIX OWN IT, NOT MS. BANNICHECK.
IF THAT'S THE CASE, 2-D, THEN I GUESS IT'S YOURS. FREE AND CLEAR.
WE'RE NOT ABOUT TO FIGHT YOU FOR IT.
AND JOHNNY SAYS "HUH?"
THE FF AREN'T A BUILDING, JOHNNY. OR MATCHING OUTFITS. OR EVEN A TEAM.
WE'RE A FAMILY. AND THAT WILL NEVER CHANGE.
HE'S RIGHT. OKAY, "ICEBERG," IF YOU GUYS ARE GOING TO USE THE BAXTER BUILDING...
...GO FOR IT. THE WORLD CAN ALWAYS USE MORE HEROES.
THAT'S PRETTY BIG A' YOU, STORM.
BUT THE MOMENT YOU SLIP UP OR FALL SHORT OF THAT LEGACY...
TSSSS
UNDERSTOOD.
WHAT HE SAID.
VALERIA!
WHA-A-AT?
YOU WERE RIGHT, DEAR. SMARTS ARE A SUPER-POWER.
TELL ME SOMETHING I DON'T KNOW.
NO BAXTER BUILDING, HUH? ANY IDEA WHERE WE'RE ALL GONNA LIVE NOW?
NOT TO WORRY. I CAN ALREADY TELL THINGS ARE LOOKING UP.
SO? ANYBODY NEED A LIFT?
HOPE YA DON'T MIND, I PULLED THIS SWEET BABY OUTTA STORAGE.
CAN'T GO WRONG WITH A CLASSIC. WHERE TO NOW, BIG GUY?
WHERE DO YOU THINK?

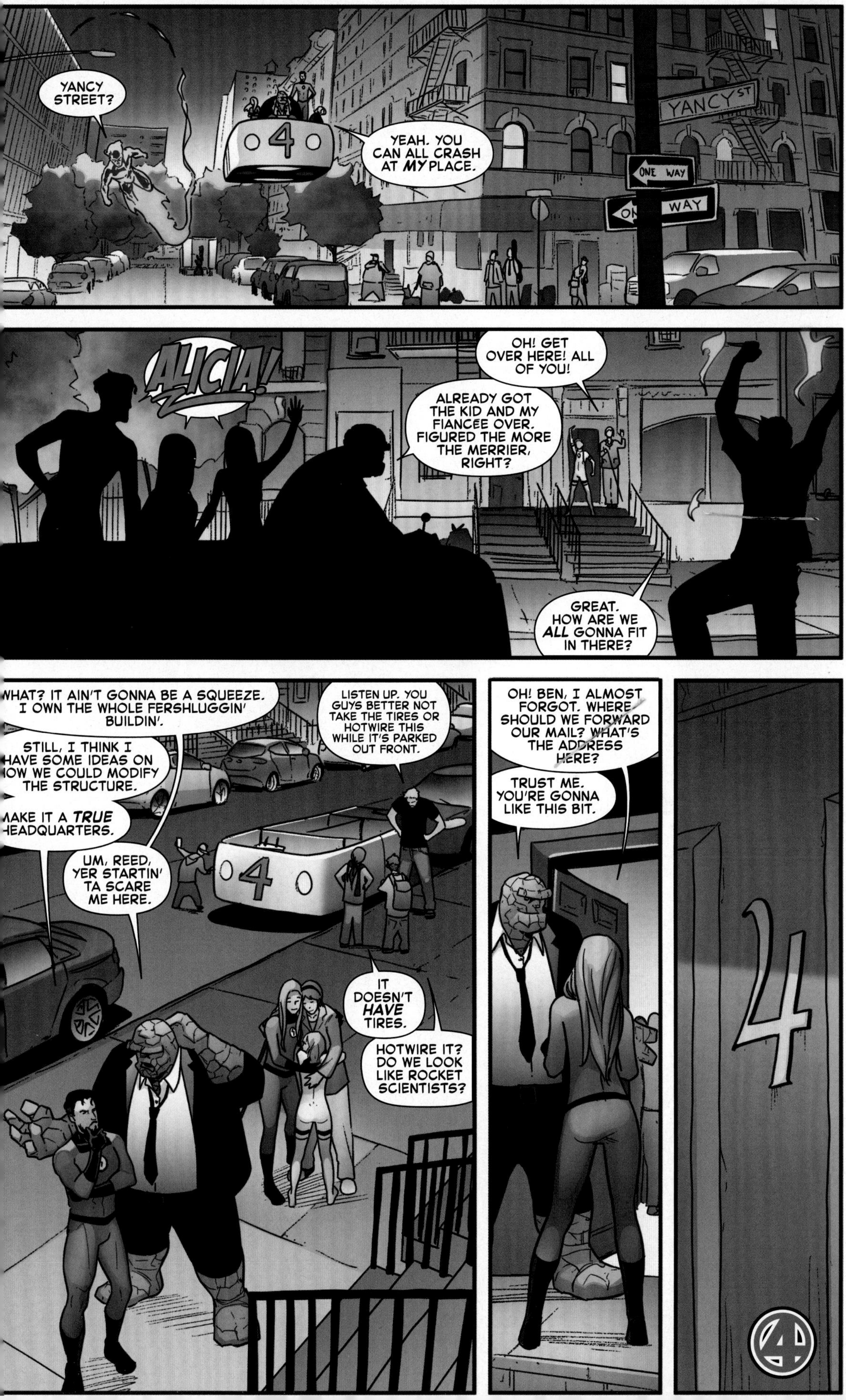
YANCY STREET?
YEAH. YOU CAN ALL CRASH AT *MY* PLACE.
YANCY ST
ONE WAY
ONE WAY
ALICIA!
OH! GET OVER HERE! ALL OF YOU!
ALREADY GOT THE KID AND MY FIANCEE OVER. FIGURED THE MORE THE MERRIER, RIGHT?
GREAT. HOW ARE WE *ALL* GONNA FIT IN THERE?
WHAT? IT AIN'T GONNA BE A SQUEEZE. I OWN THE WHOLE FERSHLUGGIN' BUILDIN'.
STILL, I THINK I HAVE SOME IDEAS ON HOW WE COULD MODIFY THE STRUCTURE.
MAKE IT A *TRUE* HEADQUARTERS.
UM, REED, YER STARTIN' TA SCARE ME HERE.
LISTEN UP. YOU GUYS BETTER NOT TAKE THE TIRES OR HOTWIRE THIS WHILE IT'S PARKED OUT FRONT.
IT DOESN'T *HAVE* TIRES.
HOTWIRE IT? DO WE LOOK LIKE ROCKET SCIENTISTS?
OH! BEN, I ALMOST FORGOT. WHERE SHOULD WE FORWARD OUR MAIL? WHAT'S THE ADDRESS HERE?
TRUST ME. YOU'RE GONNA LIKE THIS BIT.
4

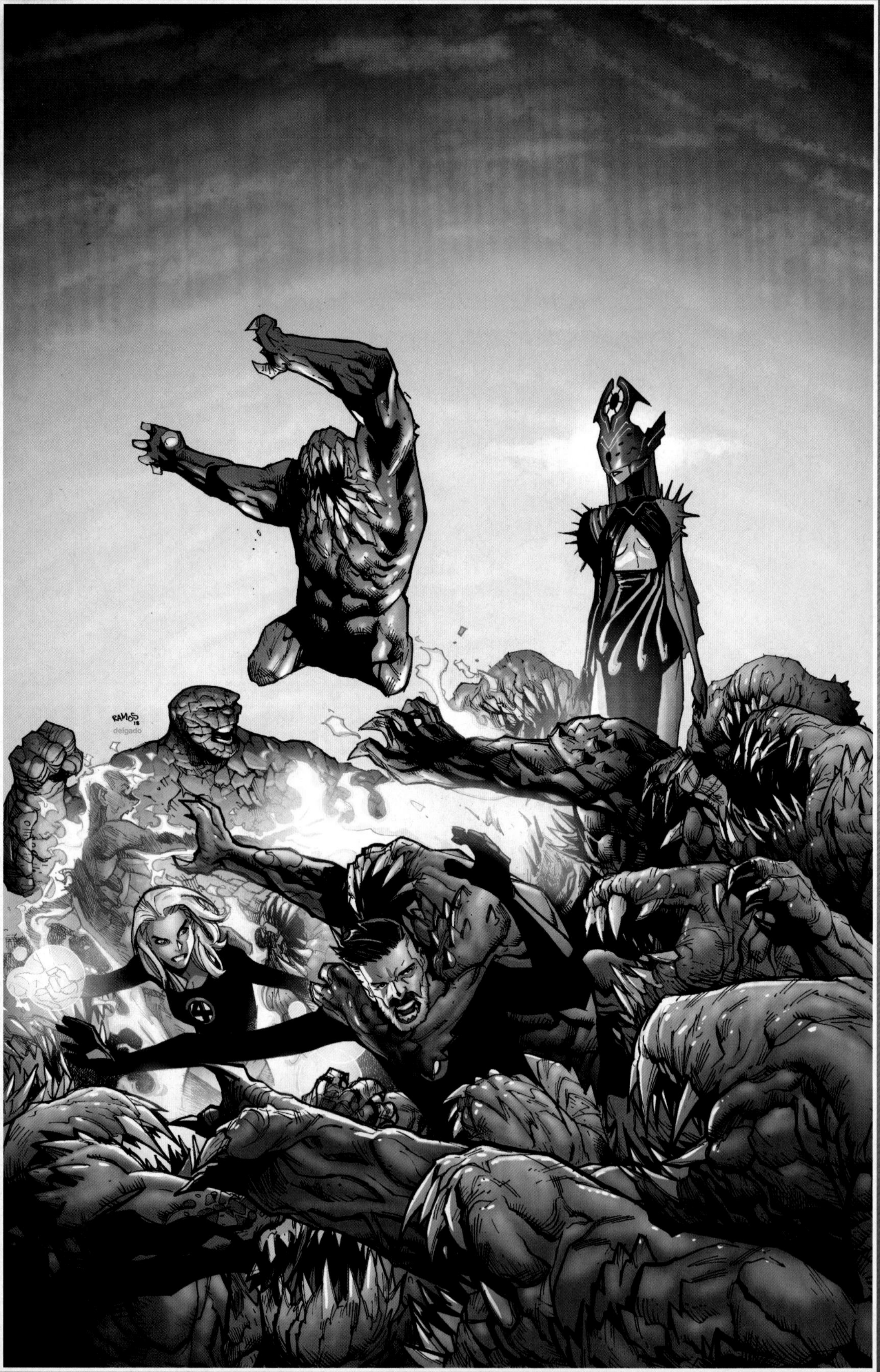
RAMOS
delgado

#1 variant by **Humberto Ramos** & **Edgar Delgado**

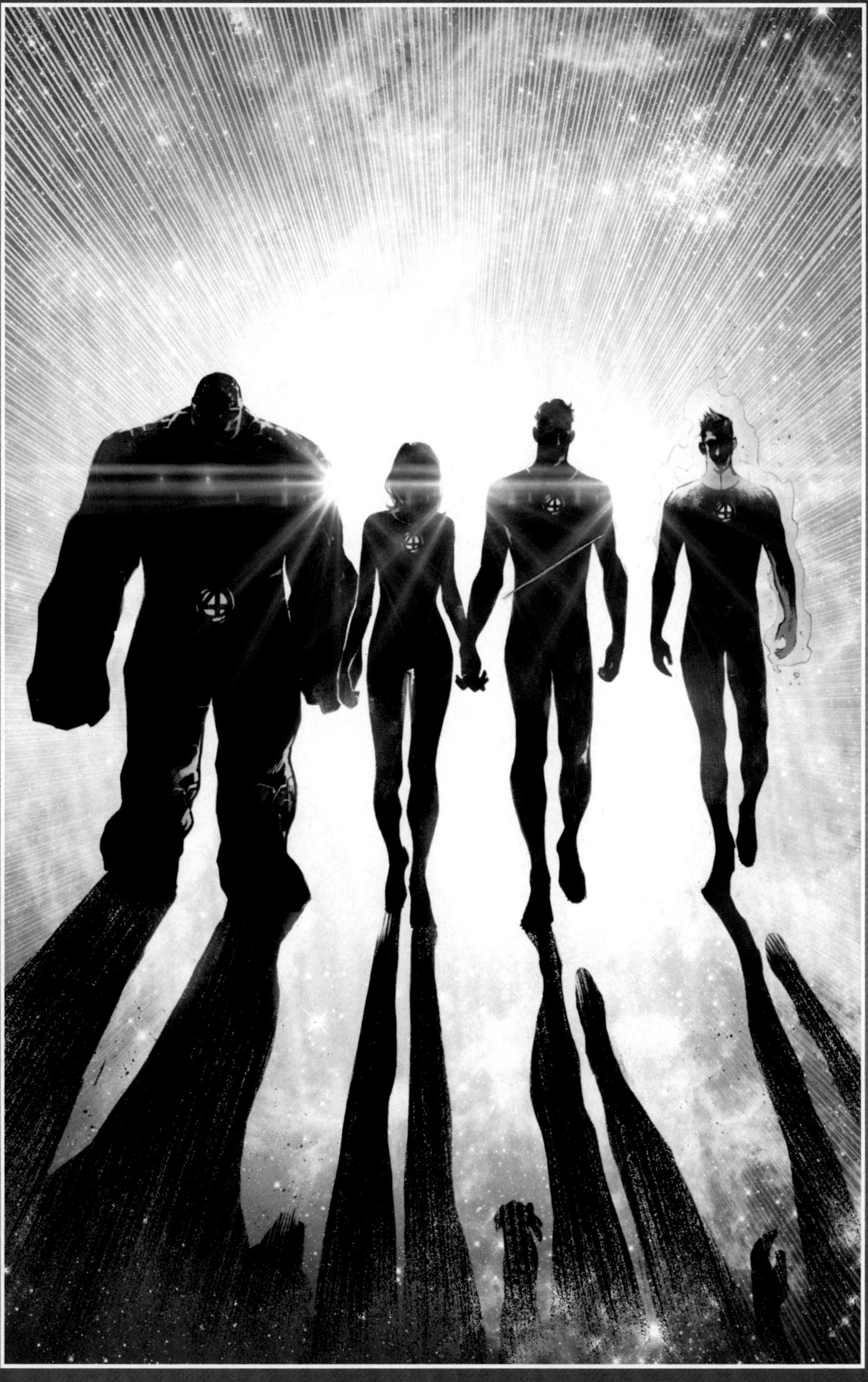

#1 teaser variant by **Sara Pichelli**

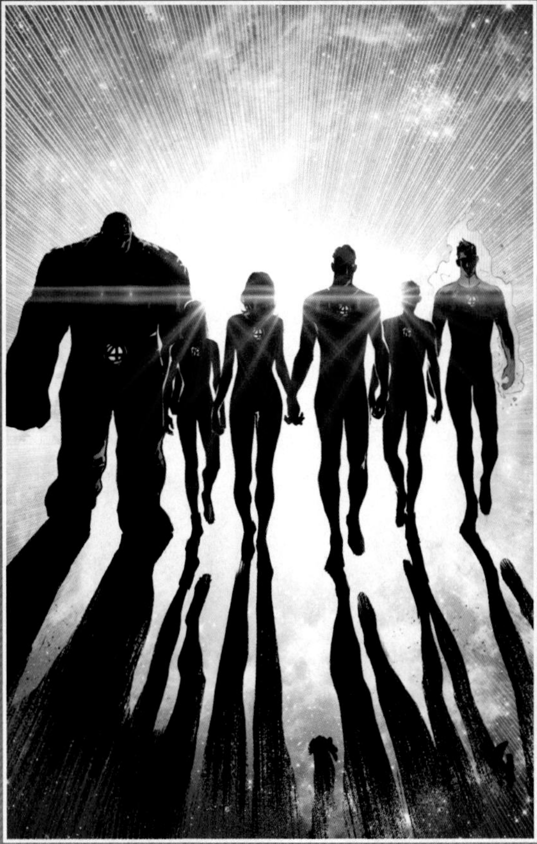

unused teaser by
Sara Pichelli

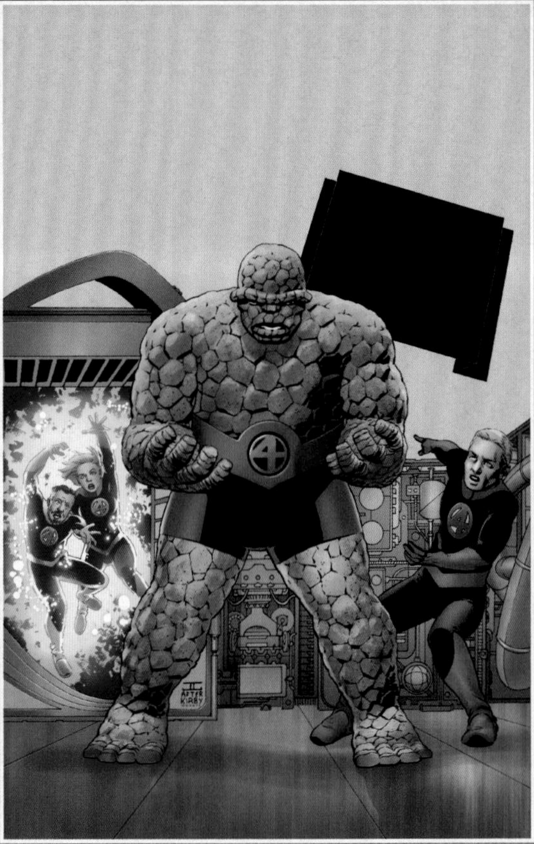

#1 variant by
John Cassaday & **Laura Martin**

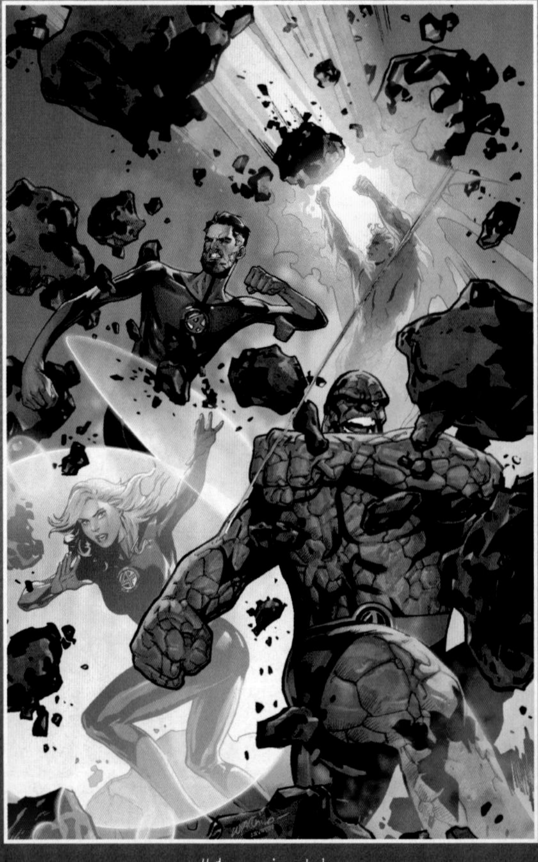

#1 variant by
Ema Lupacchino & **Jesus Aburtov**

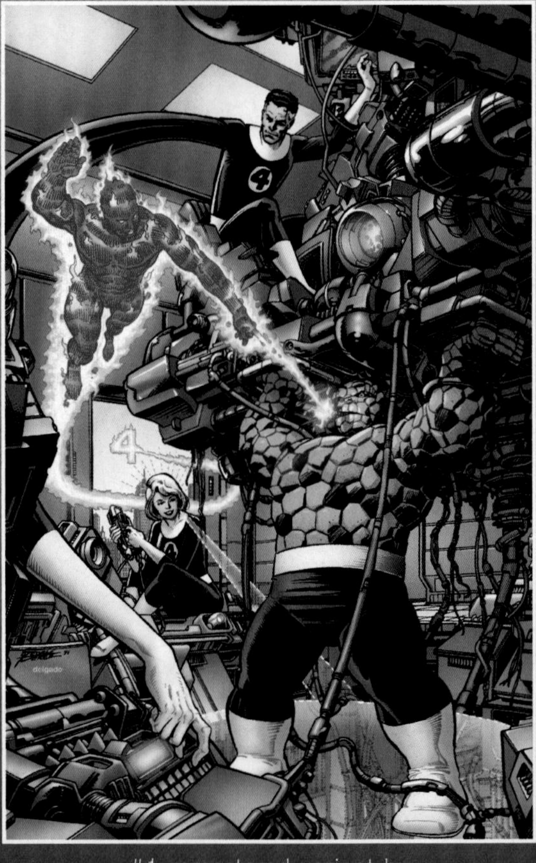

#1 remastered variant by
George Pérez & **Edgar Delgado**

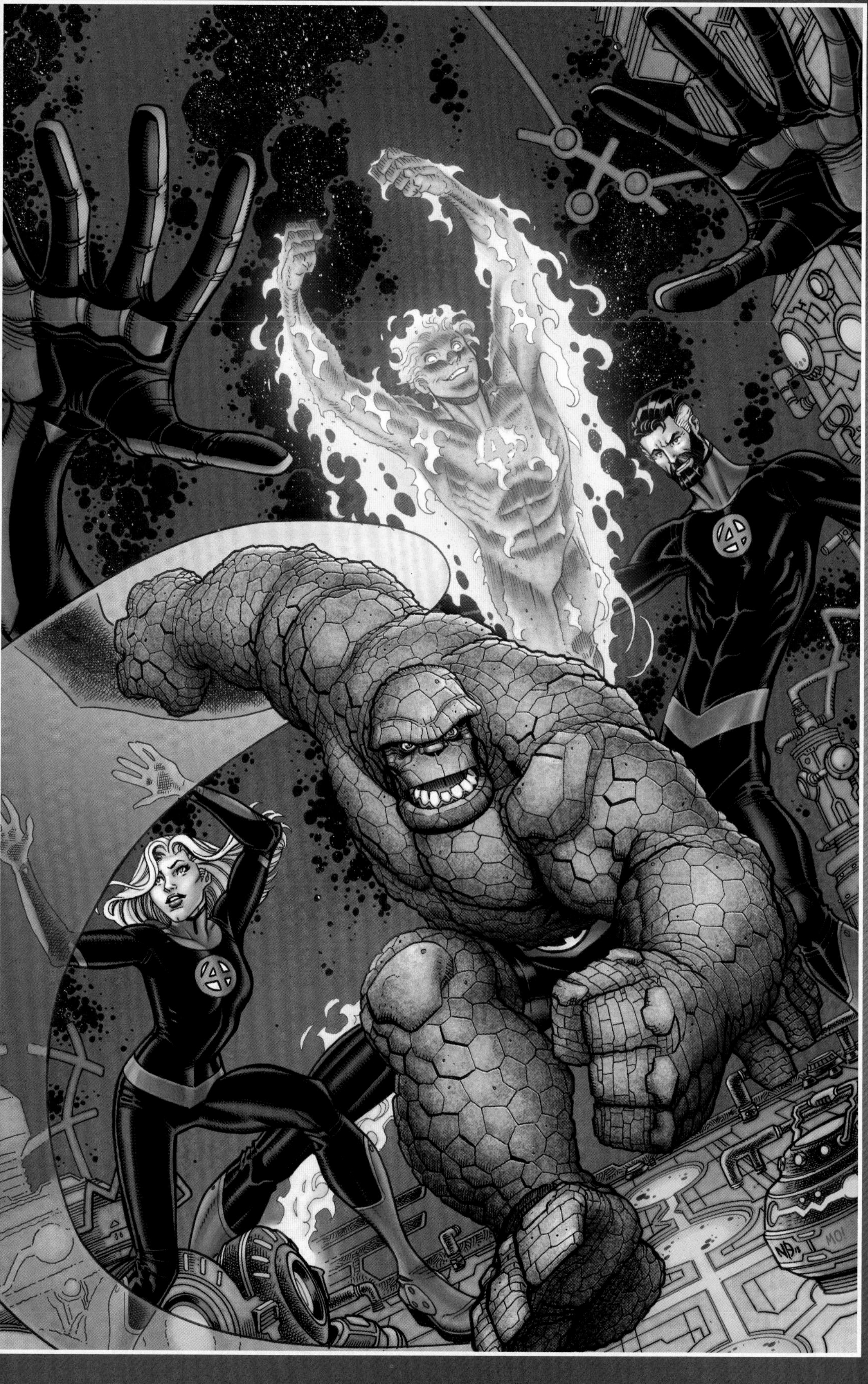

#1 variant by **Nick Bradshaw** & **Morry Hollowell**

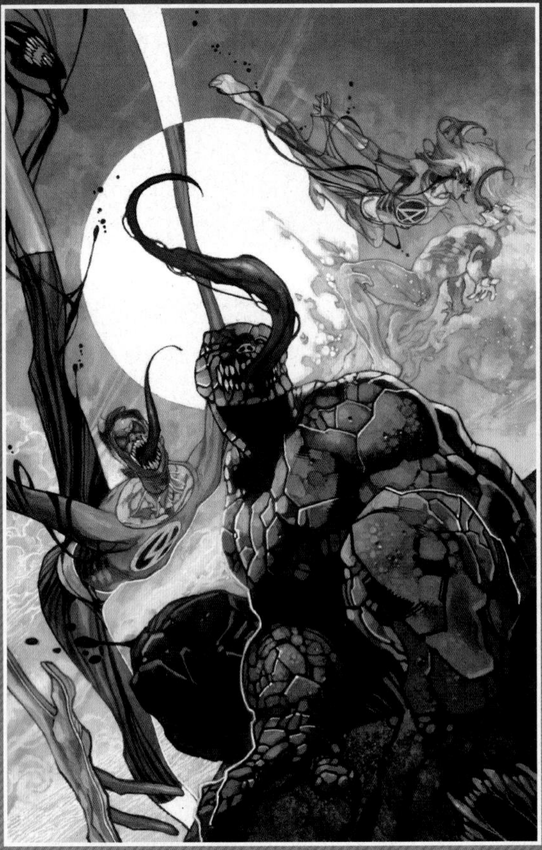

#1 variant by
Simone Bianchi

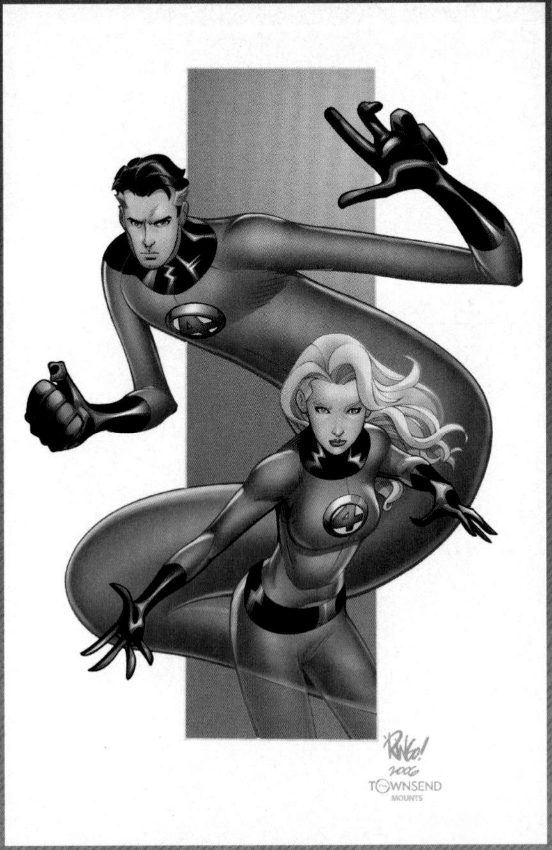
TOWNSEND
MOUNTS

#1 variant by
Mike Wieringo & **Paul Mounts**

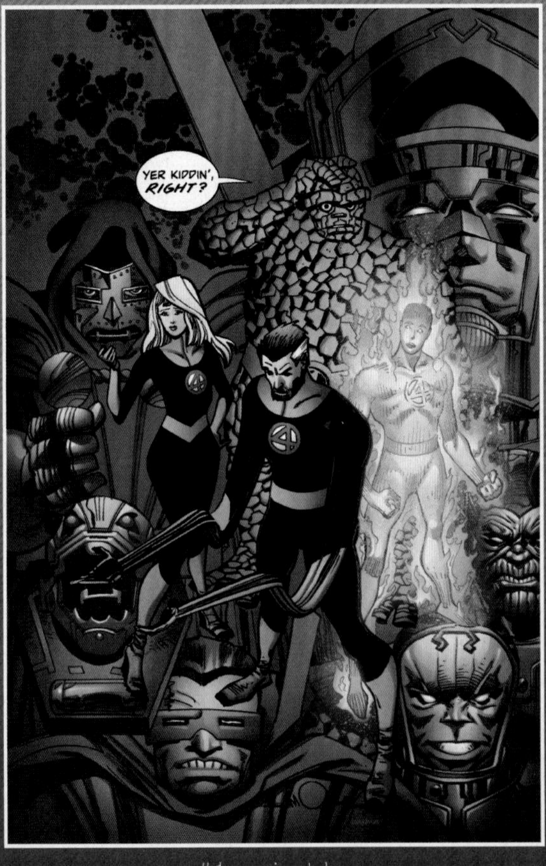
YER KIDDIN', RIGHT?

#1 variant by
Walter Simonson & **Richard Isanove**

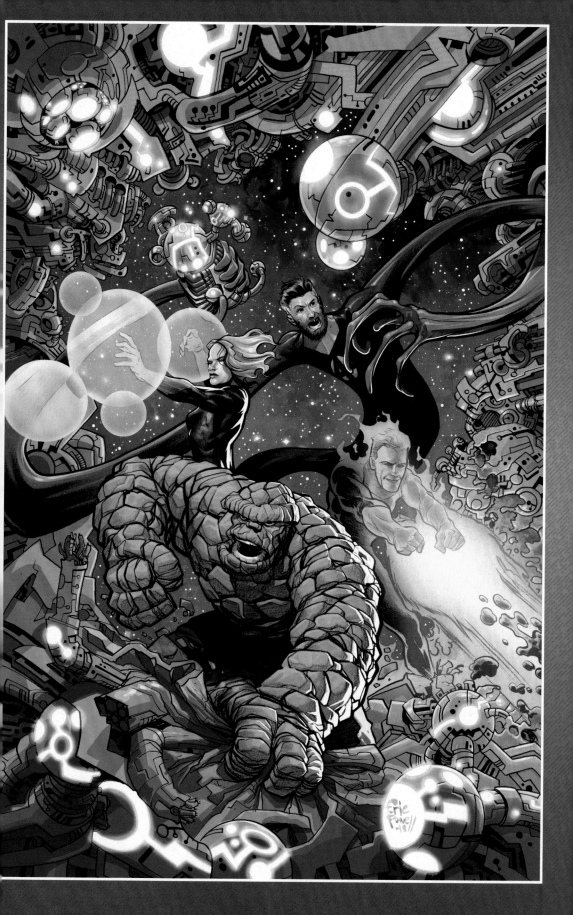

#1 variant by **Eric Powell**

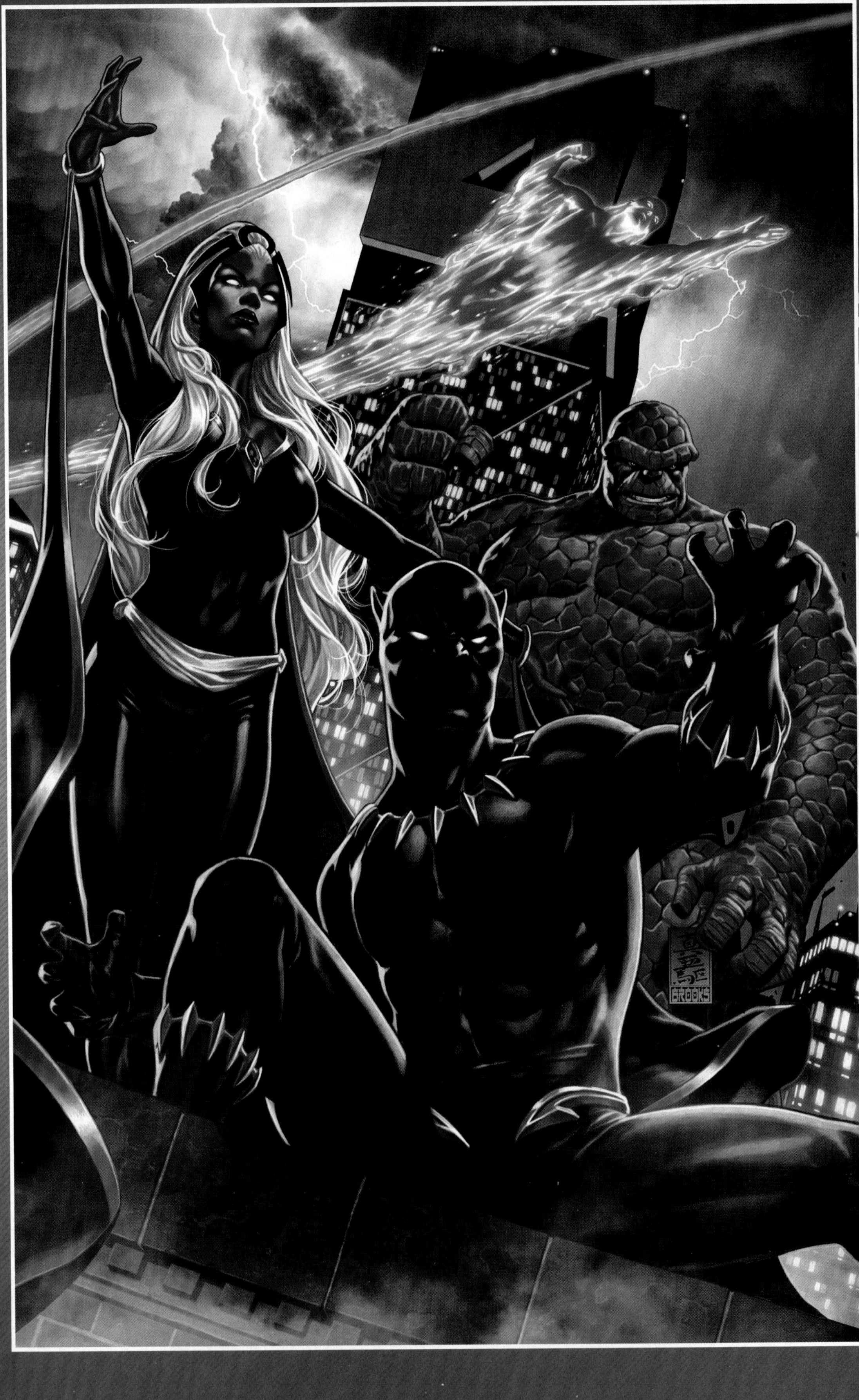
BROOKS

#1 variant by **Mark Brooks**

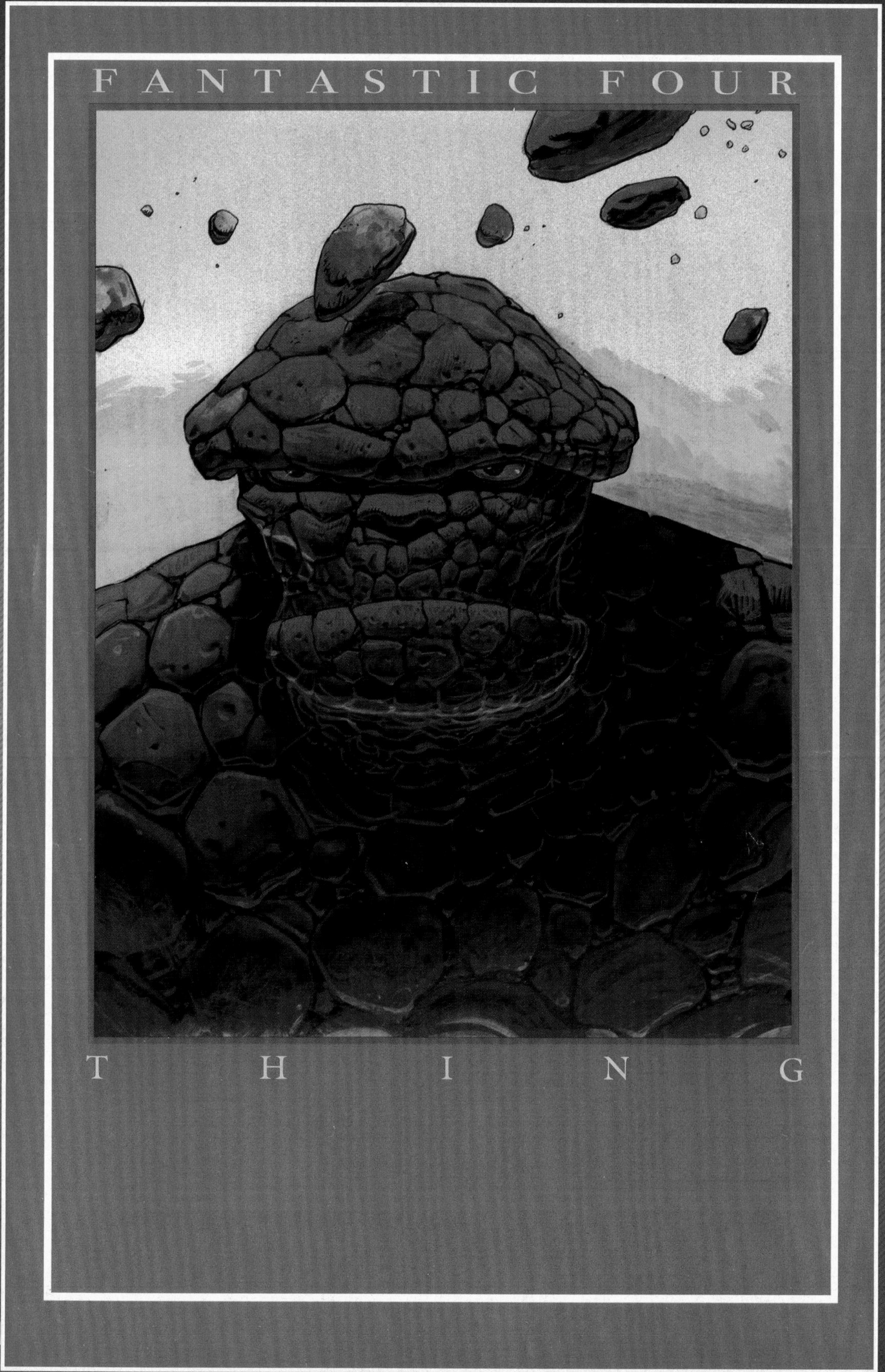
FANTASTIC FOUR
THING

#3 variant by **Moebius**

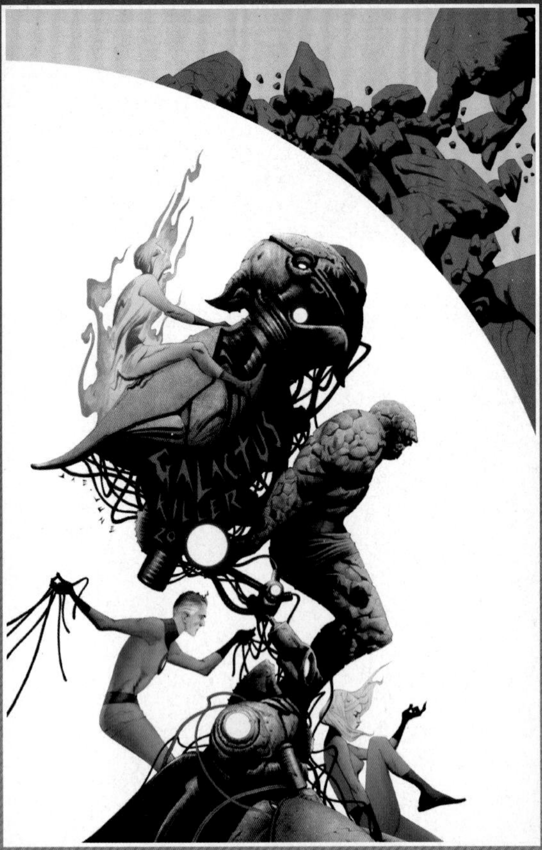
GALACTUS KILLER

#3 Marvel Knights 20th Anniversary variant by
Jae Lee

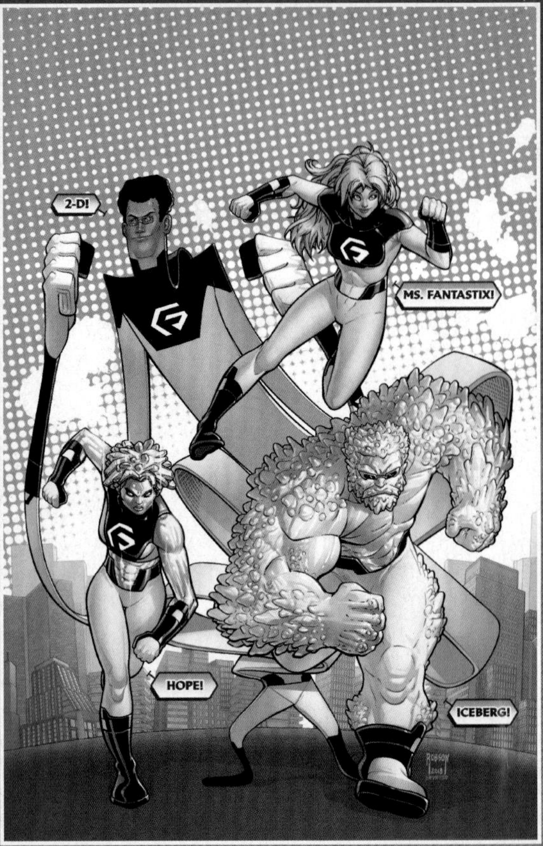
2-D!
MS. FANTASTIX!
HOPE!
ICEBERG!

#4 variant by
Wil Robson & **Jesus Aburtov**

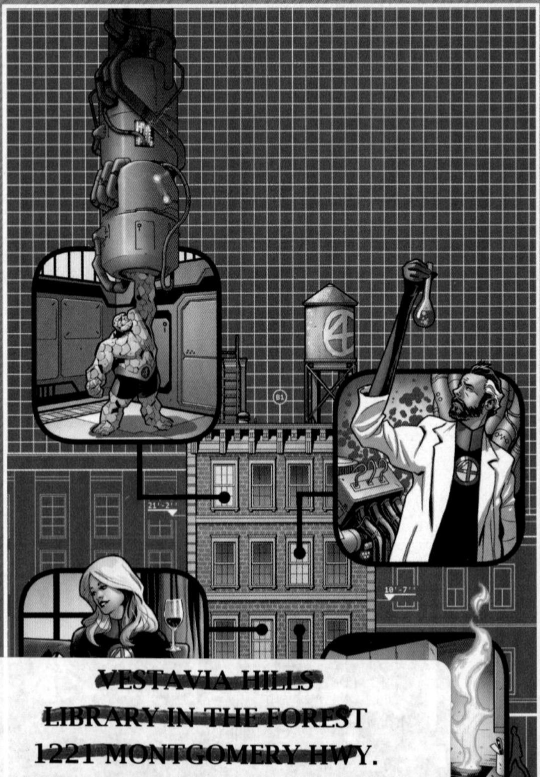

#4 variant by
Valerio Schiti & **Edgar Delgado**

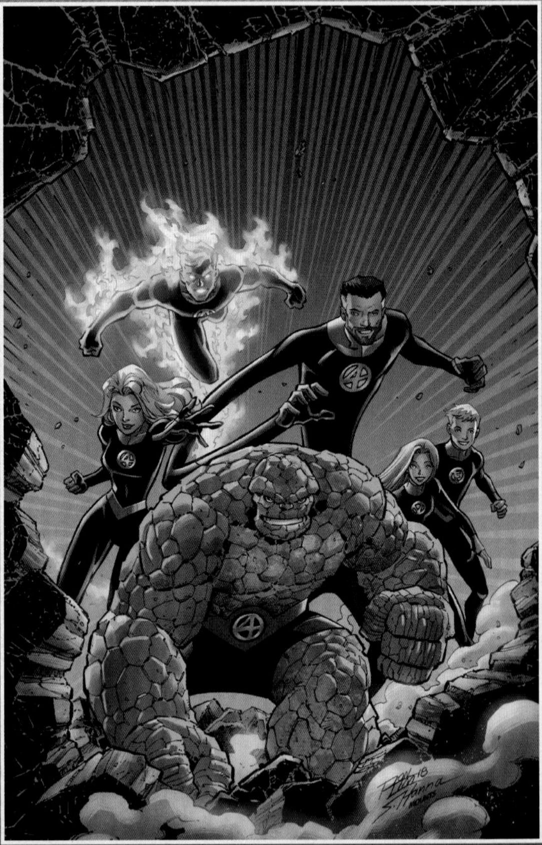

#4 variant by
Ron Lim & **Paul Mounts**